GALENA, ILLINOIS
A TIMELESS TREASURE

PHILIP A. ALEO

Aleo Publications
DUNDEE, ILLINOIS

Galena, Illinois
A Timeless Treasure

Copyright © 2015 The Galena Foundation
All Rights Reserved

Hard Cover ISBN 13: 978-0-9856081-6-3
Hard Cover ISBN 10: 0985608161

Soft Cover ISBN 13: 978-0-9856081-7-0
Soft Cover ISBN 10: 098560817X

Library of Congress Control Number: 2015917068

Published By Aleo Publications,
Division of P.F.C. Supply Co. Inc.
P.O. Box 1085
Dundee, IL. 60118

Printed in the United States of America

Printed by the Schiele Group, Elk Grove Village, Illinois

No part of this book may be reproduced or transmitted in any form or by any means, electronic or mechanical, including photocopying, recording, or by any information storage and retrieval system without permission from the publisher.

Your purchase of this book will benefit the preservation and restoration of historic Galena buildings and cultural institutions funded by The Galena Foundation, a non-profit organization founded in 1982, which has partnered with the City of Galena, the State of Illinois, Jo Daviess County, as well as local churches and community organizations on numerous projects in and near Galena.

The first major project was the restoration of the Old City Cemetery, followed by other restoration and preservation projects including work on the following:

> Fire House #1 and Fire Department Pumper
> Old High School (Green Street) Steps
> Grant Park Fountain
> Grant Park Civil War Cannons
> U.S. Grant Statue
> U.S. Grant Museum
> Galena Jo Daviess County Historical Society
> Methodist Church Steeple, Front Doors and Steps
> Belden School
> Galena Public Library
> U.S. Grant Home Pathway Project
> Elihu Washburne Home
> Grant Park Gazebo
> Old Market House
> Hess Farmhouse
> Galena Train Depot
> Turner Hall
> St. Mathew's Lutheran Church Front Doors
> Historic District Online Database at ruskinarc.com/galena

This work is made possible through the generous donations of individuals to specific projects and endowment funds managed by The Galena Foundation.

To find out how you can donate to or become a member of the foundation, visit the website at galenafoundation.org or contact the foundation at:

> The Galena Foundation
> PO Box 1
> Galena, Illinois 61036

In Memory of Alfred W. Mueller
09-10-1909 - 10-05-2004

Alfred "Alfie" Mueller was, and remains, a Galena treasure. Born in 1909, he was a part of Galena's heritage. His family came to Galena from Germany in 1850. They were working class people, the kind who built Galena. As a boy Alfie was conscientious and hard-working, traits that stayed with him his whole life. He began his career on Main street even before he graduated from high school, and lived in Galena his entire life.

But his story does not end there. Very early on, Alfie began to collect old photographs. Some were of people, some of streets, some of steamboats, but all telling the story of Galena. This passion continued until his death in 2004. But Alfie's passion still continues. His collection of over 10,000 images has become the single largest repository of Galena history.

Mr. Mueller was given an award in 1985 by the Illinois State Historical Society, and in 1989 former Galena mayor Frank Einsweiler declared May 21 to be "Alfred Mueller Day." On the same day, the library's *"Alfred Mueller Historical Collections Room"* was dedicated. The Studs Terkel Humanities Service Award was presented to him in 2000, and The Landmarks Preservation Council of Illinois honored him in 2004 with its prestigious Richard H. Driehaus award for community leadership.

A very humble man, Alfie simply wanted people to appreciate his town and its history. He was a fixture of the Galena community for 75 years. And while Alfie is now gone, his legacy continues, now and forever.

It is because of this man's passion and lifetime effort, that this book has become a reality. Over 90 percent of the archive photos in the book originated from his collection.

Table of Contents

Section	Title	Page
1	The Mound Builders and Their Descendents	1
2	Early Explorers of the Galena Region	11
3	The First Traders and Miners	15
4	The Town Is Established	31
5	Galena and the Black Hawk War of 1832	51
6	1832 -1839 — A Time of Growth	73
7	Galena's Golden Years	85
8	A Small Town's Impact on the Civil War	95
9	An Historical Time Capsule	103
	a. Business District	105
	b. Public Buildings	165
	c. Residences	207
	d. Churches	249
10	The Floods	278
11	Present Day Galena	289
	Credits and References	298
	Photo Credits	303
	Index	308

Acknowledgements

I am truly grateful for the assistance, cooperation and education provided to me by the Galena-Jo Daviess County Historical Society. Their archives had a huge impact on the development of this book. It is because of their enthusiasm and support that this book was made possible. In particular, I must emphasize the assistance of Ray Werner. Ray, thank you!

The Illinois Historic Preservation Agency was so kind in allowing me access to the Alfred Mueller Historical Photo Collection. With over 2,200 historic photos, this treasure was of unsurpassed importance in the development of this book. Terry Miller and Jamie Loso, thank you so much for your assistance and ongoing encouragement!

I wish to thank H. Scott Wolfe, Historical Librarian of the Galena Public Library, for his guidance and useful suggestions.

Thank goodness for my friends Karen Wildner and Cathy Domagalski. I truly appreciate your superb guidance and insightful editorial skills that added so much to the book.

Deborah Bertucci and the DeSoto House graciously provided me with lodging during my extended stays in Galena during the research and development of this book. Thank you so much for helping in this way. There is no other hotel in Galena that comes close to the historical significance of the DeSoto House. This was truly a blessing and a gift that I will not soon forget.

I truly appreciate the kindness and assistance of countless citizens of Galena who continued to guide me to buried historical treasures in the form of stories and photos. They certainly lived up to Galena's reputation of being the second friendliest city in the United States.

Last but by no means least, no words can be found to express the appreciation and gratitude that I have for the following individuals, businesses, and organizations that stepped up to sponsor the production of this book. Because of their open-handed generosity and appreciation of Galena's heritage and history, this book became a reality.

Amelia's Galena Ghost Tours	Galena's Kandy Kitchen	The Market House Restaurant
Baranski, Hammer, Moretta and Sheehy Associates	Ben Douglas Gay & Lene Graff	Charles & Katherine Marsden
Michael and Rachel Buckman	Grant Hill Motel	Libby Miller
City of Galena	Illinois Bank & Trust of Galena	Terry Miller
John and Marge Cooke	Susan McKeague Karnes	Ken and Ann Robb
DeSoto House	La Vie En Rose	Brian and Lisa Schoenrock, DDS
First Community Bank of Galena	LeFevre Inn & Resort	Jerry and Susan Schurmeier
Don and Carol Fouts	Jamie Loso	U.S. Historic Sites
Galena Brewing Company	Annie Lloyd Limited	Tom and Connie Wienen
Galena Candle Company	Lulu's Clothing and Gifts	Vinny Vanucchi's

Thank you!

Chapter 1
The Mound Builders And Their Descendents

Galena and the surrounding area of Illinois, located along the mighty Mississippi River, are undeniably among the most beautiful of landscapes to be found in the Midwest. The magnificent rolling hills, limestone cliffs and varying elevations located in and around Galena are attributed to the fact that this area was untouched by the glaciers that covered 85% of Illinois over the millenniums of time. In some areas of Northern Illinois, these glaciers reached a depth of 2,000 feet! The immensity and sheer weight of these glaciers moved the land they rode upon, leveling hills, filling valleys and leaving in their wake the resultant prairie land that is so prominent throughout Illinois and the surrounding Midwestern states.[1]

Undoubtedly, the beauty of the (Galena) area captivated the land's first residents just as it does us today.

The earliest inhabitants of this region were descendents of Asians that had crossed the Bering Land bridge that was located between present day Russia and Alaska. Discoveries of ancient animal bones in association with prehistoric tools on both sides of the Bering Strait show that Asian hunters followed herds of migrating caribou, mammoths and other animals across the land bridge and into North America. Over many generations, these Ice-Age nomads and their descendents, known as the Paleo Indians, followed the migrating animals through-

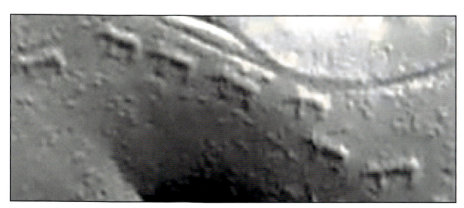

LIDAR (Light Detection and Ranging) image of the Marching Bear Mound Group, 2007. Effigy Mounds National Monument, Iowa

Courtesy of the Iowa Department of Natural Resources

out North America, traveling via corridors between the glaciers. Their food consisted of wild plants and large game including the great mammoth. Evidence shows that they were in Illinois from 10,000 B.C. to around 8,000 B.C. [2]

The Paleo-Indians were the ancestors of the Woodland Culture Indians. As early as 500 B.C., a Woodland subgroup called the Adena built earthen burial mounds in the upper Ohio River Valley. Following the disappearance of the Adenas from about A.D. 1 to A.D. 300, the Hopewell subgroup created hundreds of burial mounds and other geometric earthworks in a number of areas in the Eastern Woodlands.[3] They are noted for having developed maize agriculture, building villages and burial grounds, making pottery and also inventing the bow and arrow for hunting. The considerable time and effort they devoted to honoring and burying their dead indicates that their belief system was well defined.

After 500 A.D., late Woodland people, living at the convergence of Illinois, Wisconsin and Iowa, produced earthworks called effigy mounds in the shapes of animals. These mounds of earth were commonly shaped as birds, bears, deer, bison, turtles or panthers. There are some 284 locations in Illinois with Paleo-Indian artifacts.[4]

Although conical (cone shaped) mound building was predominate in Illinois, there are a number of sites that show that effigy mounds were also significant in this area.

More than a century ago, Professor T.H. Lewis wrote a paper titled: "Effigy Mounds in Northern Illinois," printed in the September 12, 1888 issue of *Science*. He stated:

"Mr. Lapham, in his well known work, 'Antiquities of Wisconsin' (1855), mentions mounds of the

The only known bear effigy mound in Illinois. Location - Keough Effigy Mounds, Galena, IL.
Photo Courtesy of Ronald Tigges, DigitalDubuque.com

The Thunderbird Effigy Mound in Casper Bluff Land & Water Reserve, Galena, IL. dates back to 1000 A.D. There are no other effigy mounds in the shape of a bird in Illinois. Native Americans believed the world was composed of three planes of existence. The upper world of air was considered the realm of the winged creatures, ruled by the thunderbirds. "Thunderbirds would carry the thoughts and prayers of the people to the gods, in the upper world. They also were thought to control the rain and the weather, so they were worshiped." The wingspan of this Thunderbird effigy mound measures 112 feet across. [12]

Photo Courtesy of Ronald Tigges, DigitalDubuque.com

'turtle' form on Rock River as far south as Rockford, and other animal forms on Apple River in Illinois, a few miles south of the State Line of Wisconsin."

"There was an effigy mound located two miles south of the village of Hanover in Jo Daviess County and on the east side of Apple River. The effigy's length... is 216 feet, and the average height of the body is 5 feet 6 inches. The body and head are on nearly level ground, while the legs run down the slope... Besides the animal, there are in the same group twenty three round mounds and ten embankments, as well as four round mounds..." (This is located 14 miles south of Galena).

The Keough Effigy Mounds, located just west of Galena, includes early lead mine diggings and Native American mounds, including the prize feature of the site, the only intact bear effigy mound in the State of Illinois.

The Casper Bluff effigy mounds, located near Galena, feature the majority of the Aiken mound group. This includes 51 burial mounds, with one of the highlights being the only intact bird effigy in Illinois.

Mound building would become an obsession of people throughout eastern North America for centuries to come. When Galena and the surrounding area was in its infancy, these ancient mounds still dotted the landscape. The volume titled "The History of Jo Daviess County" (1878), stated:

"On the top of the high bluffs that skirt the east bank of the Mississippi, about two and a half miles from Galena, are a number of these silent monuments of a pre-historic age. The spot is one of surpassing beauty. Standing there, the tourist has a view of a portion of three states; Illinois, Iowa and Wisconsin. A hundred feet below him, at the foot of the perpendicular cliffs, the trains of the Illinois Central Railroad thunder around the curve; the Portage is in full view, and the "Father of Waters," with its numerous bayous and islands stretches a grand panorama for miles above and below him."

"Here, probably thousands of years ago, a race of men now extinct, and unknown even in the traditions of the Indians who inhabited this region for centuries before the discovery of America by Columbus, built these strangely wonderful and enigmatical mounds. At this point these mounds are circular and conical in form. The largest one is at least forty feet in diameter at the base, and at least fifteen feet high now, after it has been beaten by the storms of many centuries. On its top stands the large stump of an oak tree that was cut down about fifty years ago, and its annular rings indicate a growth of at least 200 years. Whatever may have been the character of these mounds in other localities, these could not have been the dwelling places of their builders.[5]

The mounds on the bluff were investigated and opened in the mid 1870's by a number of the early residents of Galena, including Louis A. Rowley, W. M. Snyder and John Dowling.

These gentlemen had a deep interest in these prehistoric structures and had carefully investigated them. During their excavations, they unearthed ancient skeletons indicating a race of gigantic stature. They were buried in a sitting posture around the sides of the pit, with legs extending towards the centre. Various layers were placed over the skeletons, including soil, hard baked clay or cement, as well as layers of ashes mixed with burnt shells and bones, demonstrating an elaborate burial process. On top of these layers, a huge mound of earth was piled up over the pit, thus finishing the mound.[6]

Example of Conical Mounds.
Mound City, Chillicothe, Ohio

Many other artifacts and treasures were found buried within these earthen mounds including axes, arrows and spear-heads; a finely finished pear-shaped implement of stone, probably used for skinning animals; large pearls perforated to be strung; copper chisels and wedges; and great numbers of large bear teeth. These teeth were pierced with holes like the pearls. They also found ornaments made of copper mingled with silver, indicating that the metal came from the Lake Superior region, and copper implements somewhat resembling needles. Lastly, and most important as indicating some civilization and knowledge of arts, a piece of urn shaped pottery was found, round on the bottom and ornamented. [6]

Over time, the Eastern Woodland Culture Indians came to include the Illinois, Iroquois, Shawnee and a number of Algonquian speaking peoples including the Sauk and the Fox (Meskwaki). The Sauk and Fox Indians were prominent in the upper Mississippi region where Iowa, Wisconsin and Illinois converge. They united as one tribe in 1734.

The Sauk and Fox people lived in bark houses in small villages. One of the largest Indian villages in North America was Saukenuk, located between the Rock and Mississippi rivers in Illinois. In the early 1800's, approximately 4,000 Sauk and Fox people were living in Saukenuk.[7]

Saukenuk was located 60 miles south of Galena. Today, the Black Hawk State Historic Site located in Rock Island, Illinois sits adjacent to the original location of Saukenuk.

Saukenuk was laid out in an organized grid fashion. A main avenue ran north and south through the middle of town and was crossed by side streets going east and west. One hundred long houses faced the street. The town was divided into neighborhoods, one for each of the twelve clans. [8]

Sauk and Fox Indian Wigwam

Before the white man came and laid claim to their land, the Indians living in Saukenuk had a happy and peaceful life. It was almost like living in a paradise, where every want was satisfied. Food was plentiful and the surroundings were beautiful. The site was situated on the north side of the Rock River, at the foot of its rapids.

The Sauk and Fox cultivated hundreds of acres of land. Their cornfields extended up along the Mississippi for two miles. They also planted beans, pumpkins and squashes. The rapids of the Rock River furnished them with an abundance of excellent fish. Hunger was never an issue in Saukenuk.

The uncultivated land that was around Saukenuk was covered with blue grass. This was excellent pasture for their horses.

Sauk Indian Leader and Warrior
Black Hawk
Born -1767 Died-1838

Fresh springs flowed from the bluffs close to their village providing a constant supply of cool, clean water.

In general, the natives were deer-hunters and farmers. The men made bows and arrows, stone knives and war clubs. The women tended the garden plots where beans, corn, pumpkin, squash and tobacco were cultivated. Women also harvested these crops and prepared the food. Black pottery or wood and bark vessels were used for cooking. They dried berries, corn, fish, meat and squash for the winter. The diet of deer meat was also supplemented by other game and fish.

Water provided a means of transportation for the tribes. Birch bark canoes were fashioned by the northern tribes while the southeastern tribes dug out canoes from tree trunks. On land, the natives traveled on foot and bore their cargo on their backs, having no pack animals. Dogs were their sole domesticated animals.[10]

The Sauk and Fox people built two types of dwelling. Bark-covered dome-shaped wigwams were used during the winter, while out on the winter hunt, and larger cabin style long houses were built in Saukenuk for use in the summer.

Saukenuk was the largest city of the Sauk and Fox Indians, but there were numerous other settlements up and down the Mississippi, including the region up north where the Fever and the Mississippi rivers meet. These were the Indians that the early traders and miners met when they came to the Fever River.

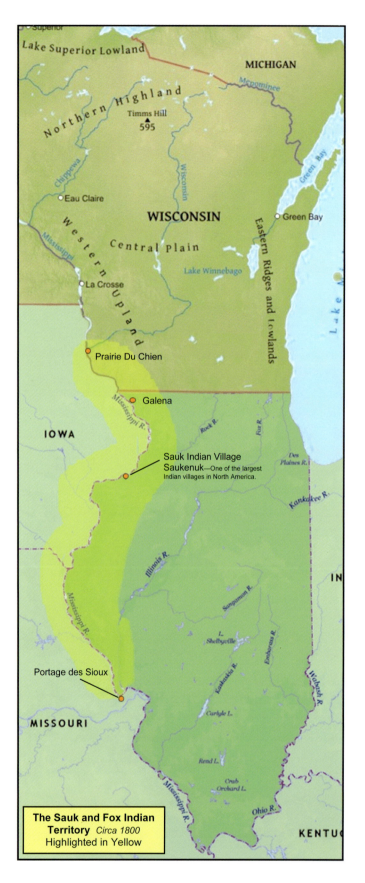

"*The History of Jo Daviess County,*" (1878), provides a number of observations that give us a good idea of how populous the Sauk and Fox Indians were in the region that became Galena.

"*The river bottoms, ravines and hillsides were thickly dotted with the wigwams of the Sacs and Foxes, who numbered at least 2,000 in this immediate vicinity.*"[10]

"*Prior to 1823, "The Point" (An early name for what would become the town of Galena) could hardly be called more than an Indian trading post. The Sacs (Sauk) and Foxes were in possession of the whole country, and had a large and populous village on the present site of the city.*"[11]

The Black Hawk State Historic Site located in Rock Island, Illinois, preserves the memories and the legacy of the Sauk Indians that called this area home until 1831.

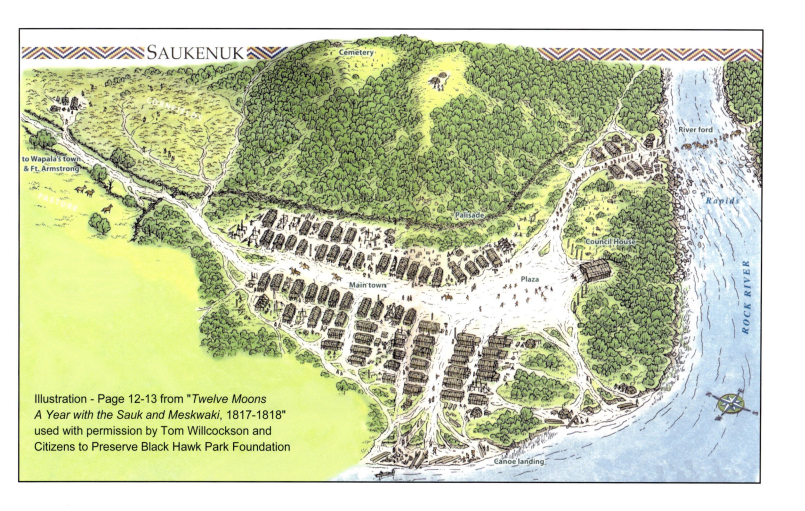

Illustration - Page 12-13 from "*Twelve Moons A Year with the Sauk and Meskwaki, 1817-1818*" used with permission by Tom Willcockson and Citizens to Preserve Black Hawk Park Foundation

Here are a number of exhibits in the Hauberg Indian Museum Watch Tower Lodge at the Black Hawk State Historic Site:

Summer Long House

The Sauk and the Meskwaki (or Fox) lived in long houses in the summer. They were sided with elm bark. Most houses measured 60 feet long by 30 feet wide. Several related families with as many as 50 people shared each house. Benches were built down the long sides and covered with reed mats and animal skins for comfort. People sat on the benches during the day and slept on them at night. Personal items were stored above and below the benches.

Winter House

During the winter months, the Sauk and the Meskwaki went to their hunting grounds and built small, 20 foot diameter and 12 foot high single family homes called *wickiups*. They were covered with many layers of cattail mats. A fire pit was dug in the center of the house, and a bed of hot coals kept the wickiups warm, even on the coldest days. Reed mats and buffalo robes were laid on the ground to provide comfort for sleeping and a buffalo robe covered the doorway.

Above: The Sauk and Meskwaki moved away from their towns in early fall and were gone all winter. The tribes divided into small bands and spread out over a wide area to secure food and fuel resources. Each band lived together in a winter camp made up of 30 or more winter houses. The men spent the winter hunting animals whose pelts were traded for goods. The women skinned the animals and dried the meat.

Below: In late February, the women, children, and elderly moved from the winter camp to their sugar maple groves. Sap from the trees was boiled down to make sugar. Sometimes the hot liquid was made into candy—a special treat for the children. The maple sugar was used all year to flavor meats and vegetables. When sugaring season was over, the people moved back to the summer towns and the cycle of the seasons started over.

Sauk Indian family photographed by Frank Rinehart (1861-1928)

Chapter 2

The Early Explorers of the Galena Region

The Galena territory remained the sole domain of the Native American Indians residing in this land, now for centuries. As time went on and exploration developed, Europeans began to venture into the North American continent.

Hernando de Soto (c.1496-1542) was a Spanish explorer who led the first known expedition into the territory of the United States and was the first to document the discovery of the mighty Mississippi River. He made this discovery in April of 1541. But his real goal was to find gold and precious gems. By the spring of 1542, de Soto had grown wear and exhausted, his search for treasure still in vain. He fell victim to disease, and died on the 21st day of May in 1542.[1,2]

Hernando de Soto

De Soto's followers, reduced by fatigue and disease to less than three hundred men, wandered about the country for nearly a year in vain, endeavoring to rescue themselves by land. They eventually constructed seven small vessels and descended the Mississippi river, hoping that it would lead them to the sea. In July, their hopes were rewarded. They came to the sea (Gulf of Mexico), and by September, reached the island of Cuba. They were the first to see the great outlet of the Mississippi, but because of the fact that they were so weary and discouraged, made no attempt to claim the country, and hardly had an intelligent idea of what they had passed through.[3]

The great river of the West had been discovered by de Soto, three quarters of a century before the French founded Quebec in 1608, but the Spanish left the country a wilderness, without any further exploration or settlement within its borders.

In 1673 the Mississippi was re-discovered by the agents of the French Canadian government, Joliet and Marquette.

Both explorers were from very different backgrounds. Father Jacques Marquette was born in Laon, France, in 1637, to a family steeped in military and civic service. He entered the Society of Jesus and studied at various Jesuit colleges in France before arriving in Canada in 1666. In Canada, Marquette became fluent in many American Indian languages and was given the task of introducing Christianity to the tribes of the Great Lakes region. He was drawn into a proposition given to his close friend Louis Joliet by the French governor, Louis de Baude Frontenac, to go on a voyage of discovery along the Mississippi River.

Louis Joliet was born in Quebec in 1645, the son of a wagon maker, and educated at the Jesuit school there. Although his parents wanted him to become a priest, Joliet wanted a life of adventure. He chose to leave the seminary after a short time to join a party of explorers heading west. Their intent was to find a more direct route from Montreal to the "Country of the Upper Lakes" and to search for copper along the shores of Lake Superior. This trip convinced Joliet to become a fur trader, a profession which would allow him a life of adventure and also provided a fairly good living.

Joliet, Marquette, and five other Frenchmen set out in May of 1673. They paddled across Lake Michigan to present-day Green Bay, Wisconsin, then up the Fox River to what is now Portage, Wisconsin. From there, they carried their canoes across land to the Wisconsin River. At this point, two Indian guides deserted them for fear of what lay ahead. They and their party pushed on alone. They paddled down the Wisconsin River until, on June 17th, they came to the broad and majestic Mississippi. They traveled down the Mississippi, passing by the entrance of the Fever River (later renamed the Galena River).

Along their journey, they came upon some Illinois Indians. During this meeting, the chief of the Illinois gave them a calumet (peace pipe).

Marquette and Joliet led their party down the Mississippi to the mouth of the Arkansas River. Strange Indians with guns suddenly surrounded them there. Only the sight of the calumet kept these Indians from attacking. Some of them became friendly enough to tell Marquette that their guns came from white explorers who were about 10 days journey farther south. These could only be Spaniards, and it would have been dangerous to go on, so the French explorers ended their trip down the Mississippi and returned to Canada by way of the Illinois River.

They passed the present site of Chicago on this part of the trip and returned to Green Bay in late September. Their four-month journey had carried them more than 2,500 miles.

The Marquette-Joliet expedition proved that the Mississippi River flowed into the Gulf of Mexico. They were probably the first white men to enter what is now Illinois.

An avenue of trade up and down the Mississippi was now opened up. Due to the efforts of French traders and missionaries, the French colonists were establishing themselves along the Mississippi with Cahokia and Kaskaskia being the earliest settlements.

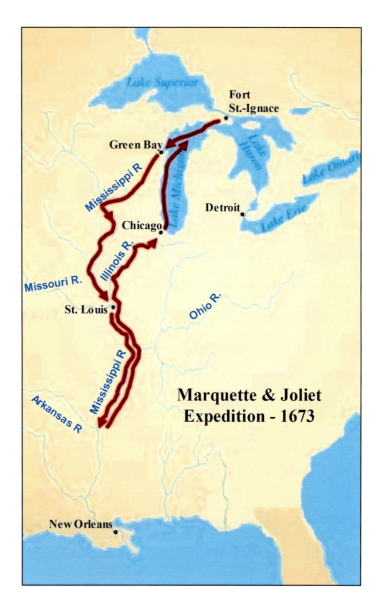

Marquette & Joliet Expedition - 1673

In 1682 the area known today as Illinois had become the possession of the French Crown, a dependency of Canada, and a part of Louisiana. Then, in 1765, the English flag was run up at the old French Fort de Chartres and Illinois was counted among the treasures of Great Britain. [4]

In 1779 it was taken from the English by Col. George Rogers Clark and "Illinois" then became a part of Virginia. It was soon known as Illinois County. In 1784, Virginia ceded all this territory to the general government, "to be cut into States, to be republican in form", with "the same right of sovereignty, freedom, and independence as the other States." [5]

The population was 12,282 in the Illinois territory in A.D. 1800. At this point in time, the only inhabitants of the northwest section of Illinois were the native American Indians. In 1804, the Sauk and Foxes, then a powerful tribe, signed a treaty in St. Louis with Gen. Harrison, the Governor of the Territory of Indiana, that ceded to the United States all their lands lying east of the Mississippi. However, Black Hawk and other chiefs who were not present at St. Louis, refused to be bound by this treaty. [6]

Based upon the treaty of 1804, all the territory north of the line drawn west from the southern extremity of Lake Michigan to the Mississippi was still in the undisputed possession of the native tribes when the State was admitted in 1818. This did not include a tract of land five leagues square (33.7 sq. miles) on the Mississippi, of which Fever River was about the centre. The United States Government had reserved this land allegedly for a military post, but in reality, it was to control the lead mines. The Government had knowledge of the existence of lead mines here, but their exact location was not known. It was thought that the entire mine region would be included within the limits of the land excluded from the Indians.

The Government intended to own and hold exclusive control of these mines. [7]

The native tribes continued to lose their land holdings, and their reservations continued to shrink. In January 1818, the Territorial Legislature of Illinois assembled at Kaskaskia and petitioned Congress for the admission of the territory as a sovereign state with a population of 40,000.

The petition was sent to Nathaniel Pope, the territorial delegate. He presented the petition to the appropriate committee and they instructed him to prepare the proposal in accordance with their wishes and requirements. The bill, as drawn in accordance with these instructions, did not embrace the present area of Illinois because it took into consideration the previously mentioned treaty. So Pope made some amendments before proposing this bill to the committee.

It was generally understood that the line established in the treaty of 1804, namely, the line drawn through the southern part of Lake Michigan, west to the Mississippi, was to be the northern boundary of the new state. But this, if adopted, would have left the "port of Chicago" (Chicago was not yet a town) in the Territory of Michigan, as well as the fourteen counties now in northern Illinois. Pope was convinced that Congress had the power and could rightfully extend the border to any location they desired. So Pope extended the northern boundary to where it is today, and used as his argument that this would provide the new State of Illinois with a good harbor on Lake Michigan. He also argued that this would generate additional funds for education and roads, based upon the sale of the additional lands. These amendments were adopted without serious opposition, and Illinois was declared an independent state. [8]

The change of the northern boundary line did not meet with the unqualified approval of the people living in the northwestern part of the new state. For many years the northern boundary of the state was not definitely known. The settlers in the northern tier of counties did not know whether they were in the state of Illinois or Michigan Territory.

Some nine years after the admission of the state, on October 27, 1827, Dr. Horatio Newhall, who had then recently arrived at the Fever River Settlement, wrote to his brother as follows: "*It is uncertain whether I am in the boundary of Illinois or Michigan, but direct your letters to Fever River, and they will come safely.*"[9]

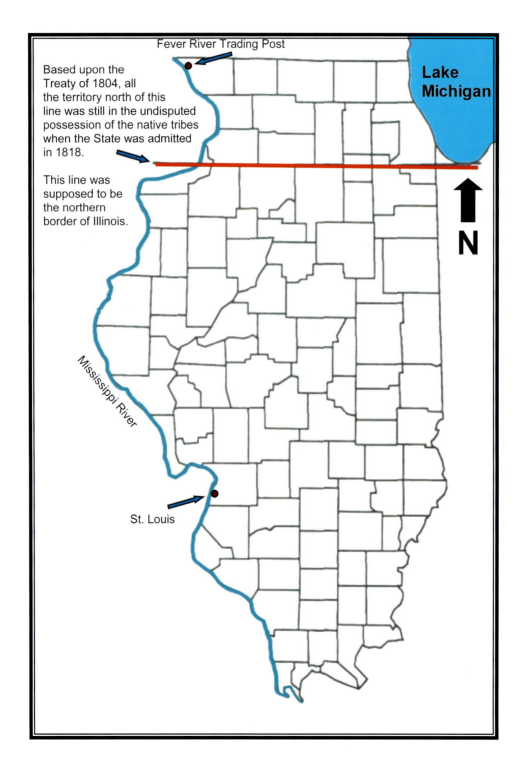

Chapter 3

The First Traders and Miners

The Catalyst of the Future

Jo Daviess County was organized on February 17, 1827, with Galena being set up as the county seat. [1]

"The earliest history and first activities of Jo Daviess County are enshrouded in almost impenetrable obscurity." However, there are records and research that were compiled in the 1870's that we, today, can glean from, that bring us much closer to the first occupation of this area. [2]

The first explorer of this region was Pierre-Charles Le Sueur, a French trader, who, on the 25th of August, 1700, while on an expedition to the Sioux on St. Peter's River (renamed the Minnesota River in 1852), discovered a small river entering the Mississippi on the right side, which he named "The River of the Mines." He describes it as "a small river running from the north, but it turns to the northeast", and he further says, "that a few miles up this river is a lead mine."

His statement leaves no doubt that he was unquestionably the first white man to ever step onto the banks of the Fever River, and visit the mines in and around what would become Galena a century later.[3]

There is also the recorded testimony of Captain Daniel S. Harris of Galena. At the time, he was the oldest surviving steamboat captain on the Mississippi and the oldest known survivor of the immigration to Galena that occurred in 1823. Harris stated:

"About 1811, George E. Jackson, a Missouri miner, had a rude log furnace and smelted lead on an island then existing on the Mississippi River, located on the east side of the main channel, a short distance below Dunleith, nearly opposite the mouth of Catfish Creek. This was the first smelting known to have been done by white men within the limits of Jo Daviess County."

Harris also stated that *"Jackson built a flat boat to float his lead to St. Louis, and had much trouble with the Indians on his way down the river."* *"He was joined,"* said Capt. Harris, *"probably about 1812 or '13, by John S. Miller, but soon after, the island was abandoned. Jackson went to Missouri, and Miller went down the river and built the first cabin and blacksmith shop on the present site of Hannibal, Mo."* [4]

The first permanent settlement by the whites in this (Jo Daviess) county, and, in fact, in all Northwestern Illinois of which any record or reliable knowledge now remains, existed about 1820 on the banks of the Fever River, now known as the Galena River. There are a number of ideas regarding how this river was named.

One tradition states that the river took its name from a Frenchman named La Fevre. Supposedly he was the first man to visit this locality, but there is no evidence to confirm this.

The most commonly accepted basis for the name comes from the Indian name for the river, *Mah-cau-bee*, which translated, means "fever," or, more literally, "fever that blisters," the Indian term for small pox.

They gave it this name, it is said, because in the early history of this county, when the extreme western frontier of the white settlements were many hundreds of miles eastward, some of the warriors from the populous Indian villages existing on the present site of Galena and on the banks of a small creek a little way southward, went to the assistance of their eastern brothers. On their return, they brought with them the loathsome disease for which they had no other name than Mah-cau-bee, "the fever that blisters." The larger river they called "*Moshuck Macaubee Sepo*," Big Small Pox River, and the smaller, "*Cosh-a-neush Macaubee Sepo*," Little Small Pox River. Hundreds of the natives died and the Indians named both streams Mah-cau-bee. The smaller one is still called Small Pox Creek to this day (at time of writing—2015), but the larger was changed by the white settlers to the rather more pleasant name of Fever, and the little frontier hamlet was known as the "Fever River Settlement," or La Pointe, until 1826-7 when the name was changed to Galena. [5]

Back in 1835, Wm. H. Snyder, a resident of Galena, spent some time with Col. George Davenport. Snyder had recently opened one of the ancient mounds on the bluff near the Portage, just south of Galena, and found an immense quantity of human bones. Mentioning this find to the Colonel, Davenport said that "when the Indians living on the streams now called Fever River and Smallpox Creek had come down with the small pox and died in large numbers, the survivors fled." Later, in about 1816, while he (Davenport) lived at the portage, they returned, gathered up the remains of the victims, and buried them in the mound Snyder had opened. From that time on, the Indians called both streams "Macaubee," hence the name Fever. (Smallpox Creek is located 3 miles south of Galena).[6]

This information helps to fill in some of the gaps regarding the infancy of Galena and the area immediately surrounding it. Davenport was living here at the portage in 1816. Let's clarify what and where the portage was. The Portage* was a narrow neck of land between the Fever (Galena) River and the Mississippi, so named because the Indians and traders were accustomed to transporting their canoes and goods across the portage. They did so to avoid the long journey down to the mouth of the Fever River, an additional distance of about two and one half miles. The distance between the Mississippi and the Fever River at the Portage was only a few rods across. Then, to make things even easier, in 1834, a channel was plowed across this neck of land at its narrowest point, thus making the Portage a navigable route of the Fever (Galena) River directly into the Mississippi.[7] This was a very convenient location for a trading post.

When "*The History of Jo Daviess County*" was being researched in preparation for its 1878 printing, some old papers were kindly placed at the disposal of the historians working on the book by William O. Gear (Son of Hezekiah H. Gear, one of Galena's earliest settlers). Included in these papers were a series of articles titled, the "*Upper Mississippi Lead Mines*," which were published in the *Galena Sentinel*, about 1843: [8]

* See footnote and photo on next page

The First Traders and Miners

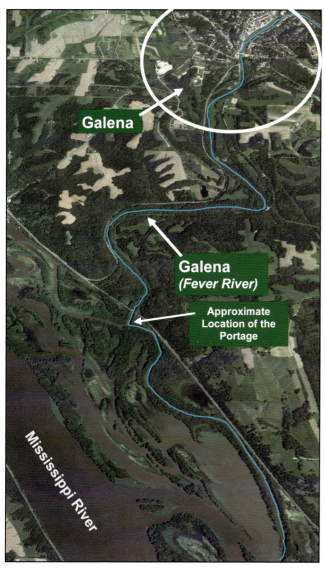

Location of the Portage

attracted the attention of traders, who came here to trade with them.

At the time, this entire region was a wilderness, occupied only by a few fur traders and roving tribes of Indians. The nearest settlements to the north were

> **"Upper Mississippi Lead Mines"**
>
> In the Fall of the year 1819, our old friend, Capt. David G. Bates, started from St. Louis, with a French crew, for Fever Riviere Upper Mississippi land mines. His vessel was a keel, the only way of conveyance then of heavy burthens on the Upper Mississippi, and the boatmen, in those days, were some of them, 'half horse and half alligator.' But the merry French, after arriving off Pilot Knob, commenced hunting for Fever River. Alter a search of three days, they found the mouth, and, on the 13th of November, after pushing through the high grass and rice lakes, they arrived safe at where Galena now stands, where they were greeted by some of the natives, from the tall grass, as well as by our old acquaintances, J. B. (W.) Shull and A. P. Vanmatre, who had taken to themselves wives from the daughters of the land, and were traders for their brethren. F⸺
> whi⸺
> territ⸺
> nativ⸺ and Dr. Muir. Capt. Bates, after disposing of, or leaving his cargo in exchange for lead, fur, etc., returned to St. Louis for another cargo."

**The *Galena Sentinel*
June 1, 1843**

This detailed account provides a picture of what this area was like prior to the founding of Galena. The area was extensively inhabited by the Indians. It was recognized, by both the Indians and the adventurous traders of the time, to be an excellent location for trade. There were a large number of Indians encamped or living here at that time, whose women and old men were engaged in raising lead from the Buck Lead, and the fame of their rude and, for them, extensive mining operations must have naturally

---

* Location of the Portage -Three and one-half miles below La Pointe (The French name for the settlement that would become Galena), between the Fever River and the Mississippi, *(The History of Jo Daviess County—(1878) Page 235)*

Dubuque's mines and Prairie Du Chien. On the east, the nearest village was Chicago, "consisting of a few rude cabins inhabited by half-breeds." [9] At Fort Clark (now Peoria), to the south, were a few pioneers, and thence, a long interval to the white settlements near Vandalia.

The relations between the Indians and the white men were not always peaceable. According to the early history of the Galena Mines by Mr. Seymour:

"The Sacs and Foxes, were noted as warlike and dangerous tribes, and had already killed several traders who had attempted to traffic among them." The paper adds: *"It was a current report among the settlers at Prairie du Chien, that a trader was murdered in 1813, at the mouth of the Sinsinawa River. His wife, a squaw, had warned him to leave the country, as the Indians meditated taking his life. Disregarding her friendly warnings, he remained, and was murdered the same night."* [10]

In 1819, when the Buck Lead* was being worked by the Indians, Mr. Jesse W. Shull was trading at Dubuque's mines (now Dubuque) for a company at Prairie du Chien. That company requested him to go to Fever River and trade with the Indians. However, he declared that it was unsafe, that the Sacs and Foxes had already murdered several traders and declined to go unless he could have the protection of the United States troops. Colonel Johnson, of the United States Army, summoned the leaders of the Sauk and Fox nations for a meeting at Prairie du Chien. When the chiefs had assembled, he informed them that the goods that Shull was about to bring were sent from their Father, the President of the United States (it was not considered a sin to lie to the Indians even then), and told them they must not molest Shull in his business.

Having received assurances of protection from the government officers and from the Indians, "Mr. Shull came to Fever River late in the summer of 1819 and erected a trading house near the river, near what would later become Perry Street." [11]

The account of Jesse Shull came from a personal interview that he gave in 1848. He was living in Green County, Wisconsin at the time. He added: "that he and Dr. Samuel C. Muir were the first white settlers on Fever River in 1819," and "during that year, Dr. Muir commenced trading here with goods furnished by the late Colonel Davenport of Rock Island." Shull also stated that: "later in the same year, Francois Bouthillier came and occupied a shanty at the bend, on the east side of Fever River, below the present limits of the City of Galena." These early traders used landmarks to find their way through the wilderness and this early frontier. The river was the major source of transportation. The landmark Bouthillier and others would look for to navigate into the Fever River off the Mississippi was known as "Pilot Knob."** This mound could be seen for miles, because of its height.

Francois Bouthillier was a French trader known at Prairie du Chien (located 60 miles north at the mouth of the Wisconsin river on the Mississippi). It is said that as early as 1812, he acted as interpreter and guide for the British troops. He undoubtedly knew of the Fever River trading point, and may have frequently visited it where he "occupied a shanty," as probably others had, prior to 1819.

---

* In 1819 the historic diggings, known for more than half a century as the Buck Lead, were being worked by the Indians. This lead took its name from "the Buck" - a Sauk or Fox chief who was encamped with his band on Fever River in 1819, and worked it. [8]

**Pilot Knob is a natural mound rising 978 feet above sea level and is located 3.4 miles south of the city of Galena, and about two miles from the Mississippi River. It was a prominent landmark to tourists and river men passing up and down the Mississippi ever since the river was first navigated. Towering above the surrounding high bluffs, it reaches an altitude of more than 400 feet above the surrounding landscape. —*History of Jo Daviess County, 1878, - Pg 818*

Aerial view of Pilot Knob Hill rising 978 feet above sea level

Photo taken from Horseshoe Mound in Galena highlighting Pilot Knob 2.25 miles away.

Importance of Lead

Lead has been in use since ancient times. Its low melting point permitted it to be used on a wide scale throughout human history. A lead statue discovered in Turkey has been dated to around 6500 BC. The Romans had indoor plumbing that was made from sheets of lead rolled into pipe. *Plumbum*, the Latin word for lead, is also the origin of the word plumber.[12]

Lead was in wide use in the United States during the 19th century. There were many types of items that were constructed of this metal. These included ammunition, burial vault liners, ceramic glazes, leaded glass and crystal, paints or other protective coatings, pewter, water lines and pipes, and more.

Because of the lead mines, the region in and around Galena was considered to be very important to the United States government, as well as the Indians, traders, and miners in the region.

The government was already aware of the fact that there were lead mines in and around the Mississippi (near where Galena would later develop) as early as 1803.

In 1807 Congress enacted that these mines could not be owned by individuals, but were to remain under the exclusive control of the government. Mining leases of three to five years were issued to various individuals to work them, but only as tenants of the United States.

In 1819 the historic diggings known for more than half a century as the Buck Lead, were being worked by the Indians, with most of the work being done by the squaws. It was the largest body of mineral then ever discovered on Fever River, and an immense amount of "galena" ore was taken out by the natives and sold to the traders before it was ever mined by white men. One estimate is that several million pounds had been taken from the "Buck Lead Diggings" by the Indians; more in fact, than was taken by white miners afterwards.

Galena Ore *

The First Miners of Note

Based upon the available records, two French traders named Stephen D'bois and Julien Dubuque were the first to come to this area with the intent to mine in 1788. Although they came to this territory together, they separated upon their arrival. D'bois established an Indian trading post on the Illinois side and Dubuque on the Iowa side of the Mississippi. Aside from the fact that D'bois is credited with being the first white man to build a cabin in what became Jo Daviess County, little more is known about him. His cabin was constructed about two miles east of Dunleith Township. [15]

Julien Dubuque

Julien Dubuque was born of Norman parents on January 10, 1762, in a small village on the south bank of the St. Lawrence, about 60 miles above Quebec. In 1788, Dubuque was a 26-year-old roaming adventurer looking for a permanent settlement. His opportunity came on the 22d day of September of that year. At a council of chiefs and braves of the Fox Indians, held in Prairie du Chien, he obtained from the Indians a grant which transformed the adventurer into a miner and trader.

Translated from French, it appears that the Foxes agreed to "…permit Mr. Julien Dubuque, called by them 'Little Night' [La Petite Nuit], to work at the mine [near Kettle Chief's village a short distance south of the present city of Dubuque] as long as he shall please…". Prior to the execution of this contract, Dubuque and his followers had established themselves at Little Fox Village and made a study of the crude mining in process there. Discovering that the river bluffs in the vicinity of Catfish Creek were rich in "Galena" or lead ore, he proceeded to acquire an influence over the natives. He made numerous presents, learned their language and adapted himself to their ways of living,

> …The traders who came amongst us (the Fox Indians) supplied us with blankets, powder, flour, and for which we gave furs, peltries, and mineral in exchange. The mineral was raised by our women and children from three of four good leads, which we had opened; this they put into sacks that would contain from 50 to 100 lbs. and carried to traders homes, and if we failed to procure a sufficiency from this source to supply wants, our young men went hunting…

The Galena Advertiser
Sept. 14, 1829

---

* Galena—The name of a common heavy mineral, lead sulfide, PbS, occurring in lead-gray crystals, usually cubes, and cleavable masses: the principal ore of lead.

flattering their vanity. He is said to have resorted to tricks of necromancy, possessing supernatural powers and supposedly having the ability to communicate with the dead, especially in order to predict the future. [16]

According to one story, there was an incident when the Indians refused to consent to one of Dubuque's demands. He threatened to set Catfish Creek on fire and leave their village high and dry. They still denied him; so one night his associates emptied a barrel of oil—or turpentine—on the water above the bend, and when it had floated down to the village, Dubuque set fire to it. In a few moments the entire creek was apparently in a blaze. The terrified Indians made haste to grant all that Dubuque had asked—and supposedly by the exercise of his will, the fire went out!

Dubuque cleared the land, built a spacious log house, opened new mines and extended the old. He erected a horse-mill and a smelting furnace—all in the vicinity of what is now known as Dubuque Bluff, where the pioneer's remains lie. The actual mining that Dubuque controlled was chiefly done by squaws and old men. The braves were above work, but not averse to profiting by the labor of others. Dubuque's white followers, now grown from two to ten, served as

**Julien Dubuque Monument—Erected in 1897 over the grave of Julien Dubuque.
Located on the bluff above Catfish Creek.**

overseers, smelters and river-men. The mining was primitive. No shafts were sunk. Drifts were run into the hills and the mineral was carried out in baskets and deposited in the smelting furnace. No gunpowder was used. The pick and crowbar, hoe and shovel, were employed instead of the engine and the complicated and costly machinery of modern mining.

In time, Dubuque obtained complete control of all the lead mines on both sides of the river. Dubuque worked at the Cave Diggings as early as 1805. These were located just a few miles north of Galena in what would become Vinegar Hill Township. He "built and operated furnaces, conducted extensive prospecting parties and controlled the boats which carried the product down the river to market. In gaining absolute supremacy over the lead industry, he displayed remarkable talent."

Dubuque made two river trips to St. Louis every year, exchanging his lead for goods for his Indian trade. The traders and people of St. Louis received the well known trader with much consideration, and his biannual visits were special events in the little frontier city. [17]

Dubuque apparently died as a result of pneumonia on March 24, 1810, at the age of forty eight. The Indians, whose confidence Dubuque had managed to retain to the last, were filled with sadness when they learned of his death. Though he used chicanery to gain title to their lands, his shrewdness, friendliness and his occasional resort to the apparently supernatural, enabled him to retain to the last, his powerful hold upon their respect and admiration. He left no heirs to inherit his estate.

The Foxes buried Dubuque with funereal honors bestowed upon a chief. Their chiefs vied with one another for the honor of carrying his body to the grave. They joined in chants and their orators bemoaned their loss and sounded his praises. For many years afterward, the Indians would visit his grave and make contributions of stones to the cairn erected over his remains.[1]

His grave was covered with a wooden and stone shelter, complete with a gable roof and open window through which Native Americans believed the soul of the departed could leave. At the apex was a wooden cross made by white friends. The stone building was still intact in 1845. [18]

Colonel James Johnson

In November 1821, the jurisdiction of the lead mines was transferred from the General Land Office to the War Department. This was the catalyst that would transform the Fever River district from a mere trading post to what it would shortly become, the booming city of Galena.

In 1822 the first mining lease was granted to two parties, James Johnson and Thomas C. Carneil. Four additional leases were provided to different parties that same year. Nine leases were granted in 1823.

James Johnson came from Kentucky and was a brother of Colonel R. M. Johnson, of historic renown as the slayer of Tecumseh.[19]

Johnson came with a company of 100 men for the purpose of mining. Up until this point, the only white men that had come to Fever River were traders.[20]

Johnson also built a furnace for smelting the ore that he mined. The *"History of Jo Daviess County"* stated that this "smelter" was built "very nearly on the present site of H. F. McCloskey's store on the levee on the west side of Main Street, directly

Slavery in the Mines

It is noteworthy that negro slaves were working here in Galena and working in the lead mines in the early 1800's. Many of the early miners were from slave-holding states and brought their slaves with them.

When Captain Harris arrived in 1823, there were between 100 to 150 slaves here. Under the ordinance of 1787, slavery was forever prohibited in the Northwest Territory, but Illinois sought to evade this organic law by the enactment of statutes by which these slaves could be held as "indentured" or "registered servants." These statutes were known as the Black Laws. As late as March 10, 1829, the commissioners of Jo Daviess County ordered a tax of one half per cent to be levied and collected on "town lots, slaves, indentured or registered servants" etc. [22]

As of 1887 there was still living in Galena, "a venerable old colored man," Swanzy Adams. Born a slave in Virginia in April 1796, he moved to Kentucky and in April 1827, to Fever River as the slave of James A. Duncan." His master "hired him" to Captain Comstock, for whom he worked as a miner. He subsequently bought himself (paid for his freedom) for $1,500 (although he quaintly stated: *good boys like me could be bought in Kentucky for $350*). He discovered a lead of lead that paid his debt, but he was compelled to serve five years longer as a slave and was once kidnapped and taken to St. Louis. "Old Swanzy," as he was familiarly called, was the sole survivor of the slaves held under the Black Laws of Illinois. Eventually Swanzy secured a comfortable home and competence against want in his declining years (Note news article and footnote on page 24).

As the miners made their way to Galena and the lead mines, so did the traders.

> . . . In the spring of 1822, Col. James Johnson, of Kentucky, a brother of Col. Richard M. Johnson, of Tecumseh notoriety, with a company of 100 men, came here for the purpose of mining. . . No white man had been here except traders, and if they would mine peaceably, they must make new treaties with those Indians who were mining here. At this time the were mining in what is now termed the Buck and Doe range (north of the city), so called for the Indian chief and his wife who discovered it. We might here state that it is said by some, that Doe, the wife of the chief, was out on the side hill digging roots and accidently found some "float" mineral, which, of course, set them all to digging. A great deal of mineral was obtained by them, and Johnson made a purchase of these diggings by paying several hogsheads of tobacco, a few barrels of whiskey, and a few trinkets. As soon as the bargain was concluded the Indians gathered together for the purpose of having a "big drunk." (This ended in a fight which drove Johnson's men to their boats.)

Galena Daily Courier
August 29, 1860

opposite the foot of Bouthillier Street."

According to a letter dated April 12, 1822, Captain Marston, at Fort Edwards, wrote to Mr. Farrar, at Fever River, that "the Johnsons of Kentucky have leased the Fever River Lead Mines and are about sending up a large number of men including a large number of negro slaves."[21]

H. F. M'CLOSKEY,
WHOLESALE
Grocer, Forwarding & Commission Merchant
No. 32 LEVEE,
GALENA, IL.

Liberal Advances Made on Consignments.

1865 Advertisement

A Trader's Village

Based upon the article printed in the *Gazetteer of Illinois and Missouri* in 1822, there were already "ten or twelve houses or cabins" in the "Traders Village" located here.

Among the traders that we have record of is Amos Farrar. By August or September of 1821, Farrar was already managing a trading post on Fever River near the Portage as an agent for the American Fur Company, and was living here with his Fox Indian wife.

On the 1st of June 1825, Farrar received a permit signed by Charles Smith, the acting sub-agent of U. S. Lead Mines, permitting him to occupy five acres of government land for cultivation and to build a cabin thereon, situated near the Portage. He was to "comply with all regulations concerning cutting timber." [23]

Farrar and his wife had three children. His wife died prior to Amos, and he remarried in or about 1830. His second wife was Sophia Gear, sister to the noted Captain H. H. Gear. Amos Farrar died of consumption at his residence within the Galena stockade on July 24, 1832. [24]

Thomas H. January was trading at The Pointe as early as 1819. He became a permanent resident in 1821.

Other settlers starting to arrive at the Fever River Trading Post included Mr. B. Symmes and James Connor, and perhaps, David G. Bates, who has always been considered among the earliest settlers arriving in the mining region.

Still Remembered by Old Timers

Another who is still remembered by the older men and women was Swanzy Adams, black slave owned by one of the early gamblers here. Swanzy had been prospecting in the hills and had almost purchased his freedom when his master suffered serious financial reverses and decided to sell Swanzy down the river. At the last minute some of Swanzy's friends made up the difference, and purchased his freedom. Swanzy, legend relates, was defrauded of his freedom later, and finally struck a good lead of lead that bought him off again.

He worked here for many years at odd jobs. Finally, he became proprietor of the town's water cart, carrying buckets of water to the homes of citizens. An early directory lists Swanzy as "superintendent of the Galena water works."

During the days before the war between the states, a free Galena negro named Jerry Boyd was persuaded by some men from Mississippi to accompany them south to work in a hotel. From the suspicious manner in which they traveled Jerry believed that the was being sold into slavery. When he resisted his captors, they murdered him and went on with Jerry's wife and daughter, who, in some way, were able to send word back to Galena of their capture. Samuel Hughlett, a settler from Kentucky, and a companion immediately went to Missouri where they found Mrs. Boyd and her daughter and brought them back to Galena.

One of the most important figures in the town's social life during the early days was the negro, Barney Norris, who had served John Quincy Adams as a footman and who came to Galena in 1829 with Captain Legate as his servant. For many years Barney was hired by the prominent citizens to act as butler at their formal parties. In 1848 he accompanied Colonel William S. Hamilton, son of Alexander Hamilton to California. When Hamilton died at the gold mines, it was Barney Norris who buried his body. Later Barney returned to Galena, marking the end of a colorful era with his passing years later.

Freeport Journal-Standard (Freeport, Illinois)
Friday, September 24, 1937

This was the catalyst that would transform the Fever River district from a mere trading post to the booming city of Galena.

The presence of white men on the Fever River had become permanent.

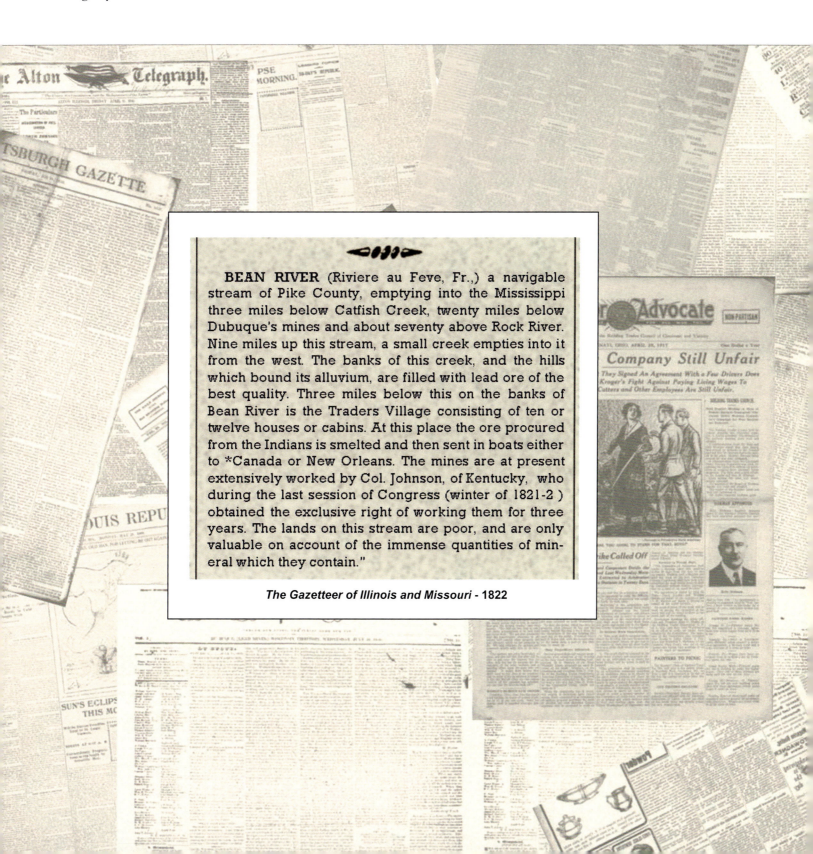

BEAN RIVER (Riviere au Feve, Fr.,) a navigable stream of Pike County, emptying into the Mississippi three miles below Catfish Creek, twenty miles below Dubuque's mines and about seventy above Rock River. Nine miles up this stream, a small creek empties into it from the west. The banks of this creek, and the hills which bound its alluvium, are filled with lead ore of the best quality. Three miles below this on the banks of Bean River is the Traders Village consisting of ten or twelve houses or cabins. At this place the ore procured from the Indians is smelted and then sent in boats either to *Canada or New Orleans. The mines are at present extensively worked by Col. Johnson, of Kentucky, who during the last session of Congress (winter of 1821-2) obtained the exclusive right of working them for three years. The lands on this stream are poor, and are only valuable on account of the immense quantities of mineral which they contain."

The Gazetteer of Illinois and Missouri - 1822

Hundreds of mines were established in and around Galena in the early 1800's. The photo above is the Cleveland Mine, located south of Galena. Photo below shows miners at the opening of a mine.

**Above: The Kennedy Mine, located near Galena.
Below: Men moving a mine boiler with a steam powered tractor**

The Black Jack Mine was discovered in 1854 by Stephen Marsden, a farmer who lived three miles south of Galena. After penetrating the side of a hill to drain a spring on his property that had become clogged, he found a large cave with an abundant deposit of mineral blende and pyrite.

The blende, zinc in natural form (commonly called black jack), was at first thought to be worthless. But once its value was determined, the mine was intensively operated. The first ton sold for $12. In the period from 1853 to 1859, approximately 3,000,000 pounds of zinc, an enormous quantity for the primitive mining methods of the time, was taken from the district, and most of this came from the Black Jack. Marsden eventually sold the mine to the Illinois Zinc company of Peru. It was purchased in 1913 by the Mineral Point Zinc Company, which operated it until it closed in March 1927, after taking out more than one million tons of minerals.

The underground cavity of the Black Jack was extraordinarily large. Compared with coal mines in which workers could hardly stand erect, the Black Jack was in many places more than ninety feet high. It was 200 feet underground and more than three-fourths of a mile long.—*The Freeport Journal Standard,* March 17, 1927

The First Traders and Miners

An early Galena log cabin with frame additions.

Chapter 4

The Town is Established

June of 1823 marked an important event in the history of the Fever River Settlement. Dr. Moses Meeker of Cincinnati, Ohio, who had prospected on Fever River during the previous year, organized a colony and embarked on the 20th day of April 1823, on the keel-boat* *Col. Bomford*. There were 30 men besides the women and children; 75 tons of freight, consisting of a complete mining outfit, and merchandise and provisions sufficient to subsist the party a year after their arrival. [1]

Among the passengers were Dr. Moses Meeker; James Harris and his son Daniel Smith Harris (15 yrs. old); Benson Hunt, his wife and children; John Doyle, with his wife and child; Maria Bunce (Mrs. Doyle's sister) and her two brothers; Maria Rutherford; Thomas Boyce; Israel Garretson; John Whittington (the steersman) and Wm. Hewlett. [2] These families and individuals were the earliest arrivals at the Fever River Settlement aside from the traders and miners.

They traveled 400 miles down the Ohio River and another 150 miles up the Mississippi until they reached St. Louis. Once there, James Harris left the boat, purchased a number of cattle for Dr. Meeker and drove them across the country to Fever River. He arrived two or three weeks after the *Col. Bomford*, which arrived on the 20th of June, having made the trip in sixty days. At the time this was regarded as a remarkably quick passage, averaging a little over nine miles per day. The Mississippi was very high and had overflowed its banks, and the crew were often obliged to resort to warping and bushwhacking.** [3]

At Grand Tower, located south of St. Louis, the *Col. Bomford* was passed by the steamer *Virginia*, probably commanded by Capt. John Shellcross, on her way from Pittsburg to Fort Snelling with supplies for the troops stationed there. She was the first steamboat that ever ascended the Mississippi above the mouth of the Illinois River, and she was certainly the first steam propelled boat that ever parted the waters of Fever River in June, 1823. [4]

---

* A keel-boat was similar to a modern barge only its hull was lower. These boats were from 50 to 80 feet long, and from 10 to 15 feet wide, having a hold of only 2 to 2-1/2 feet deep.

** The keel-boat was propelled by sails, by rowing, poling, bushwhacking, cordelling and warping. When the water was high or the boat was running close to shore, the crew would grasp the bushes growing on the bank and pull the boat up river. This was "bushwhacking." Sometimes a long line or rope would be attached to the mast and the crew, walking on the shore with the other end, towed the craft up stream. This was "cordelling." At other times when cordelling was impracticable in crossing rapids, a long line would be carried ahead and made fast to a tree or rock, the crew in the boat, taking the line over their shoulders and holding the rope tight, would walk from the bow to stern, drop the rope, then walk back on the other side to the bow in a continual circle of men, take it up again, in the rear of the others, thus keeping the boat in motion. This is called 'warpng'.

Upon the arrival of his party at the Fever River Settlement, Dr. Meeker found less than 100 men mining and trading with the Indians. Among them were Dr. S. C. Muir; Thomas H. January; Amos Farrar; Jesse Shull; F. Bouthillier; A. P. VanMatre; D. G. Bates; John Coney; John Ray; J. Johnson; N. Bates; J. Connor; B. Symmes; E. Rutter; J. Hardy; R. Burton; Stephen Howard; Israel Mitchel; J. and C. Armstrong, and others. [5]

Moses Meeker stated: *We (Meeker and party) pushed up the river without any annoyance worth noting, and entered the Fever River on Sunday… On arriving, I found Col. James Johnson had arrived before me, accompanied by Gen. Simrall from Kentucky, with a few men… I was at my destination port, which was no small job… the timber was on the opposite side of the river… I spent the first year building houses, furnaces, and stables, and in digging a well. In the month of August, I had the census taken; there were 74 persons, men, women and children, white and black…* [6]

Upon Meeker's arrival at the Fever River Settlement, they found a few structures including Amos Farrar's trading post, which was a double log cabin on the bank of the river, between what is now Perry and Franklin, in the middle of Water Street. Nearby was a cabin built by Farrar, to accommodate his Indian customers. Thomas January had constructed a double log cabin and a warehouse on The Point bearing his name. These few log cabins were all the dwellings and places of business of the entire white population at the time of their arrival, but the river bottoms, hillsides and ravines were thickly dotted with wigwams of the Sauk and Fox Indians, who numbered about 2000. [7]

The Indians were peaceable and treated the whites kindly. They spent their time hunting and fishing and supplied the whites with large portions of meats, consisting of venison, game, fish and other foods. Other Indians came to this area to trade as well. The Winnebagos and Menominees were among these. Their home was then farther north in Michigan Territory. The Menominees are represented as being the most pleasant and friendly, while the Winnebagos were prone to be insolent, hot-tempered and disorderly. [8]

It's interesting to note that at the time of the early settlement, the present location of the DeSoto House (at the corner of Main and Green Street) housed a large pond that extended some distance northward, east of Main Street. Here, the boys, both white and Indian, used to come to fish for years. During the high water in 1828, a catfish weighing 106 pounds was caught at the present site of the DeSoto House. [9]

The arrival of Dr. Meeker and his companions marked a new era in the history of the mining district. It gave impetus and growth to the little remote settlement which until then was scarcely more than an Indian trading post. It was almost unknown except to roving traders and frontiersmen.

It required enthusiasm, energy, bravery, perseverance and patient endurance of toil and privations, unknown in later years, to venture into the very heart of the Indian country and make a permanent settlement in the midst of a populous Indian village.

Dr. Meeker possessed all these characteristics to a remarkable degree as did Mr. James Harris, his foreman, confidential counselor and friend. These two men became the head and soul, so to speak, of the new settlement, and to them, perhaps more than to any others, it owes its rapid development and growth. Only six years after their arrival on the spot where they landed, a town was laid out by the United States authorities. [6]

The *Virginia* was called the *Clermont* of the upper Mississippi. It was a small stern-wheeler of 109.32 tons, built at Wheeling, Virginia in 1819 and owned by Redick McKee, James Pemberton, and seven others. It was 118 feet long; 18 feet, 10 inches wide; and its depth was 5 feet, 2 inches. It had a small cabin on its deck, but no pilot house, being run by a tiller at the back, and it lacked both mast and figurehead. According to its enrollment at the Port of New Orleans dated December 21, 1822, it was the fifty-first boat built and documented on western waters. During the course of its first journey on the upper Mississippi in 1823, it was commanded by two men. [10, 11]

The first steam powered boat to reach Galena was the *Virginia* in 1823. Its passengers included a Kentucky family bound for the lead mines at Galena ...*with their arms and baggage, cats and dogs, hens and turkeys, the children too had their own stock*.

This marked the beginning of a lengthy run of steam powered vessels that would run up the Mississippi to Galena. There were numerous steamboats in port at Galena on a regular basis and by 1837 there were 359 steamship arrivals and departures in one season.

The following photos are examples of steamboats that came to Galena.

The *General Barnard* docked in front of the Belvedere House in Galena on June 22, 1899

The construction of the *General Barnard* began in November of 1878. The boat was 218 feet long, had a 37 foot beam and was 65 feet in width overall. The cost to build the ship was $20,963.00. The *General Barnard* left the Howard Shipyards of Jeffersonville, Indiana on April 12, 1879 and arrived at Rock Island on the 22nd. It was initially used by the government to perform work on the Mississippi.[12]

Galena, Illinois

Photo—The U.S. Mail Steamboats—*New St. Paul* and *Nominee* docked in Galena in 1852.
The ***New St. Paul*** was a side-wheel, built at New Albany, Indiana in 1852. It weighed 225 tons. The ***Nominee*** was a side-wheel, built at Shousetown, Pa. in 1848. It weighed 213 tons. Daniel Smith Harris of Galena, was the Captain of the ***Nominee*** in 1850. In 1853 the ***Nominee*** made 29 trips from Galena to St. Paul. Note that on the side-wheel of both ships is the word *Packet*. These were the most common and versatile boat types on the inland rivers from the 1840's until after the Civil War. In its early English usage, "packet" referred to the carrying of mail, but these boats were all purpose vessels that carried freight and passengers, along with mail.

These workhorse boats could be either stern-wheelers or side-wheelers (or occasionally center-wheelers) and had at least two decks.

Packet steamers became the classic icon of the river. They were of shallow draft, usually no more than four feet on a large boat and sometimes as little as eighteen inches on a small one, with a flexible wood hull, low-pressure condensing steam engines and one or two boilers. They had one or more cabin decks, a pilothouse, and paddle wheels on the sides or at the stern. The side-wheeler was more versatile and more easily maneuvered then a stern-wheeler, as the wheels permitted the boat to turn more quickly and in a shorter space. One wheel could be reversed so that the boat could be turned almost "on a dime." [13]

Galena, Illinois

The Sidney was built at Murraysville, West Virginia and completed at Wheeling, West Virginia in 1880. It was sold to the Diamond Jo Line in 1882 and ran from St. Louis to St. Paul until she was purchased by the Streckfus Line to replace the original JS (1901) and converted into an excursion boat. The **Sidney** was rebuilt in 1921 at Mound City, Illinois and renamed **Washington**. It remained in operation until 1937 and was dismantled in 1938.[14]

Galena, Illinois

Boating excursions were very popular in Galena during the 1800's. The two photos on this page are examples of these excursions. Photos c.1890's

The Town is Established

Right: The *Morningstar* Interior

Above: Postcard of the *Morningstar* on the Mississippi River.

Left: Advertisement found in the *True Republican* Newspaper, May 28, 1913

The Northern Steamboat Company was organized on May 10, 1910 in Davenport, Iowa. It's first President was William A. Blair. Blair was born in Galena on November 17, 1856. His entire life was devoted to ships and the river.

Lower: Photo of the *Morningstar*, built in 1911.

The Helen Blair—Built in 1896 at Marietta, Ohio, this steamship was originally named the *Urania*. Captain Blair bought the *Urania* in 1901 and used her at Burlington, Iowa to run local trades. On September 5, 1901 she burned her texas (officers' cabins) and pilothouse off at Muscatine, Iowa. When rebuilt that winter, she was renamed to honor the daughter of Captain Blair. On July 13, 1910 while proceeding downstream about 3 1/3 miles below Davenport, Iowa, she hit an obstruction in the channel and was sunk in seven feet of water. She was raised and repaired; amount of damage was $2,500. On April 27, 1913, the *Helen Blair* was the first steamboat to come to Galena, Illinois in years. Over 40 excursionists from Rock Island, Davenport and Dubuque were on board. They were given automobile tours of historical sites including the Grant House as well as other sites. As the photo below indicates, many Galenians came out to the dock to welcome the ship and its passengers. [15]

The *Helen Blair* at Galena
April 27, 1913

In earlier years, large steamers like the *Northern Light* or the *Grey Eagle*, each 250 feet long, could turn around in the Galena harbor. By 1913, because of the fact that the river had been filled up and silted with the soil from cultivated hills over the years, the *Helen Blair*, at only 180 feet long, had to back all the way out of the river and turn in Harris Slough, five miles below the town and at the mouth of the Mississippi. [16]

This was the last steamship to ever come to Galena.

Mrs. Meeker died in December 1829, at age 39. In 1833 Dr. Meeker moved to Iowa County, Wisconsin and resumed his practice. He died there on July 7, 1865, at 75. His remains were brought back to Galena and laid in the Old Cemetery Park on the hill. Mr. Harris lived but a few years to witness the results of his labors, as he died suddenly in 1829, and he too, lies near his old friend in the midst of the scenes he loved so well. [17]

The permanent occupation of the area was well under way by the fall of 1824, when Lieutenant Martin Thomas transferred the federal lead agency from St. Louis to the Fever River Settlement. He was authorized to grant permits for occupying and also improving city lots. These lots were not owned, but leased because of an act passed by the United States Government in 1807 that reserved mineral lands in the public domain. These permits included a clause that the U. S. Agent could reclaim the land at any time with just a 30 day notice! This clause and the severe limitation of private land ownership in the Fever River district (soon to be named Galena) remained in effect until 1836.

In 1825 Lt. Thomas instituted new rules governing the lead production in the Fever River district. Miners were only allowed to sell their lead to licensed smelters.

Licensed smelters had the responsibility of paying a 10 % lead tax to the government. This arrangement proved beneficial for the miners, as well as the smelters. Other rules were also implemented by Lt. Thomas that included a ruling on timber.

One of Lt. Thomas regulations stated: *No timber is to be cut within one hundred yards of the Fever River bank, from one mile above its mouth to and one mile above the point where January's cabins are situated.*

An early pioneer's daughter, Charlotte Gear Girdon (Capt. Gear's daughter), gave the following account of father's efforts to build a home for his family. She stated:

He cut his logs on a steep bluff on the banks of Fever River, rolled them into the water and towed them, one by one, upstream half a mile to the site he had selected, by tying one end of a rope around the log and the other end around his body, and walking up, sometimes in the water, sometimes on the bank. When he had thus collected a sufficient number of logs, the miners in the vicinity helped him raise his cabin. The roof of this cabin was thatched with long prairie grass and covered with sods. [18]

In July of 1826, the Lieutenant mapped out the upper street of the town. It was named Bench Street because it formed a natural "bench" running parallel to Main Street. By this time Galena was home to fifteen to twenty houses and a half dozen business establishments. The settlement had started to grow in importance as a smelting center and a commercial depot for the mining population scattered throughout the countryside.

No timber to be cut within one hundred yards of Fever River bank, from one mile above its mouth to and one mile above the point where January's cabins are situated.

M. THOMAS,
Lieut. U. S. Army and Supt. of Lead Mines.

The Fourteenth Regulation for Miners:

Any miner who shall disobey or go contrary to any of these regulations, shall forfeit his permit to dig or mine; and should he attempt to cut timber, mine, farm, cultivate land or build cabins, without written permission from the agent, he will be prosecuted as a trespasser on United States land.

1826 was a remarkable year of growth and development for the settlement and the mining region. The mining of lead in this region was gaining major public awareness and interest throughout the country. Many men came to mine "seasonally." They would come in the spring and leave in the fall. These "seasonal" miners were given the nickname *"Suckers"*, a name that would eventually designate the State of Illinois as the "Sucker State." This is a positive title, as shown in the newspaper article printed on page 44.

The number of miners in 1826 aptly demonstrated the importance of the region during this period. As of January 31, 1826, the number of diggers was 163 with 29,185 pounds of lead being manufactured. In April, 1826, the number of diggers increased to 287 and the amount of lead manufactured to 78,528 pounds. May had a rapid increase in the number of diggers to 350, but only 6,927 pounds of lead was reported as manufactured. The growth continued. In June there were 406 diggers; 173,479 pounds of lead. July, 441 diggers; 140,781 pounds of lead. October, 548 diggers; 269,405 pounds of lead.[19] This influx of miners in the surrounding countryside generated growth for the town of Galena.

Among those prominent in the early history of this region who arrived in 1826, are Maj. T. B. Farnsworth; M. C. Comstock; Charles Gear with his son William T. Gear and sister Sophia Gear; John Turney; William Smith; John Dowling and his son Nicholas; Capt. Allenwrath; Capt. Abraham Hathaway; Lemon Parker; William P. Tilton; R. P. Guyard; James H. Hammett; John Campbell; William Townsend; Louis Chetlain and many others.[20]

Charles Gear was an enthusiastic Mason and was undoubtedly instrumental in organizing Strangers Union Lodge No. 14, the first Masonic organization in the mines under the jurisdiction of the Grand Lodge of Missouri. Sophia Gear, his sister, opened the first school taught by a female in 1827, and subsequently married Amos Farrar. Allenwrath struck the lead called "Allenwrath Diggings." John Turney was the first lawyer to settle here. Hathaway was a butcher for some years, but later moved to Guilford. Lemon Parker, William P. Tilton, D. B. Morehouse and Robert P. Guyard organized the firm of Parker, Tilton & Co. later known as the Galena Mining Company.[21]

The little frontier hamlet was known as "Fever River Settlement," or La Pointe, until 1826-7, when the name was changed to Galena. A number of accounts are listed as to how the name "Galena" was selected. The *History of Jo Daviess County*—1878 states:

It is said that the name 'Galena' was given to it at a meeting of the settlers held probably in 1826, at which thirty-three persons were present. At this meeting it is said that it was first proposed to call the new town "Jackson", but this was lost by one vote. A proposition to call it "Jo Daviess" was rejected by a majority of eight. Mr. R. W. Chandler proposed the name of "Harrison", and this was accepted by only three majority, but in view of the differences of opinion, Mr. Chandler afterwards suggested the name "Galena" as being one upon which all could agree, as well as being very appropriate, and that name was unanimously adopted.

However while I was digging into old newspapers, I came upon another source that puts a twist on the origin of the name selection. Published in 1838, this was recorded four decades earlier than the above mentioned book. Quoting the *Galena Gazette*, this source states that following the selection of the name "Harrison" as also stated in the *History of Jo Daviess County*, that an individual, writing to the Post Master General, took it upon himself to choose the name Galena! The article from the *Times-Picayune Newspaper* of New Orleans is reproduced on the following page for you to read yourself.

> ORIGIN OF GALENA.— The Galena Gazette gives an account of the origin of that place. It seems that it was founded in 1826 by thirty-three persons, who had some difficulty in fixing upon a name. The first proposition was to call it "Jackson" — vetoed by a majority of one. "Joe Daviess" was next tried—lost. The third proposition was, to call it "Harrison"— carried by a majority of three votes. A committee was appointed to write on to the Post Master General to have a Post Office established; but the person who drafted the letter took the responsibility of choosing a name himself. He accordingly called it by the appropriate title of "Galena," which signifies sulphuret of lead, and which it will doubtless continue to bear as long as the lead mines hold out—in other words, to the end of time.

The *Times-Picayune* (New Orleans, Louisiana)
Sunday, June 17, 1838

The birth of the first white children in all of Jo Daviess County occurred in Galena on October 9, 1824. A son, James Smith Hunt was born to Benson Hunt, and within hours, John S. Miller had a daughter whose name was Mary S. Miller. These two children were the first to be born in the Fever River Settlement. [22]

The town's growth was increasing at a rapid pace. One visitor's experience was recorded in the *Adams Sentinel* — Gettysburg, Pennsylvania, on June 27, 1827. Regarding his experience in Galena, he stated:

"The rise of the place is astonishing. This is the grand point of emigration in the western country. Every body seems flocking here; each steamboat brings up to 100 passengers, and lands them on shore."

Because of this great influx of people and the limited resources available, living costs were skyrocketing. He went on to say:

One house, of a single story, containing two rooms, lets for $6,000 per ann. You can get no kind of rooms for less than $24 or $25 per month.

To put these figures into perspective, agricultural laborers averaged just $0.48 cents to $0.58 cents per day in the 1820's. Common laborers averaged just $0.75 cents to $1 per day! [11] Comparing these incomes to the housing costs in Galena in 1827, the extremely disproportionate costs are an understatement.

> *Extract of a letter from a young Bostonian, at Galena, Fever River, to a relationship of his in that city, dated April 22, 1827:*
>
> "This town has grown in a few months. The rise of the place is really astonishing. This is the grand point of emigration now in the Western country; every body seems flocking here; each steam boat brings up to 100 passengers, and lands them on shore. How they live I do not know, for there are no shelters for them. Provisions they are obliged to bring with them, as the place is very barren. Many persons return, but they bear no proportion to those who remain—those who follow mining do well. A great deal of lead is manufactured here, and many are making money rapidly. The log buildings (and there are no other here) rent at extravagant rates. One house, of a single story, containing two rooms, lets for $6000 per ann. You can get no kind of rooms for less than $24 to $25 per month. I board at the principal tavern. It is a log building with three rooms, and a loft over the whole for a grand sleeping chamber. I went up to examine it, and saw from 20 to 30 beds, with pallets and buffalo robes between them. A few nights since, from 150 to 200 persons slept in this house. This loft is open to the weather in a thousand places. We have nothing but salt pork, hams, potatoes and sour crout. The taverner tells me that there have been no fresh provisions in this place for four weeks but he calculated fresh provisions will be a drug in the course of two or three weeks. The country appears to be a miserable one. A month before I left St. Louis every tree was in blossom but here it is still winter, and there are no signs of vegetation. A great many die here from intemperance. This place is about five hundred miles above St. Louis."- *The Adams Sentinel (Gettysburg, Pennsylvania) - June 27, 1827*

The *Adams Sentinel* (Gettysburg, Pennsylvania)
June 27, 1827

From the Prairie Argue

THE SUCKERS.

That part of Fever river on which Galena stands is called the "Sucker Shoot." This "shoot" extends from the Rapids above the city down to the Mississippi. In this stream up to the very rocks over which the water falls, in old times especially, and even to this day, that species of fish called "Suckers" during the spring season and early summer, collect from the Mississippi in merry schools, counting by their millions. Year after year, as sure as the season changed and spring followed the winter, up swarmed the suckers into "Sucker Shoot." No adversity of fortune, caused by the inroads of civilized or savage fishermen—no change of water craft, from the Indian canoe and the miner's barge, to the loud breathing steamboat, frightened the suckers from "Sucker Shoot;" but, true to instinct, and glorying forever in water-falls, rocks and dashing cataracts, the steady, tireless, pioneering 'Sucker" bravely lodged himself amidst the rocks and foam of the Fever river rapids.

Well, in old times, when solitude enwrapped in the shadows of the wilderness, on the banks of the Mississippi, it was noised about in the forts at Vincennes, Massac and Pittsburgh, at Kaskaskia, Ste. Genevieve, and all the "lower country," as well as the "old colonies," that in the vicinity of "Sucker shoot," in the upper Indian country," were mines of silver and lead—of lead exhaustless as the bosom of the mountains.—Time went by—and soon the mines of Galena came to be known in commerce. Barges, rowed by oars, or set up against the mighty current of the "Father of Waters," by poles, leant against the broad shoulders of sturdy men, now and then, in early spring time, set out for the lead mines of Galena; and as the ice and snow left it, the *suckers* and the *miners* entered "Sucker shoot" together.

Each were perform the work of a spring and summer. The suckers in the domestic pleasures and cares of propagating their species; the miners in the steady toil of digging from the earth the rich metals of the mine. And when fall came with his cool winds, and falling foliage, and threatening ice, each returned down the stream they had ascended, to come back together, when the ice of winter should again disappear. So it continued year after year, and season after season—the "miners of Illinois" and the suckers of "Sucker shoot," kept jolly, profitable, and steady companionship. The thing came at last to be noticed, and as all things mortal rise from the loss of the greater, so as the number of *sucker fish* grew less, and that of the *miners* of "Sucker shoot" grew larger, the name of the steady pioneer of the *water*, was transferred to the pioneers on *land*, and the people of the territory through which "Sucker shoot" run, were called and known as Suckers. And when the said territory became a State, by the universal acclamation of the west, that name at first generic, and applied from the Falls of St. Anthony to Skunk river west, and to Lake Michigan east, and south to Galena, became the political soubriquet (nickname) of the people of Illinois.

Such is the true and well authenticated origin of the name "Sucker," and its application to the people of Illinois. *Whether* we consider the character of the fish whose name we bear, or the interesting incident of the story of "Sucker school," the title is a fine one, noble and creditable in its origin; and we believe now, since the battle of Buena Vista, our people, our people have won for themselves the highest point of the character of the Sucker—and that is, an iron disposition to go as far man can go, and to stay there until they choose to retreat. This is the noble point in the character of the *sucker fish*— it is also the glorious boast of the *Sucker soldier.* What power can drive the sucker from the very base of the cataract, where amidst rocks and raging whirlpools he lodges his home! What other fish shows such steadiness of purpose, such fixed resolve! Mark the fitness of the names given to the heroes, whose shouldered together when Hardin and Bissell led them on the stormy, bloody field of Buena Vista.... Then welcome the title "Sucker" for the noble sons of Illinois, It comes to us a title of steady, sober and brawny industry. Its history points out the location and prosperity of one of our most flourishing cities, and the growth of one of the chief sources of national wealth; and as we have worn it in the civil lists of States with credit, it has become inexpressibly dear on the field of battle, and immortal with the fame of a Hardin, a Bissell, a Morrison, a Pope, a Warren, and a Weatherford.

Alton Telegraph (Alton, Illinois)
May 14, 1847

Galena was a mining town. Lead was the key factor fueling its growth. Mining was taking place despite the fact that the Indians lived in close proximity. The Indian tribes' lifestyle and customs were misunderstood by the majority of whites who had recently migrated to the area. Because of this, the whites were always on the lookout for trouble. In July of 1827, the Winnebago Indians were reported to have been harassing the settlers up north in Prairie Du Chien and the nearby mining districts. The inhabitants took refuge in the fort and were preparing themselves against an attack. Down in the Fever River district (Galena) fifty miles south, the local miners were also alarmed by this news and were most certainly preparing themselves. Thankfully, matters settled down and normalcy resumed for the time being.

The white man continued his march West. Stories about Galena were frequently in the news papers back East. Its prosperity and potential for new wealth enticed countless numbers of people to make their way to this enterprising location.

February 5, 1829 was a special date for Galena. The Senate and the House of Representatives of the United States ratified an Act authorizing the laying of a town on the Bean (Fever) River in the State of Illinois. This would speed up the rate of growth and development in Galena, the fastest growing town in Illinois. In February of 1830, a newspaper in Maryland ran an extensive article detailing the beauty and the richness of the Galena region. The writer compared the *climate of this region to that of Italy,* and stated... *the streams of this region, copious and briskly gliding over pebbles of cornelian, topaz, agates, opal, and quartz, are as pure as crystal*.

Galena began to attract settlers in addition in addition to lead miners. Within a short time, the early European pioneers realized that their original belief that this prairie region of the country was too far north to be an agricultural country was not true.

This proved to be an unexpected blessing for the miners in 1829-30. During this period, the price of lead dropped to a serious low. The miners were compelled to plant or starve. Their efforts, combined with the rich soil, produced more than ample provisions to sustain the population in the mining district during this period.

An article originally printed in the *St. Louis Times* in 1830 stated:

> Galena Potatoes—A year or two ago, potatoes were carried from this place to Galena, and sold at one dollar and fifty cents per bushel. At this time, potatoes, not of the same kind, but far superior in flavor and mellowness, were brought from Galena and sold in this place at one dollar per barrel. Our country increases in natural wealth as we advance towards the extremities—*Saint Louis Times,*

**Reprinted in the *Pittsburgh Gazette*,
June 11, 1830**

The first farms to be cultivated in the mining district of Fever River were that of James Harris and Moses Meeker in 1824. The Harris farm was located on the Mississippi River, a few miles south of Galena, at what was originally named Anderson's Slough. It began to be called Harris' Slough after Harris settled there and occupied the cabin that had been abandoned by Major Anderson. Anderson had been sent to this locale in 1822 by the Ordinance Department and stationed there as a surveyor.[23] Until this day, this area is still named Harris Slough.

Dr. Meeker's farm was located about two and one half miles north of Galena. His close friend James Harris planted its first crops. The first orchard in the county was planted here on the Meeker farm in 1824.[24]

These were the first of many farms that would be established in this region. In describing Galena, the *Miners' Journal* of May 1832 stated that... *fine farms are to be seen in every part of the country.*

Galena, Illinois

Approved, 5th of February, 1829

An Act authorizing the laying off a town on Bean river in the State of Illinois, and for other purposes.

Be it enacted by the Senate and House of Representatives of the United States of America in Congress assembled, That a tract of land in the States of Illinois, at and including "Galena" on Bean river, shall, under the direction of the surveyor of the Public Lands for the States of Illinois and Missouri, and the Territory of Arkansas, be laid off into town lots, streets, and avenues, and into out-lots, having regard to the lots and streets already surveyed, in such manner, and of such dimensions, as he may think proper. *Provided,* the tract so to be laid off shall not exceed the quantity contained in one entire section, nor the town lots one quarter of an acre each, nor shall the out-lots exceed the quantity of two acres each. — When the survey of the lots shall be completed, a plat thereof shall be returned to the Secretary of the Treasury, and within twelve months thereafter the lots shall be offered to the highest bidder at public sale, under the direction of the President of the United States, and at such other times as he shall think proper. *Provided,* that no town lot shall be sold for a sum less than five dollars; and *provided further,* that a quantity of ground of proper width of the said river, and running therewith the whole length of the said town, shall be reserved from sale for public use, and remain forever a common highway.

Sec. 2. Be it further enacted, That it shall be the duty of the said Surveyor to class the lots already surveyed, in the said town of Galena, into three classes according to the relative value thereof, on account of the situation and eligibility for business, without regard, however, to the improvements made thereon; and previous to the sale of the said lots as aforesaid, each and every person, or his, her, or their legal representative or representatives, who shall heretofore have obtained from the agent of the United States a permit to occupy any lot or lots in the said town of Galena, or who shall have actually occupied and improved any lot or lots in the said town, or within the tract of land hereby authorized to be laid off into lots shall be permitted to purchase such lot or lots, by paying therefore, in cash, if the same fall within the first class, as aforesaid, at the rate of twenty-five dollars per acre; if within the second class at the rate of fifteen dollars per acre; and if within the third class, at the rate of ten dollars per acre; *Provided,* that no one of the persons aforesaid shall be permitted to purchase by authority of this section more than one half acre of ground; unless a larger quantity shall be necessary to embrace permanent improvements already made.

Approved, 5th February, 1829

The *Raleigh Register*
(Raleigh, North Carolina) Mar 3, 1829

By 1832 Galena had much to offer for individuals from all walks of life. Miners, manufacturers and merchants all flourished here in Galena. There was also a solid establishment of Catholic, Methodist and Presbyterian churches to serve the residents. The town was very civilized and boasted a temperance society of 75 members, all having pledged to abstain from ale, porter, wine, ardent spirits as well as all other intoxicating drinks. There was even a juvenile temperance society in Galena with 45 members by 1832.

The future was looking bright for the prospering inhabitants of Galena and the surrounding mines. This, however, was not the case with the native Indians. They were feeling the effects of the "Pale face" and were not happy.

The Sauk Indian leader, Black Hawk, provided personal insight on Indian life prior to the arrival of the white settlements. He stated: *Our village was situated on the north side of the Rock River, at the foot of its rapids, and on the point of land between Rock River and the Mississippi. In its front, a prairie extended to the bank of the Mississippi; and in our rear, a continued bluff, gently ascending from the prairie. On the side of this bluff we had our corn-fields, extending about two miles up, running parallel with the Mississippi; where we joined those of the Foxes, whose village was on the bank of the Mississippi, opposite the lower end of Rock island, and three miles distant from ours. We had about eight hundred acres in cultivation, including what we had on the islands of Rock River. The land around our village, uncultivated, was covered with blue-grass, which made excellent pasture for our horses. Several fine springs broke out of the bluff, near by, from which we were supplied good water. The rapids of Rock River furnished us with an abundance of excellent fish, and the land, being good, never failed to produce good crops of corn, beans, pumpkins and squashes. We always had plenty —our children never cried with hunger, nor our people were never in want. Here our village had stood for nearly a hundred years, during all which*

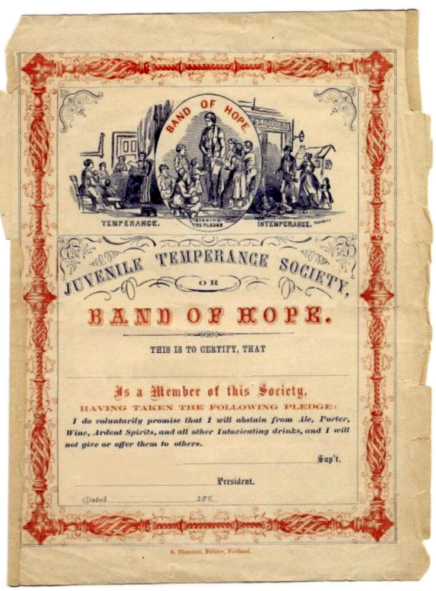

Juvenile Temperance Society Member Certification Form from the 1860's

time we were the undisputed possessors of the Mississippi, from the Ouisconsin to the Portage des Sioux, near the mouth of the Missouri, being about seven hundred miles in length. [25]

As the white men moved in and built settlements, this had a negative effect on the native Indians. Black Hawk went on to say: *We were not as happy then in our village as formerly. Our people got more liquor than customary. I used all my influence to prevent drunkenness, but without effect. As the settlements progressed toward us, we became worse off, and more unhappy. Many of our people, instead of going to their old hunting grounds, where game was plenty, would go near to the settlements to hunt— and, instead of saving their skins to pay the trader for goods furnished them in the fall, would sell them to the settlers for whiskey! And would return in the spring with their families, almost naked, and without the means of getting anything for them.* [26]

Because of the Treaty of 1804, enacted in St Louis, between the United States and four individuals of the Sauk Indians, all the land of their forefathers east of the Mississippi was ceded over to the United States. This was done without the knowledge or authority of the tribes or nation.

By 1831 Black Hawk and the Sauk and Fox tribes were uprooted and forced to leave their homes, their cultivated lands for crops and the burial sites of their forefathers. They were relocated west of the Mississippi.

This painting (circa 1872) by John Gast, called *American Progress*, is an allegorical representation of the modernization of the new west. Here Columbia, a personification of the United States, leads civilization westward with American settlers, stringing telegraph wire as she sweeps west; she holds a school book as well. The different stages of economic activity of the pioneers are highlighted and, especially, the changing forms of transportation.

The Town is Established

THE FAR WEST REGION

The following highly interesting letter, descriptive of the Region far West, is from the pen of Caleb Atwater, Esq, who was connected with the Agency for making the Indian treaties lately ratified by the Senate.

Washington, Jan 1, 1830

"The treaties with certain Indian tribes, for the cession of the mineral country, on the upper Mississippi, are ratified by the *unanimous consent of the Senate*. By these treaties the United States has acquired 8,000,000 acres of land, equal in all respects to any in the Union. The climate of this region is equal to that of Italy, such is the purity of the air. When traveling along the road from Dodgeville, (twelve miles south of the Wisconsin) to Galena, on Fever River, I could distinctly see a wagon and a team five miles off, with the naked eye. This purity of atmosphere may be attributed to the total absence of marshy ground, and the elevation of the country, which, after leaving the Wisconsin and Mississippi rivers, and ascending to the common level of the country, is, by my computation, about 200 feet above the sea. The absence of dense forests all the way to the Rocky Mountains, and to the Frozen Ocean, to which it may be added, that the mineral country is beyond the influence of the great northern lakes-may, in part account for the purity of the atmosphere.

The streams of this region, copious and briskly gliding over pebbles of cornelian, topaz, agates, opal, and quartz, are as pure as crystal. Originating in springs, they are cool enough for drinking in the hottest day in August. The Mississippi, from Rock Island to the mouth of the Wisconsin, a distance of two hundred miles and upwards, and which forms the Western boundary of the ceded territory, is, on an average, about three fourths of a mile in width. The fish are abundant, of fine flavor, and furnish food for the Indians on the western shore of that beautiful river."

**The *Torch Light & Public Advertiser*
(Hagerstown, Maryland) Feb. 18, 1830**

The miner, the smelter and the merchant all transact a cash business. Fine farms are to be seen in every part of the country. Mills are built on almost every stream. Machines are in operation for the rolling of lead and for the manufacture of leaden pipes. A shot tower is being built at Helena. Laborers receive from $15 to $20 per month and their board. There are three churches in the town of Galena a Catholic, a Methodist and a Presbyterian. There is a temperance society of seventy-five members, and a juvenile temperance society of forty-five members. Education is encouraged and promoted. Justice is regularly administered. Numerous crimes common in older settlements are here wholly unknown. Most persons sleep with unbarred doors, and sleep in safety. A jail has been finished three years, and during all that time has not been occupied a single week. The people of Galena are generally well dressed, polite and sociable, and if there is a place where a respectable stranger finds pure, unalloyed hospitality, it is at the Upper Mississippi lead mines. One hundred and two steamboats* and seventy-two keel-boats have arrived in a single year, and the annual product of lead has increased to 13,343,150 pounds.

* (At times you see fifteen or twenty large Mississippi steamboats in the river at a time.)

***Miners' Journal*
May 9, 1832**

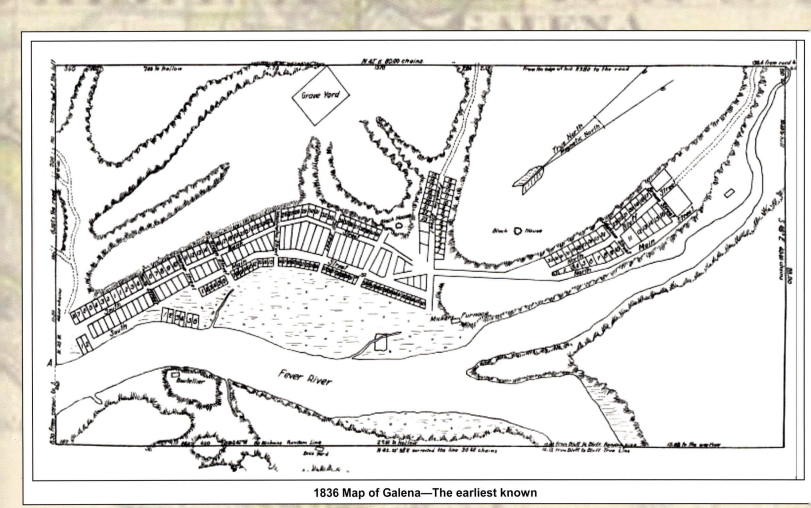

1836 Map of Galena—The earliest known

The first 'official' survey map of the old lead mining town of Galena was authorized in 1836 by the three commissioners appointed by the United States Congress. The plat resulting from this survey is dated March 28, 1838, and is the earliest map of Galena on file in the General Land Office at Washington or in the county courthouse at Galena. At the time of this survey, Galena had grown to be a town of 400 to 500 buildings and boasted a population of between 2,500 and 3,000. Both sides of the stream had been occupied, the swamps along the stream had been platted and partially developed, and the town had expanded beyond the river flood plain up the bordering bluffs onto the upland.—Source: *The Wisconsin Magazine of History* Vol. 23, No. 1 (Sep., 1939), pp. 40-43, *"The Earliest Map of Galena, Illinois,* by Glenn T. Trewartha.

Chapter 5

Galena and the Black Hawk War of 1832

In order to understand the developments that led to the Black Hawk War of 1832, we need to go back to August of 1804. This topic could fill volumes. This chapter will provide a brief overview of the events leading up to the war.

Before making an attempt to elaborate on this topic, it is important to note that there are always different perspectives, viewpoints and opinions. "History" is really two words, "His and Story." History is therefore often, if not always - tainted, as it is usually written by the "victors".

This *his-story* is written from the standpoint of the Sauk Indians. Much of the information came from the autobiography of Black Hawk. So, the accuracy, or should I say *his-story*, may not always coincide with the written history of the victors.

Who was Black Hawk? Black Hawk was born in the Sauk Indian Village of Saukenuk in c. 1767. He was not born into a family of chiefs, but was a member of the Sauk warrior class. When just 15 years old, he wounded his first enemy in battle. Time and again he proved his courage, bravery and skill in battle. He came to be a trusted leader of large war parties.

Fact 1. The year is 1804. Four Indians representing the Sauk and Fox had gone to St. Louis to meet with General William Henry Harrison, then Governor of the Territory of Indiana. (At this time, the entire region that would become the state of Illinois was included in the Territory of Indiana.) Their purpose was to ease the tension created when some of their young warriors had murdered a number of white settlers.[1]

Fact 2. They signed a treaty that included a number of provisions intended to promote peace, friendship, order, and trade between the two parties. However, in Article 2 of this treaty they unknowingly and without proper authority ceded over to the United States all of their nation's lands east of the Mississippi. These four men were not important chiefs of the Sauk and Fox, nor had any of them been authorized by the tribal councils to negotiate a land cession.[2]

Fact 3. Because of this, Black Hawk and others did not recognize or accept the validity of this treaty.

Black Hawk's home, Saukenuk, was located about sixty miles south of Galena on the Mississippi. This was one of the largest Indian villages in North America and had been occupied by the Sauk Indians since 1735.

In spite of the newly signed treaty, life in the Indian village of Saukenuk continued on as normal in 1804 and many years following. The influx of white settlers was just a trickle during the first decade of the 19th century and therefore, didn't really impact the native Indians living hundreds of miles north of St. Louis.

In the 1820's the increase of white settlers began to encroach upon the Indians living in the Territory that had become the State of Illinois in 1818. Trading posts like Galena and Chicago were developing into towns. Numerous forts had sprung up on the Illinois frontier. These included: Fort Dearborn-1803, Fort Lamotte-c. 1810, Fort Massac-1812, Fort Clark-1813, Fort Johnson-1814 and Fort Armstrong in 1816.

The Indians living in Saukenuk were starting to feel the effects of the settlements of the white settlers, as ramifications of the treaty of 1804 were now affecting their village. Fort Armstrong, built in 1816, was just a few miles north of their village.

Black Hawk stated in his autobiography ...*we found that troops arrived to build a fort at Rock Island. This, in our opinion, was a contradiction to what we had done—"to prepare for war in time of peace." We did not, however, object to their building the fort on the island, but we were very sorry, as this was the best island on the Mississippi, and had long been the resort of our young people during the summer. It was like our garden (like the white people have near to their big villages) which supplied us with strawberries, blackberries, gooseberries, plums, apples, and nuts of different kinds; and its waters supplied us with fine fish, being situated in the rapids of the river. In my early life, I spent many happy days on this island.* [3]

As had been the custom for decades, every fall the Indians living in Saukenuk would leave to go to their winter hunting grounds in Iowa and then return to Saukenuk in the spring.

In mid May of 1828, the Indian agent, Thomas Forsyth, told the Sauk that this coming summer was going to be the last summer that they were going to be permitted to live in their village of Saukenuk. He reminded them that they no longer owned the land their village rested on, and that it had been sold to the U.S. Government years earlier. The time had come for them to resettle elsewhere.

Many of the Sauk leaders angrily reacted to these assertions and demanded that they would not move from the place where the bones of their ancestors lay and that they would defend themselves against any power that may be sent to drive them away.

The summer months passed in Saukenuk. The Indian squaws planted and harvested their crops as usual, stored away a portion of the corn and seeds for the coming year, and after their normal preparations, the Sauk Indians departed Saukenuk for their winter hunting grounds. During their absence, squatters were told that the Sauk were not going to return to the village, so a number of them moved in.

Rumors that white settlers were occupying their village reached the Sauk Indians while they were out on their winter hunt. Black Hawk, although 61 years of age, traveled alone through the cold, snow-filled countryside to see for himself. Black Hawk stated: *During the winter, I received information that three families of whites had arrived at our village and destroyed some of our lodges, and were making fences and dividing our corn-fields for their own use... I immediately started for Rock River, a distance of ten days travel, and on my arrival found the report to be true. I went to my lodge, and saw a family occupying it.* [4]

Black Hawk attempted to speak to these "intruders" but, with the language barrier, was unable to do so. He left for Rock Island to see the Indian Agent, but because he was not there, spoke to an interpreter and told him what he wanted to say to the squatters who had overtaken his village. He told the interpreter to tell the people that *they were not to settle on our lands—nor trouble our lodges or fences—that there was plenty of land in the country for them to settle upon—and they must leave our village, as we are coming back to it in the spring.*[5]

Black Hawk left the region and went back to the Sauk Indian winter hunting grounds located west of the Mississippi, feeling confident that his requests would be respected.

In the spring of 1829, the Sauk and Fox Indians of Saukenuk returned to their village. The white settlers who had taken up residence in Saukenuk had not left. Tensions were running high. Many of the Indians decided that this would be their last year east of the Mississippi. They felt that they could not resist the United States by force and felt that removal to the west of the Mississippi was necessary. A key leader and rival of Black Hawk, Keokuk, was among these. This caused a division among the Indians, and those who acquiesced to relocating west of the Mississippi considered those who opposed as "mutinous."

Black Hawk and other Sauk and Fox warriors and families did return in the spring of 1830 and, after another year of increased tension, again in the spring of 1831.

The few hundred who returned that year (1831) did so because they viewed it as a sacred place and a home that could not simply be abandoned without being removed by force. They were living in Saukenuk with the white settlers who had moved in.

This was the "straw that broke the camel's back," so to speak. The Illinois Governor, John Reynolds, had reached his limit and would no longer tolerate the actions of these "mutinous" Indians. Reynolds informed Superintendent Clark that he had decided to call out a militia force of seven hundred mounted soldiers, who would remove the Sauks and Foxes *dead or alive, over to the west side of the Mississippi.*[6]

Clark immediately passed this letter on to General Edmund Pendleton Gaines, the commander of the Western Division of the U.S. Army. By early June of 1831, Gaines had moved his headquarters to Rock Island, within a few miles of Saukenuk, and had begun meeting with the Sauk and Fox chiefs and leading warriors. The chiefs still claimed that they had never ceded the land north of the Rock.

Their claims fell on deaf ears. Gaines was not even willing to allow them to stay long enough to harvest their corn. He did, however, agree to Keokuk's proposal of providing the Sauks and Foxes corn for the coming winter. Because of this, many families moved across to the west side of the Mississippi.

The Sauks and Foxes, who remained into mid-June, insisted that they would not leave the homes of their forefathers. Black Hawk angrily told Gaines, *My fathers were great men*, and he also stated, *I wish to remain where the bones of my fathers are laid.*

For a moment, try understand Black Hawk's position. He was an aged man of 64 years and this was the home where he had lived his entire life. All the happy memories of his youth were here. His children were born and grew up here, his parents, grandparents and great grandparents were all buried here. Over his lifetime he witnessed the entire subjugation of his people by the white man. This man wasn't a "savage." He was a human being who had feelings, honor and pride, and also a love for his home. What was happening was really a travesty to his people.

On June 25, 1831, Governor Reynolds arrived near Rock Island with 1,400 men of the Illinois Militia. With this mighty force, Gaines had more than enough force to easily remove Black Hawk and his supporters. Gaines sent the armed steamboat, *Winnebago* up the Rock, placed his artillery near Saukenuk, and readied his troops.

Black Hawk realized the seriousness of the situation. He could easily see that he would not be able to oppose this mighty force. Above all, he didn't want to see his people hurt. To avoid a confrontation, during the night, Black Hawk and the remaining Sauks and Foxes crossed the Mississippi back onto the western banks.

This wasn't good enough for Gaines. He demanded that they come to Fort Armstrong for a council meeting. On June 30, Gaines and Reynolds forced Black Hawk and the chiefs of the British Band* to sign "Articles of Agreement and Capitulation." A total of 28 chiefs and warriors signed these papers. Under this agreement, the humiliated Black Hawk agreed to remain west of the Mississippi, to stop visiting British posts in Canada, and "to submit to the authority of the friendly chiefs & braves," including Keokuk. The Sauk were to cross the Mississippi and never return to Saukenuk.

One would hope that this would be the end of tensions and trouble for both the Indians and the white settlers — that now both the Indians west of the Mississippi and the whites to the east could live in peace. Unfortunately, that was not to be the case. Black Hawk left the State of Illinois, leading his people to Iowa. Here they found little food and starvation began to set in. Even though all the Sauks and the Foxes of Saukenuk were now removed to the west bank of the Mississippi, tensions still ran high during the summer and fall of 1831.

There was a huge wave of anti-native sentiment raging throughout Illinois and the western frontier. As soon as Black Hawk left, the American militia moved into the old village of Saukenuk and burned many of the lodges. The volunteer soldiers also vandalized the Sauk cemetery and desecrated the native burial mounds. There were reports of settlers beating native men and, without reason, shooting at native livestock.

The once proud and independent, but now beaten Sauk and Fox who had been forced to leave their village resented this. They grew even more frustrated when the government failed to follow through and provide adequate corn for their survival during the winter. This was probably one of the factors that caused a small number of Indians, in the fall of 1831, to cross over to the east bank of the Mississippi to harvest whatever corn, beans and squash they could glean from their old fields. All this did was cause new conflicts.

Governor Reynolds (who was no ally of the Indians) stated in July of 1831, "If I am again compelled to call on the Militia of this State... I will place in the field such a force as will exterminate all Indians, who will not let us alone." [7]

Black Hawk was not aware of this clear intent of Governor Reynolds. If he would have been, it is highly improbable that he would have led nearly 1,000 Indians across the Mississippi in the spring of 1832.

Some factors that moved him to make this decision included the invitation of White Cloud** to make a new settlement at his village on the Rock (now Prophetstown, Ill.). Although it wasn't Saukenuk, it was in close proximity, some 35 miles northeast. He was also given false information that would have emboldened him. A young Sauk chief, named Ne-o-Pope, had visited the British at Fort Malden in Ontario, Canada in the summer of 1831. He falsely claimed that they had pledged to provide aid including men, guns, powder, and shot—if the Americans

---

* "British Band" was a name given to Black Hawk and his followers. Black Hawk had an alliance with the British that dated from the War of 1812. Because of his alliance with the British that spanned decades, he and his group were called this colloquial name.

** White Cloud was a Winnebago Chief, spiritual councilor and prophet of his followers.

tried to drive them (the Sauk and Fox Indians) off by force. On top of this, White Cloud told Black Hawk that, if the Americans attacked the Sauks and Foxes, they would be joined by other tribes and by a British force that would come down Lake Michigan.

With this information in hand, along with a longing for his homeland, Black Hawk crossed the Mississippi on April 6, 1832, with approximately 400 Sauk warriors, old men of the tribe, Indian squaws and children. It is a fact "that no Indian warriors ever went on the war path encumbered in that way." This was NOT a war party. Without a doubt, if Black Hawk would have known what was to follow, he would not have crossed over the Mississippi.

Black Hawk's band proceeded up the Rock to White Cloud's village. Along the way, it is noted that they caused no disruption. In fact, a Mr. H.S. Townsend of Warren, Illinois, stated ...*that in one instance, at least where they took corn from a settler, they paid him for it.* Capt. W. B. Green is on record, stating, ...*I never heard of Black Hawk's band, while passing up Rock River, committing any depredation whatever, not even petty theft.* Frederick Stahl, of Galena, stated that he was informed by the veteran John Dixon, that ...*when Black Hawk's band passed his post, before the arrival of the troops, they were at his house. Ne-o-Pope had the young braves well in hand, and informed him that they intended to commit no depredations, and would not fight unless they were attacked.* [8]

Everything was about to change on May 12, 1832. As there are war-mongers today, so was the situation in 1832. Major Isaiah Stillman was among this number. He had a "fixed determination to wage a war of extermination" against this group of Indians. With about four hundred well-mounted volunteers, he was prepared for battle. He and his men were encamped at White Rock Grove, about thirty-five miles from Dixon. Unbeknown to Stillman, he was in very close proximity to Black Hawk. Black Hawk was not preparing for war. To the contrary, he was preparing a truce for peace.

That evening many of Stillman's volunteers got drunk. They were boisterous and anxious for battle. The *Galenian* (the Galena newspaper) reported ...*they were all eager to get sight of an Indian, and were determined not to be happy until each had the gory scalp of a Sac dangling at his belt.*

Unaware of these motives and with the intention of pursuing peace, when Black Hawk learned of Stillman's presence, he sent a small party of his braves to Stillman's camp with a flag of truce to invite them to his encampment. On their approach, they were discovered by some of the men who, without reporting to their commander and without orders, hastily mounted and dashed down upon the approaching Indians. The braves, not understanding this sudden movement, retreated towards the camp of their chief. The whites fired, killing two and capturing two more, but the others escaped, still pursued by the reckless volunteers. When Black Hawk and his war chief, Ne-o-pope, saw them dashing down upon their camp, their flag of truce disregarded, and, believing that their overtures for peace had been rejected, they raised the terrible war-whoop and prepared for battle. Black Hawk decided that if he was going to die, he would die fighting. Rallying his warriors, they made a suicidal attack against the larger force. They ran shouting into certain death, and then, to their surprise, the American volunteers broke and ran. Thus began the Black Hawk War of 1832.

Following their victory at Stillman's Run, Black Hawk led his warriors through the countryside, burning farmsteads and taking scalps. This was just the beginning…

The intention of Governor Reynolds was very clear. He had one response: "Crush Black Hawk." This action was even supported by the President of the United States, Andrew Jackson. The Indian Agent at the time, William Clark (of Lewis and Clark fame) wrote: *A War of Extermination should be waged against them. The honor and respectability of the Government requires this: — the peace and quiet of the frontier, the lives and safety of its inhabitants demand it.* [9]

The War's Effect On Galena

Initially, the residents of Galena weren't overly concerned when Black Hawk first crossed the Mississippi in late April. In fact, by coincidence, some United States troops arrived at Galena from Prairie du Chien on the 1st of May, at about the same time Black Hawk had commenced his march up Rock River. They (the soldiers) were en route to Fort Armstrong down by Rock Island.

About that time, three Galenians, J. W. Stephenson, John Foley and Mr. Atchison, returned from a scouting expedition and reported that the Indians had dispersed among the neighboring tribes.

The *Galenian* of May 16th, printed before the tidings of Stillman's fiasco had reached Galena, said: *It is already proved that they (the Indians) will not attempt to fight it out with us, as many have supposed.* The paper then raised the question: *Will the temporary dispersion of Black Hawk's band among their neighbors cause our troops to be disbanded?*

On the evening of the 15th of May, Capt. James W. Stephenson arrived at Galena with the startling news of Stillman's disastrous defeat and the commencement of bloody hostilities by the Indians. This created intense excitement among the people in Galena. The ringing notes of the bugle called the settlers and miners together on the old water race on the bottom near the river, near the foot of Washington Street, Galena, and a company of mounted rangers was organized, with James W. Stephenson for captain. [11]

At 3 o'clock on the morning of Saturday, May 19, Sergeant Fred Stahl (a respected citizen of Galena) with a party of five, left Galena on a scouting expedition. They had traveled approximately fifty miles when they were ambushed by Black Hawk and the Indians.

Stahl and the survivors of this ambush returned to Galena on Sunday, the 20th. He added to the alarm of the people by reporting that his party had been ambushed by the Indians just on the edge of Buffalo Grove, now in Ogle County, fifty miles from Galena, at about 5 o'clock p.m. on Saturday afternoon. He sadly informed them that William Durley was instantly killed and left on the spot (Note photo on following page). Stahl received a bullet through his coat collar, and James Smith afterwards found a bullet hole in his hat,[12] showing just how close of a scrape they had with death.

Horatio Newhall, a resident of Galena wrote a letter to his relative, Isaac Newhall, on this day. He painfully wrote:

2 o'clock P.M., awful news has this moment arrived. Our Express which we sent to the main army yesterday has this moment returned. It consisted of six men, fine young men who volunteered their services, when within twelve miles of Dixons' ferry where the main army is supposed to be, they were suddenly surprised by a party of Indians, who fired on them. Mr. Durley was shot dead. He exclaimed "O God" and died. Mr. Smith had a ball pass thro' his hat half

On Saturday, May 19th, 1832 about 5:00 p.m. William Durley was killed during an ambush by Black Hawk and his braves. This marker is located northwest of Polo on Galena Trail Road in Ogle County, Illinois.

Indians must be exterminated or sent off.

On May 19 a stockade began to be constructed near the centre of the town. A blockhouse was erected near the corner of Elk and Prospect Streets, on a spot selected by Lieut. J. R. B. Gardenier. This was manned by an artillery company.

On Monday May 21, Col. J. M. Strode, commanding the 27th Regiment Illinois Militia, proclaimed martial law in Galena and required every able bodied man to work on the stockade from 9 a.m. to 6 p.m. Strode's proclamation also prohibited the sale of spirits at any of the groceries or taverns in Galena from 8 o'clock a.m. until 7 o'clock p.m., and all persons were positively prohibited from firing guns without positive orders, unless while standing guard to give an alarm. [14]

an inch above his head. They have just arrived, all but poor Durley. He was a good young man, and of a very respectable family. He was my friend; if tears were of use I could shed them for months. I have known him for ten years. His little nephew is now at my elbow weeping for the awful death of his uncle. If there is anything on earth I now most desire, it is to kill Indians enough to avenge the death of Durley. I have no doubt the main army is completely surrounded by Indian Spies. No communication can go from them to us, or from us to them. We have satisfactory evidence of the fact. Our fort here goes on bravely. Today is Sunday, but all hands are at work. As the boat will not start until morning, I leave my letter unsealed for further news. [13]

The town of Galena and the lead mines in the surrounding area were adversely affected. All civil process came to a standstill and mining business was suspended.

The *Galenian,* of May 23, 1832, stated: *The tomahawk and scalping knife have again been drawn on our frontier. Blood of our best citizens has been spilt in great profusion within the borders of Illinois. The*

The town of Galena stood in readiness for what seemed to be inevitable, an outright attack by Black Hawk and his warriors.

People were streaming in from the countryside seeking a place of refuge and safety. To their dismay, they weren't provided for as they thought they should be. The Black Hawk War was an event that the majority of citizens had never before experienced. They were all in a state of alarm, had their own business to manage, and right or wrong, left their country neighbors to fend for themselves. Numbers of them were encamped on the bottom near the river for some time, no provision for them having been made within the stockade. Miners refused to come into town for this reason. They said, "We may as well remain at home as to go to the Point, where no

BLACK HAWK WAR STOCKADE GALENA, ILL. 1832

"The United States government erected two block houses in Galena, forts or stockades as they were called, on opposite hill tops. The most important was erected one hundred fifty feet above what is now Bench and Perry streets. It was commanded by Colonel Strode of the 27th Regiment of the Illinois Militia. The block house was garrisoned by one hundred fifty regular soldiers. From this vantage point, the country for miles around could be seen. The fort was supplied with cannons, guns and ammunition to fight the invader.

Colonel Strode proclaimed martial law for the district on May 31st, 1832. Every able bodied man regardless of occupation or position, was ordered to work on a run-way from the block house to the large underground room in Amos Farrar's log house, the logs placed upright according to the French plan of building. This room was excavated from the rock hillside. It was walled with limestone and upheld by giant oak timbers rudely cut from the virgin forests near by.

The men worked day and night to build the run-way from the blockhouse to the stockade in the Farrar place of refuge. The run-way was made by digging a deep trench and placing timbers upright in it. These timbers were six to twelve inches in diameter and from ten to fifteen feet in height. They were "cemented" together after being placed in the trench with clay mud and in so doing, formed a solid wall of wood with port holes on either side so that guns could be used by the people if they were attacked from the outside." *Information taken from—Galena's Old Stockade, written by Florence Gratiot Bale, c.1944*

Galena and the Black Hawk War of 1832

Located within the stockade, the home of Amos and Sophia Gear Farrar was used as a refuge for the women and children of the Galena area during the Black Hawk War. Today, the home is a museum and a Galena landmark.

arrangements have been made for us." A feeling of jealousy or bitterness sprang up because of this.[15]

On Monday night, June 4, 1832, the alarm that the town was under attack was sounded at midnight. *The scene was horrid beyond description. Men, women and children flying to the stockade.* Dr. Newhall, who wrote of this incident to his brother in a letter dated June 8, 1832, stated that *he calculated seven hundred women and children were there within fifteen minutes of the alarm gun being fired. Some with dresses, some with none—some with shoes and some barefoot. Sick persons were transported on others' shoulders. Women and children were screaming from one end of the town to the other.*

To the initial relief of all, this was a false alarm. However, they soon found out that this was a "planned" false alarm under the direction of Colonel Strode.

The next day, when the people learned how cruelly their fears had been played upon, their indignation knew no bounds. All business was suspended. Col. Strode and his associates fled the town and an impromptu meeting was held at Swan's tavern, at which strong denunciatory resolutions were passed. Within a few days, the people calmed down and Colonel Strode returned. Although his motive was good, the means he adopted were questionable.[16]

On Tuesday night, July 24, a fire broke out in a stable located within the Galena stockade, killing two horses. It was said that there was powder stored in the stable, so this caused another major scare, but this time the stampede was from the stockade, not into it.

Black Hawk   b.1767— d. October 3, 1838
Sauk Indian Leader and Warrior

Amos Farrar, one of the original settlers who arrived in Galena in 1823, died at his house in the stockade the same night as the fire. On his deathbed, he declared that *the Indians were not to be blamed, that if they had been left alone, there would have been no trouble.*[17]

Galena never came under attack, although skirmishes and isolated battles and confrontations were taking place in close proximity.

By September, the band of Black Hawk's warriors were experiencing heavy losses. Friendly Sauk and Fox Indians were supporting the soldiers and were sent out to follow the trail of Black Hawk. The Sioux Indians were also supporting the soldiers and had killed or captured a number of Black Hawk's warriors. Five or six of his principle chiefs and warriors had already been captured and taken to Fort Armstrong. The war was nearing its end.

The casualties of the war were serious to Black Hawk and his band, but more so was the hunger of his people, the women and children. They were

The Apple River Fort
(Elizabeth, Illinois)

Photo of the current day replica of the original Apple River Fort, located in Elizabeth, Illinois

When the settlers of the Apple River Settlement (located at present day Elizabeth, 12 miles east of Galena) heard of Black Hawk's rout of the Illinois militia at the battle of Stillman's Run on May 14, 1832, they quickly set about building a fort for their protection. They chose one of the settler's cabins for one corner of the fort, and another structure, perhaps a log out-building, for the opposite corner. The settlers then felled trees, dug a 2-foot to 3-foot trench connecting the two buildings, and erected a palisade of 14 to 15-foot logs, thereby creating a fort 50 x 70 feet.

The settlers turned the out-building into a blockhouse by adding a second story that projected out over the lower story some two feet. At the two corners opposite the buildings, they erected firing stands. The fort's defenders could now see in all directions and, from the blockhouse and firing stands, stop anyone who might be trying to climb the wall or set the fort on fire.

Although Galena didn't experience any battles, there were a number that came quite close. The small town of Elizabeth, located just 12 miles east of Galena did see battle. At the time, it was called the Apple River Settlement. On June 24, 1832, four messengers, Fred Dixon, George W. Herclerode, Mr. Kirkpatrick and Edmund Welsch, who were en route from Galena to Dixon, stopped at the fort. After a brief visit, they continued on their way, only to encounter Black Hawk's band on the ridge some 300 yards from the fort. The Sauk opened fire, wounding Welsch in the thigh and knocking him from the horse. The other men managed to pick him up and hurried back to the fort.

Moments later, some 200 warriors swooped down on the fort. Although there were only 45 people in the fort, 22 men and 23 women and children, they all rallied together in the fight. The men scrambled for their guns, leaped to the firing benches and took their places at the blockhouse portholes. The women and children at first huddled near the back cabins. Then Elizabeth Armstrong rallied the women. They loaded guns and musket balls so that the men could keep up a steady stream of fire. The battle raged for about 45 minutes. Then Black Hawk, thinking that the fort was heavily armed, abandoned the battle, raiding nearby cabins for supplies as he and his warriors departed. Considering the ferocity of the fighting, the casualties were light. Two men were wounded and only one man was killed, George W. Herclerode. He was shot in the neck and instantly killed as he was standing on one of the firing benches. It is not known how many Indians were killed, although some blood was afterwards seen in a deserted cabin.

The *Galenian* newspaper of June 25th, 1832 stated: "The women were all occupied as well as the men — girls of eight years took their part, some made cartridges, some ran bullets, some loaded muskets, all were engaged, and God grant that America may never have greater cowards in her armies than the ladies in Apple River Fort." [22]

The Apple River Fort's interior closely resembles the original fort that was built in 1832 to protect the settlers from attack. The size of the fort and location of the structures are based on archaeological investigations of the site which revealed information about the layout and settlement at the original fort.

starving to death. They had resorted to butchering horses, digging for roots and scraping the trees for bark.[18]

On July 21, 1832, Black Hawk was overtaken at the Wisconsin River. His braves fought in order to enable the women and children to cross the river. Known as the Battle of Wisconsin Heights, a Mr. Townsend stated that *they (Black Hawk's band) were badly whipped by our troops, and worse whipped by starvation.*

The first Indian killed was discovered walking ahead of the troops with a pack of meat on his back. A soldier fired but missed him, he turned and immediately threw down his gun, but was bayoneted after his surrender.[19]

The fighting continued on throughout the day and did not cease until about 10 pm that evening. Despite being vastly outnumbered and sustaining heavy casualties, Black Hawk's warriors managed to delay the combined government forces long enough to allow the majority of the women, children and aged in the group, approximately 700 in all, to escape across the Wisconsin River.

The following morning, about daybreak, according to Captain Daniel S. Harris,* *the camp of soldiers was alarmed by the clarion voice of the Prophet* (Black Hawk's friend White Cloud) *from a hill nearly a mile away. At first we thought it was an alarm, but soon found that the Prophet was pleading for peace. Although he was so far distant, I could hear distinctly every word, and I understood enough to know that he did not want to fight.* The interpreter stated that *the Prophet had said that they had their squaws and families with them and were starving; that they did not want to fight any more, but wanted peace and would do no more harm, if they could be permitted to cross the Mississippi in peace.*

"Mr. P. J. Pilcher, a resident of Elizabeth, who was also there, stated that they were awakened by the shrill voice of the chief, and that he plainly understood: *Ne-com, P-e e-1 o-o-o; Friends, we fight no more.* Mr. Pilcher told General Henry what the Indian said, but Henry said *...pay no attention to any thing they say or do, but form in line of battle.* The Winnebagos in camp also informed the officers of the meaning of the Prophet's message, and *early in the morning,* says Pilcher, *they went with us to the spot where the Indian had stood, when he proclaimed peace, and there we found a tomahawk buried* - an emphatic declaration that so far as Black Hawk and his band were concerned, hostilities were ended.

No attention was paid to this second attempt to negotiate peace. It was said that the officers had no interpreter and did not know what the Prophet said until after the war ended. This excuse is invalidated by the direct and emphatic testimony of Capt. Harris and Mr. Pilcher. *The starved and dying Indians must be exterminated,* this was the view of the war mongers that were intent on ridding the land of the native Indians.

The next morning, not an Indian remained on the east side of the Wisconsin. The Battle of Bad Axe was the final battle of the war. Located near the present town of Victory, Wisconsin, this battle took place on August 2, 1832. This was a sad day in the history of humanity. Since the 1850's this battle has been called a massacre.

On the first day, *for eight miles* reported Townsend, *we were skirmishing with their rear guard, and numbers of squaws and children were killed.* Mr. Town-

- Captain Daniel S. Harris was one of the original pioneers to come to Galena back in 1823. He and his brother, R. S. Harris, built the first steamboat ever built on the Fever River, at the Portage, and called her the *Jo Daviess*.

send said he passed one squaw who had been shot and fallen on her face. On her back was strapped a child. The same shot that killed the mother had broken the child's arm, but in spite of this, the child was sitting on the back of the dead parent gnawing in its ravenous hunger, the raw flesh from a horse bone. [20]

The following day would mark the end of the war, and the actions of the soldiers would result in this battle being called a massacre. When the soldiers, under the direction of General Henry, met up with the main body of the Indians, a desperate bayonet and musket battle followed. Women and children fled the fight into the river, where many drowned immediately. The steamship *Warrior* * arrived on the scene at about 10:00 a.m. and joined in the slaughter, despite the fact that the elderly Black Hawk was again waving a white flag and attempting to surrender.

The slaughter on the eastern bank of the river continued for eight hours. The soldiers shot at anyone--man, woman, or child--who ran for cover or tried to swim across the river. They shot women who were swimming with children on their backs; they shot wounded swimmers who were almost certain to drown anyway. Other women and children were killed as they tried to surrender. The soldiers scalped most of the dead bodies. From the backs of some of the dead, they cut long strips of flesh for razor straps.[21]

Battle of Bad Axe engraved by Henry Lewis 1819-1904

* The steamboat *Warrior* was both privately built and owned. The 111-foot (33.8 m) boat was built by Joseph Throckmorton, who also owned the vessel in a partnership with Galena resident William Hempstead. At the Battle of Bad Axe, the vessel was armed with a 6 pound cannon, 3 crew and 23 soldiers: (2 officers, 15 federal Army troops and 6 volunteer militia).

U.S. forces captured an additional 75 Native Americans. Of the total 400 to 500 Sauk and Fox Indians at Bad Axe on August 2, most were killed at the scene, others escaped across the river. Those who escaped across the river found only temporary reprieve as many were captured and killed by Sioux warriors acting in support of the U.S. Army. The Sioux brought 68 scalps and 22 prisoners to the U.S. Indian agent Joseph M. Street in the weeks following the battle. Most of the Sauk and Fox were shot in the water or drowned trying to cross the Mississippi to safety.

In 2007 Kerry A. Trask published his book titled, *Black Hawk: The Battle for the Heart of America*. Trask commented that the hideous and inhuman viewpoint held by one of the soldiers at Bad Axe, a Mr. John Allen Wakefield, was a viewpoint held by

The Battle of Bad Axe engraved by Ernest Heinemann (1848-1912)

nearly all the militia members. Wakefield's statement was: *I must confess, that it filled my heart with gratitude and joy, to think that I had been instrumental, with many others, in delivering my country of those merciless savages, and restoring those people again to their peaceful homes and firesides."*

The battle of Bad Axe terminated the war, and brought about Black Hawk's surrender.

Dead Indian Mother and Her Child
Scene from the Massacre of Bad Axe
Source: *Illustrated life of General Winfield Scott* (1847), Barnes and Co., New York
D.H. Strother (illustrator)

1832
Historical Documents
Author: Sauk Indian Warrior and Leader, Black Hawk

"Black Hawk Surrender Speech"

Black-Hawk is an Indian. He has done nothing for which an Indian ought to be ashamed. He has fought for his countrymen, the squaws and papooses, against white men, who came, year after year, to cheat them and take away their lands. You know the cause of our making war. It is known to all white men. They ought to be ashamed of it. The white men despise the Indians, and drive them from their homes. But the Indians are not deceitful. The white men speak bad of the Indian, and look at him spitefully. But the Indian does not tell lies; Indians do not steal.

An Indian, who is as bad as the white men, could not live in our nation; he would be put to death, and eat up by the wolves. The white men are bad school masters; they carry false looks, and deal in false actions; they smile in the face of the poor Indian to cheat him; they shake them by the hand to gain their confidence, to make them drunk, to deceive them, and ruin our wives. We told them to leave us alone, and keep away from us; but they followed on, and beset our paths, and they coiled themselves among us, like the snake. They poisoned us by their touch. We are not safe. We lived in danger. We are becoming like them, hypocrites and liars, adulterers, lazy drones, all talkers, and no workers.

We looked up to the Great Sprit. We went to our great father. We were encouraged. His great counsel gave us fair words and big promises; but we got no satisfaction. Things were growing worse. There were no deer in the forest. The opossum and beaver have fled; the springs were drying up, and our squaws and papooses without victuals to keep them from starving; we called a great council, and built a large fire. The spirit of our fathers arose and spoke to us to avenge our wrongs or die. We all spoke before the council fire. It was warm and pleasant. We set up the war-whoop, and dug up the tomahawk; our knives were ready, and the heart of Black-hawk swelled high in the bosom, when he led his warriors to battle. He is satisfied. He will go to the world of spirits contented. He has done his duty. His father will meet him there, and commend him.

Galena, Illinois

The following newspaper articles, written in 1832, are from all over the country. They provide a glimpse into the news of the day, and the interest of the public regarding the western frontier.

Indian Hostilities.— We have been favored with the following extract of a letter from Belleville, Illinois, to a gentleman in this city. The letter is dated May 3d.

"The papers will have informed you of the return of the hostile Indians, Black Hawk's band into our State, and the prospect of bloodshed. The troops left us some days since. Information by steamboats from Galena just received, announces that the band consists of about two thousand, that one hundred head of cattle have been captured by the Indians, who killed the animals and dried the flesh, that our Indian Agent resident in that quarter had been taken prisoner, and that the Winnebago's had ransomed him at a high price. We are all anxiety to hear from our troops. I will write you soon as I hear of their arrival at Rock river. The miners have all come in, and it is truly afflicting that we should again at this busy season be called from our homes. No doubts are entertained that there will be fighting as soon as our troops reach Fort Atkinson. Gov. Reynolds has gone on with the militia."

The Globe of yesterday gives the annexed extract of a letter, received from the Head Quarters of General Atkinson, dated 27th April:

"That the conduct of Blackhawk and his associates, renders it necessary that he should take the field, and, as far as possible prevent them from doing any mischief: that Mr. Gratiot, Indian Agent, has just arrived from the Prophet Village. Blackhawk and his party were there. Yesterday they set out, in company with the Prophet's bank, for the purpose of taking a position on Rock River, some fifteen or twenty miles above Dixon's Ferry, where they are determined to hold out in defiance of any force that can, they say, be sent against them. They have the British flag hoisted, under which the war dance is constantly exhibited. They must be checked at once, or the whole frontier will be in a flame. General Atkinson proposes moving be Galena and taking a position at Dixon's Ferry on the Fort Clarke road and await the arrival of Governor Reynold's mounted force, when the General presumes, the hostile party can be put down.

To a mild talk sent by General Atkinson to Black Hawk, he returned an answer that his heart is bad and that he will fight any force sent against him.

Great distress is already felt on the frontiers. The inhabitants have abandoned their farms and are falling back for safety."

The *Evening Post* (New York, New York)
May 18, 1832

The Indians.— We have received nothing definte from the troops gone to the protection of the frontier, but rumors are as wild as they are numerous. One report is that the Indians in the vicinity of Galena have evinced a spirit of hostility, and had driven the miners from their labors, into the town. They made Mr. Gratiot, of Gratiot's Grove, a prisoner; he was, however, delivered to a party of friendly Indians on the payment of a few pounds of tobacco. Another rumor, and one on which we place the most reliance, is, that the Indians, aware of their inferiority, have hoisted the white flag in token of peace, and are preparing to recross the Mississippi.— *Alton (Illinois Spec. May 4.*

The *Evening Post* (New York, New York)
May 23, 1832

From the Seat of War.—From an intelligent gentleman who arrived yesterday (6 days) from Galena, we learn that the Indians, principally the Sacs, Foxes and Winnebago's, continued in hostile bands to rove the country, and alarm the Illinois frontier. They were estimated by him to be in force from two to three thousand men. General Atkinson and Governor Reynolds had not at their disposal a sufficient force to pursue them.—Martial law has been proclaimed at Galena. General Atkinson was fortifying his position at Dixon's Ferry.—The Indians had sent their women to Turkey village. Every appearance seemed to indicate continued and prolonged hostilities. It is the opinion of our informant that the marauding Indians cannot be driven back or dispersed for some months. On the 24th May, the Indian Agent, St. Vrain, was killed— his companions made their escape. The inhabitants of the mineral country have generally broken up their settlements and have sent their families to the interior of Illinois. The alarm is great, and much injury to the settlements is apprehended.

Black Hawk is represented by our informant as being a warrior of undoubted bravery and great influence in his tribe. He is not however, a regularly constituted chief—but a Bravo, who by his deeds, courage, and talents, has acquired an unbounded ascendancy over a large portion of his nation. He is ferocious, cruel and revengeful. The Sacs and Foxes are at war at present not only with the whites, but with the Menominee's of the north, and with other tribes westward.

The *Evening Post* (New York, New York)
June 13, 1832

On Friday, the 18th May, a party of five men commanded by Mr. F. Stahl, set forth from Galena on a scouting expedition thro' the country supposed to be occupied by the enemy. They had gone about fifty miles, in the direction of the station of the militia of Illinois, without meeting any obstruction, when they were suddenly attacked by a small ambuscade of Red men. The whites had passed the ambush, when the Indians arose and fired; and the first knowledge the surprised party had of the immediate presence of the foe, was the discharge of the murderous rifle. The Indians were painted green, and lay concealed in the grass on a slight declivity. One of the whites, a Mr. Durley, was killed instantly, and two others had parts of their clothing pierced by the balls. After the first fire, the whites perceiving the Indians to be superior in force, turned and fled—and made their way back to Galena without any further loss.

Star and Banner
(Gettysburg, Pennsylvania) June 19, 1832

Accounts have been received at New-Orleans from St. Louis, to the 26th May, by which we learn that the steamer Chieftain had arrived there from Galena, with the last of the women and children, all the mining business having been suspended. The Chieftain reports that a detachment of eighteen men, commanded by Lieut. Hamilton, had been cut off near Fort Clark.

Boston Post (Boston, Massachusetts)
June 21, 1832

In short, that whole section of the country was pervaded by a general sentiment of alarm. At Galena, civil process had been suspended by a military order from the commanding officer of the militia in that district, and Stockades and Block houses were erected for the protection and defense of the town.

The *Evening Post* (New York, New York)
June 11, 1832

GALENA is under martial law. On Monday, the 21st ult. (says the Galenian,) such was considered the danger of the town, that Col. Stode, commanding, issued his proclamation, declaring Martial Law. By this proclamation, every man who cannot produce a certificate from the surgeon, is to labor from 9 o'clock A.M. to 6 o'clock P.M. on the stockade erecting for the defense of said town. All persons are prohibited from selling or giving away spirituous liquors before seven o'clock P.M. All persons are prohibited from firing guns without orders, unless while standing guard to give the alarm. The proclamation was received by the people with much satisfaction. They have a company of rangers, mounted riflemen, of 75 men, a company of artillery, a volunteer company of riflemen, and two companies of infantry.

Fortifications for the defense of Galena are rapidly progressing. On Saturday, the 29th, a stockade was commenced near the centre of the town, on two angles of which block houses are to be erected.

The *Sandusky Clarion* (Sandusky, Ohio)
July 4, 1832

Galena, Illinois

Extract of a letter dated:
Galena, June 8, 1832

"The Indian war has assumed an alarming character. On Monday night last we had an alarm at midnight, that the town was attacked. The scene was horid beyond description. Men, women and children flying to the stockade. I calculated seven hundred women and children were there within fifteen minutes after the alarm gun was fired—some with dresses on and some with none—some with shoes and some barefoot. Sick persons were transported on others' shoulders. Women and children were screaming from one end of the town to the other. It was a false alarm; had there been an Indian attack, I believe the people would have fought well.

"It is now ascertained here where the main body of the Indians are. In two or three weeks an attack will be made that will be decisive. All the hostile Indians will be slain, or thousands of Americans will be scalped. The Indians have already taken about forty scalps in the whole.

The *Evening Post* (New York, New York)
June 29, 1832

Indian War.— General Scott, at the last dates, was at Fort Armstrong, with six companies. Colonel Eusno, with the column left by General Scott at Galena, was encamped on Rock river, four miles below the Fort, in consequence of the existence of a few cases of the cholera, all of a mild type among the troops.

Parties of the friendly Sacs and Foxes had been sent out to follow on the trail of Black Hawk's band, about 100 of whom had been killed or taken by the Sioux, since the action of the Ioway. Five or six of his principle Chiefs and Warriors had been brought into Fort Armstrong, and parties of the Sioux and Menomonee's had been ordered to scour the country; the latter under the command of Col. S.C. Stambaugh. Nothing certain is yet known of the fate of Black Hawk.

There can be little doubt that the war has closed; but General Scott has yet much to do in arranging terms of lasting peace; in these duties Gov. Reynolds of Illinois has been associated with him, and he will have the benefit of the experience of General Clark, of St. Louis. —*Globe.*

The *Evening Post* (New York, New York)
September 11, 1832

Chapter 6

1832 – 1839
A Time of Growth

The conclusion of the Blackhawk War in 1832 opened up a period of unparalleled growth and development in Galena and the surrounding territory. The white settlers no longer carried the undercurrent of anxiety and fear of the Indian in Illinois. *The Pittsburgh Gazette* of January 30, 1836 discussed life in Galena, Illinois in detail. It stated:

"...But four years ago (1832), Galena, with 4 or 500 inhabitants, was under arms, and the surrounding country was the theatre of bloodshed.—At length, however, the cause of danger has been removed, and the inhabitants enjoy the most permanent security. The rifle being laid aside, the implements for digging have taken its place."

By late 1833 Galena boasted a population of 500 to 600 inhabitants. There were thirty-six stores and groceries, four blacksmith shops, four carpenters, two tailors, two saddlers, two shoe makers, one silversmith, one wagon maker, one tanner, four taverns, four practicing lawyers, four physicians, two ministers of the gospel, one Presbyterian and one Methodist Chapel and a respectable Academy. [2]

To have this wide range of talents and business in this far western town provided proof that this wasn't just an outpost, but an established and civilized community that settlers and families could move to and thrive.

The *Evening Post Newspaper (New York)* printed in October of 1833 stated:

"Any necessities and luxuries of life could be had in Galena and be easily attained as well. Transportation from New York to Galena only took 30 days in 1833. The cost to ship this distance was $1.63 per hundred pounds." This was considered a "nominal" expense for merchants at that time. [3]

> CHICAGO.— We have had the pleasure of a conversation with Mr. Frederick Stahl, of the firm Johnson & Stahl, of this place, who returned from Chicago on Tuesday last. He informs us that he ordered goods from N. York, which were shipped on the 10th, and arrived at Chicago on the 30th August. The charges for transportation from New York to Chicago, including commissions and storage, is only $1.63 cts. Per 100 pounds. Insurance 3 - 4 per cent in the fall, and 1 - 2 per cent at other seasons of the year. The country from Dixon's Ferry, on Rock river, to Chicago is smooth and level, and with little improvement, an excellent road may be made. An ox team could make a trip from thence to Galena, with great ease, in ten days. Thus we see, that merchandise can be brought from New York to Galena in thirty days, and at an expense merely nominal.

The *Evening Post* (New York, New York)
Saturday, October 26, 1833

In 1834 meetings were held in Galena to discuss the introduction of a system of common schools* into the region. The resolution was passed, approving the system and recommending the adoption of measures to promote its establishment. [4]

* Common Schools—Note foot note on following page

Galena purchased two "Selye Pumpers" in 1836. Each was capable of throwing water 100—150 feet at 200 gallons per minute. The two fire engines were originally named Cataract and Neptune.

A major concern of all towns in the 1800's was the threat of fire. In August of 1835, Galena secured funds to purchase a "first class" fire engine.[5] Evidently, funds were sufficient to purchase two engines, rather than just one, and so the new fire engines named the *Cataract* and the *Neptune* arrived early in September, 1836. The engines were manufactured by the Selye Fire Engine Company of Rochester, New York and were designed to throw water 100 to 150 feet. These "engines", as they were called at the time, were equipped with tools used in this era including drag-ropes, suction hose, wrenches and axes. Galena purchased the largest "engines" available at the time. These were manned by twenty men each and could pump up to 200 gallons of water per minute.[6]

On Tuesday, November 8, 1836, two fire companies were organized: Galena Fire Associations No. 1 and No. 2. *The Gazette and Advertiser* of November 12,

---

* From page 73: "Common school" was the name used for public schools in the United States and Canada in the late 19th century. Unlike the modern public school, a common school was locally funded and managed. Common schools were developed to give free secular education to all children regardless of socio-economic status, gender, religion, or national origin, and attendance was compulsory until the eighth grade.

1836 contained the following: "We congratulate our citizens upon the organization of two fire companies. The meeting on Tuesday night last was well attended and great unanimity of feeling prevailed in the election of officers, etc. Both engines are well manned, and by men, too, that can be depended upon in case of fire."

Visitors to this region of the country often times related to the citizens living back east, what it was like to visit the far west. At times, remarkable experiences were printed in the newspapers. *The Evening Post* of New York on June 18, 1833, printed the article "*Fishing On Skates.*" Who has ever thought of the idea of running down fish on skates? This was a sport in Galena on the Fever River back in 1833.

From the Sporting Magazine.
FISHING ON SKATES!
Kaskaskia, Randolph Co. IL. March 27, 1833

MR. EDITOR:

Seeing an invitation in your useful and very interesting Magazine, to us of the "far west," to give your eastern readers an account of some our amusements, I avail myself of it, and send you the following; novel in itself, and I believe peculiar to this region. It is no other than catching fish by running them down! We have all heard of running down foxes, wolves, and other wild animals; but few, I believe, have ever thought that the finny tenants of the flood can be taken in the same manner. But they are frequently, and in great quantities; and the sport is as lively and exhilarating as can well be imagined.

The citizens of Galena often amuse themselves in this way on Fever river, on which the town is situated. The water on that stream is very clear, and the ice there, (N. lat. 42° 25) forms in one night, two or three inches thick, as pure as crystal itself. Through it, the fish can be seen to the depth of eight feet or more, and at a distance of ten or fifteen feet. Those who are fond of the sport, prepare their skates, equipped with a gig* and a tomahawk, and each man looks out for his game. Having discovered a pike, muskellunge, or sturgeon, he gives chase, and watching the motions of his game, he can, upon his skates, adopt his own movements to them; and in a pursuit of something less than three hundred yards, performing various evolutions, the fish becoming exhausted with fear, and his exertions to escape, stops. The sportsman, with his tomahawk, blocks out about six inches square of the ice, and with his gig brings his prey to air, pierced by its prongs. What is remarkable, while the ice is cutting the fish shows no symptoms of alarm, nor do they attempt a further escape.

Thus are two of the most delightful amusements combined, skating and fishing. It is only however, for one or two days in a season, that this sport can be enjoyed, for after the first freezing the ice loses its transparency, so that the fish cannot be discovered through it, its surface no longer resembling that of the polished mirror.

The kind of fish taken in this way, are the common pike, weighing from half a pound to three pounds, the muskellunge of about the same size, both very delicious, and an inferior kind of sturgeon. A Mr. J. J. C. merchant of this place, was one of the skating party of four on Fever river, who ran down and captured in one day, almost four hundred fine fish, of the description mentioned above. Fishing on skates is a novelty I doubt not, to most of your readers, but in the west, it is often enjoyed, and you are assured, that it wants no one ingredient of "right excellent sport," though my description of it is tame and frigid.

The *Evening Post* (New York, New York)
Tuesday, June 18, 1833

> Many houses are framed here, and all prepared ready for "putting together," and in that state shipped to the Illinois, Upper Mississippi, or wherever the emigrant may choose to "cast his lot."
>
> It seems to us that building houses for the Far West might be a regular and profitable branch of business in this city, where all the necessary materials are cheaper than in any other city of the Union. The freight on a two story house, 16 by 30 feet, including all the wood work, nails, glass, &c., from Pittsburgh to Peoria, Galena or any intermediate point on the Illinois or Upper Mississippi would not exceed one hundred dollars, according the rates above mentioned. ***Advocate.***

The *Pittsburgh Gazette* (Pittsburgh, Pennsylvania)
Thursday, May 2, 1839

> ***The Lead Trade.*** — One of the most important items of western commerce is the lead from the Galena (Ill.) mineral region. We learn from the St. Louis Republican, that in 1839, there were received in that city 275,000 pigs, in 1840, 352,000; and in 1841, thus far, 395,000. This nearly all goes to New Orleans. At the latter city there were received in 1839, 300,000 pigs; in 1840, 352,000, and in 1841, up to the middle of November, 340,000. A pig of weighs about 60 pounds, which estimated at 3 1/2 cents, give the value of this trade alone at $947,325.

Southport Telegraph (Southport, Wisconsin)
Tuesday, February 22, 1842

Other newspapers of the time printed articles that have been helpful in understanding what life was like out in the then far western regions of the country. Recall Chapter 4 stated, that timber located on the east side of the Mississippi was reserved for use by the smelters. This was because trees were locally rare. This made it difficult to obtain building materials for homes as well as business. An interesting article found in the May 2, 1839 *Pittsburgh Gazette* identifies one of the solutions that was used to remedy this situation.

It states that in the 1830's, homes were being framed and prepared ready for "putting together" in Pittsburgh and then were being shipped to Illinois! This was profitable for all parties involved because building materials were in abundance in Pennsylvania and thus, less expensive. The costs for shipping a two story home, (including all the woodwork, nails, glass, etc. measuring 16 feet by 30 feet) from Pittsburgh to Galena would not exceed one hundred dollars.

Perhaps the most significant catalyst for growth was the fact that the price of lead had risen significantly. The value of lead mined from the Galena lead mines in 1841 had a value at that time of $947,328.00. In today's dollars by comparison, this would amount to over twenty two million dollars ($22,000,000.00).[1]

The *Pittsburgh Gazette* dated January 30, 1836, ran an extensive article detailing life in Galena, Illinois. Emphasizing the highlights of the area, it stated: *"...the quantity [of lead] was inexhaustible, and that it*

The mining district lies principally south of the Wisconsin, and north of Rock river. Dubuque's and other rich mines are west of the Mississippi. The amount of lead made from 1821 to 1823, was 58,634,488 pounds, from which the government received, as rent, 5,246,839 pounds. The rent has since been reduced from 10 to 6 per cent. The lead is inexhaustible, and must ever prove a source of wealth to the country. Money is plenty here, and all who are industrious can live like kings. Nor is the soil of the mining district inferior to that of the other parts of the state. The land is much more undulating than in the interior, being thickly interspersed with bluffs, which add greatly to the beauty of the country. Few if any of these bluffs are so high or difficult, as to prevent cultivation. The vegetables produced in this country are unparalleled. I have been credibly informed that eight hundred bushels of potatoes have been taken from one acre of ground, without any attendance on them after they were planted. Wheat is said to produce better here than in the interior of the state; and the country is peculiarly congenial to oat crops. There appears to be but one difficulty to the farmer, which is the apparent scarcity of timber; but the introduction of hedging will remove the difficulty on the one hand, and coal, which is found in abundance in parts of the state, will remove it on the other. Timber is on the increase, and will soon be plenty. I have been thus particular, because we want enterprising farmers.

The climate of the mining district is congenial to health, which is emphatically, the "poor man's riches, and the rich man's bliss." There are physicians, but they are only called upon to check those diseases which are incidental to mankind in every situation. The winters are cold, but no more so than in many parts of Pennsylvania. The country abounds with the purest limestone springs, and the springs are interspersed with the most inviting mill seats. The facilities for roads are great, and the hills abound with the most valuable stone quarries. The materials for brick are to be found in almost every direction; and the apparent deficiency of timber, so far from operating against the country, will form an incentive to call these treasures into action, which otherwise might lie unobserved.

Thus has nature bestowed upon the "Mininh District," in the most "luxuriant profusion," its richest blessings. The hills are made the depositories of the richest treasures, the streams abound with fish, the groves are filled with game, the soil is productive of the sweetest luxuries; and every wind blows health and prosperity to the industrious inhabitants.. Nor do they degenerate into the licentiousness and voluptuousness which are generally the attendants of easily gained affluence.; but they continue proverbial for their habits of industry.

In the midst of this highly favored region, is situated the flourishing town of Galena, which is the grand emporium of the far North West. It was first settled in 1826, and was an outpost of 3 or 400 miles advance in the wilderness, N.W. of St. Louis. It is 326 m. N.N.W. from Vandalia, about 350 from St. Louis, and 990 from Washington. It is situated on the Fever river, three miles from the Mississippi by land, and seven by water. When the navigation is open, which has just closed for the present season, boats arrive and depart almost every day. The average number of inhabitants is 2,000, though the number may be less at present, as the 'suckers' have taken the 'shoot.' The location of Galena is truly romantic, and the rising bluffs around give quite an ancient aspect. The name is derived from the mineral "Galena," signifying a native sulphuret of lead.

The enterprise and intelligence of the place deserve a notice. In the population of 2,000, there is not one family that is unwilling or incapable of supporting itself. The buildings, though not extravagant, are neat and convenient, and even superior, for a new country. The public building consist of one Methodist and one Presbyterian church, and a courthouse. A Catholic chapel is in progress, and a lot has been procured for the erection of an Episcopalian house. There is no jail, which, so far from arguing a want of enterprise, reflects favorably the morals of the place. There are upwards of forty stores, including groceries, besides a respectable number of mechanics. Nor foes the intelligence of the place fall short of its enterprise. It supports two weekly periodicals, one of which, for size and appearance, would do honor to any of the eastern cities. There is an excellent assortment of books for sale in the place, and many valuable private libraries. A "Library Association" has been formed, and a library about being purchased, with which it is contemplated to connect a Lyceum.

In points of advantages, few, if any places in the western country, can boast of superiority over the town of Galena; and yet no town is more painfully misrepresented. It is considered, by persons not a thousand miles distant, in the possession of the Indians, and the theater of savage barbarity and excess. A more polite, intelligent, and enterprising

Article continues on next page

The *Pittsburgh Gazette*
(Pittsburgh, Pennsylvania) Saturday, Jan 30, 1836

set of people, I never met with. Since my residence here I have not seen an Indian. The history of Galena is short and interesting:-For many years the Indians and the French hunted and traders had been accustomed to dig lead in this region, which they sold to the traders. In 1821, arrangements were made to prosecute the business of smelting, by the late Col. James Johnson, of Great Crossings, Ky., and brother to the Hon. R. M. Johnson.

In 1828 the country was almost literally filled with miners, smelters, merchants, speculators, gamblers, and every description of character. Such was the record of adventurers, in 1829, to this hitherto almost unknown and desolate region, that the lead business was greatly overdone, and the market for a while nearly destroyed. Fortunes were made almost upon the turn of a spade, and lost with equal facility. The business has since revived, and must remain prosperous, as the mines will be worked in proportion to the demand for lead, and the rest of the time devoted to tilling the soil. But four years ago, Galena, with 4 or 500 inhabitants, was under arms, and the surrounding country was the theatre of bloodshed.—At length, however, the cause of danger has been removed, and the inhabitants enjoy the most permanent security. The rifle being laid aside, the implements for digging have taken its place.—*Pittsburgh Conference Journal*

- The "suckers" are those Illinoisan's who come up the Mississippi every spring for the purpose of mining, and return in the fall; and they derive their name from the fish which instinctively pursues the same course.

The *Pittsburgh Gazette*
(Pittsburgh, Pennsylvania) Saturday, Jan 30, 1836

would "ever prove a source of wealth for the country." "Money is plenty here and all those who are industrious live as kings." "The vegetables produced in this region are unparalleled. …. 800 bushels of potatoes have been taken from one acre of ground." "Wheat is said to produce better here than in the interior of the state. The climate of the mining district is congenial to health, which is emphatically, 'the poor man's riches, and the rich man's bliss.' The country abounds with the purest limestone springs… the materials for brick are to be found in almost every direction. The streams

Horrid Affair. — A murder, of the most atrocious character was committed near Dubuque, last Thursday, by Patrick O'Conner. He killed his own partner, by the name of O'Keaf, and then shot another man, but did not kill him.

The same man formerly lived in Galena, and during his residence here, he was well known to be one of the vilest wretches on earth. He was frequently guilty of the commission of crimes, for which the gallows, was cheated out of its lawful and just rights. He set several houses on fire, in this town, and was *screened* from justice, that is the *halter*, by availing himself of the claim to have had the *mania a potu*.

No sooner had the country opened at Dubuque, and beyond the reach of law, then he availed himself of the *glorious privilege* of locating where he could *burn* houses, *kill* men, *steal, rob, plunder*, and no legal tribunal to bring him to just punishment.

Thus we have daily evidence of the indispensable necessity of the immediate organization of a new government, on the west side of the river.

In the mean time, we hope the people there will, in the present case, organize a special court among themselves, and try the offender, and, if found guilty, give him the **HEMP**.

We learn, since writing the above, that a court was called, and the murderer tried, convicted, and sentenced to be hung, on the 20th inst. —*Galenian, May 2.*

The *Pittsburgh Gazette*
(Pittsburgh, Pennsylvania) Saturday, June 21, 1834

The above is a brief narration of all the circumstances relating to the unfortunate affair at Dubuque, which terminated the life of O'Conner on the 20th inst.

At 12 o'clock, on the day of execution the prisoner was taken from his place of confinement, under a guard of a company of volunteers, commanded by L. Wheeler, to the place of execution, where had assembled about 1,500 citizens. He was placed on a cart, the rope was made fast to the gallows, when the cart was driven away, leaving the prisoner suspended between the heavens and the earth.

The whole proceedings were carried on with the utmost regularity and good order. By mutual consent, every coffee house was kept closed, and not a drop of spirits was sold until after the execution.

The *Pittsburgh Gazette*
(Pittsburgh, Pennsylvania) Saturday, July 12, 1834

Galena was called the "Grand Emporium of the Far North West." Emporium is defined as *a place, town, or city of important commerce, especially a principal center of trade.* New York is one of the world's great emporiums.

Although the "picture" painted by the article above highlighted the opportunities and the many blessings of life in Galena and the surrounding region, this was still considered the far west at the time. There were obstacles and dangers that had to be overcome.

New settlements often lacked a judicial system and law enforcement. The criminal element knew this and often took advantage of such situations. Newspaper articles dating back to the 1830's posted here, detail a number of criminals, their lawless actions and also speedy justice. Incidents such as this aptly demonstrate that Illinois was the "Wild West" in the 1830's, and that Galena was at the far corner of the northwest frontier. Despite these and many other challenges, the 1830's proved to be a time in which Galena flourished and expanded.

Transportation was continuing to develop. In 1839, an article appeared in Pittsburgh that said "distance should be measured in hours rather than miles." It boasted of how newspapers arriving from New York some 660 miles away were arriving there within 3-1/2 days. It explained how a traveler leaving Pittsburgh could arrive in Detroit within 8 or 10 hours and from there (Detroit), reach Galena within six days.

The activity on the Mississippi and the Fever River was also remarkable. There were so many steamboat arrivals in Galena on some days, and with these arrivals, an ever increasing number of inhabitants, that the town was said to present the appearance of a seaport.

The immense forests of pine found on the Upper Mississippi and its tributaries had been under the possession of the Indians until the late 1830's. This

> John B Smith, who shot Woodbury Massey, some months ago, at Dubuque, and who escaped legal punishment for want of jurisdiction in the Courts of the United States, was shot down and killed, in the streets of Galena, on the 13th ult., by Henry L. Massey, a highly respectable brother of the deceased. An eye witness of the occurrence informs us, that Smith was shot with a pistol at the distance of fifty yards.—Massey has since left the country.—*Louisville Journal*

The *Pittsburgh Gazette* (Pittsburgh, Pennsylvania)
Tuesday, March 22, 1836

> It is not of physical wonders, alone, that the great West is productive. There is a kind of indigenous ferocity in some of the *people* of that country which is as peculiar as the fertility of the soil, the immense size and volume of the rivers, and the vast prairies, which distinguish it from other regions. A singular instance of this spirit is now before us. In the town of Dubuque, Illinois, some three or four weeks ago, *Henry L. Massey* had an encounter with an old gentleman named *Smith*, whom he shot with a pistol. About two weeks after, Miss *Massey*, a sister of the first named homicide, shot *William Smith*, son of the deceased. The feud, no doubt, will be kept up, men, women and children mingling in the melee, until the hostile clans have been all, in western phrase, "used up."

The *Weekly Raleigh Register*
(Raleigh, North Carolina) Tuesday, April 26, 1836

abound with fish, the groves are filled with game and the soil is productive of the sweetest luxuries." …. "The location of Galena is truly romantic, and the rising bluffs around give quite an ancient aspect. The buildings, though not extravagant, are neat and convenient, and even superior for a new country. In points of advantages, few, if any places in the western country, can boast of superiority over the town of Galena."

> *Traveling.*— Distance in these days should be measured in hours, not miles. Newspapers are now received here from New York in 3-1/2 days— distance 660 miles. From this to Chicago, one may travel by a good steam boat in 4 days; distance by the rout, about 800 miles; or to Green Bay in 3 days; distance, 630 miles. Or the traveler may go from this to Detroit in 8 or 10 hours and thence by rail road, stages, and steam boat to Chicago; and by stage to Galena, going the whole distance in six days.
> New York to Cleveland, distance 3-1/2 days.
> Cleveland to Chicago, by lake, 4 "
> Cleveland to Green Bay, " 3 "
> Cleveland to Detroit, " 10 hours.
> Detroit to Galena, 6 days.
> —*Cleve. Herald*

The *Pittsburgh Gazette* (Pittsburgh, Pennsylvania)
Monday, May 27, 1839

> Of all the older settlements, if the term may be used even with reference to that place— Galena (Illinois) has been, of late, subjected to the most astonishing improvements. There are so many steamboat arrivals-there some days, and such accessions to the number of inhabitants, that the town is said to present the appearance of a seaport. The papers of the place represent the increase of the population as far beyond the supply of houses or even lodging for their accommodation, not withstanding the builders' implements are kept untiringly in operation. For the industrious mechanic it provides a heart-cheering harvest; for the lazy workman, we should suppose, it would be any thing but a pleasant situation. —

The *Sun* (Baltimore, Maryland)
Thursday, May 30, 1839

> *Upper Mississippi Pineries.*— The immense forests of pine found on the Upper Mississipppi and its tributaries, just begin to yield their riches to the whites, having until quite recently been in possession of the Indians. Several large rafts have arrived at Galena from above, and timber dealers in St. Louis are now looking to Wisconsin for future supplies. Lumber from the Ohio has heretofore supplied the market.— *Cleve. Herald.*

The *Pittsburgh Gazette* (Pittsburgh, Pennsylvania)
Tuesday, June 4, 1839

was now yielding its "riches" to the settlers. Timber dealers up and down the Mississippi would no longer be sourcing their lumber from Pittsburgh and the Alleghany Mountains.

Even though wood was becoming readily attainable, the dangers of fire were always of great concern in the frontier towns. This is probably a major factor making brick the most important and popular building material in Galena. In 1837, full-scale production of bricks began, making them available for building houses in Galena.

The Northwestern Gazette and Galena Advertiser of May 20, 1837, ran this article:

> Captain Orren [sic] Smith has now a patent machine for making *Bricks* in full operation, within a short distance from town. It is said to work to admiration. The clay is put into the machine in a dry state, and by means of a horse power, the way it is pressed out in the shape of smooth, handsome bricks, is not slow; which without further trouble or preparation, are carried to the kiln, to undergo the fiery ordeal.

Because brick was used rather than wood, having "fire proof" buildings proved to be a major factor leading to the preservation of so many of these old structures down to this day. At the time of writing (2014), the Galena Historic District contains nearly 1,000 buildings, all constructed before 1900. The boundary of the historic district includes any area, place, building, structure, work of art, or other object within the "original city" and all subdivisions added before December 31, 1859.

During the 1830's there was no doubt that Galena was, and would continue to be, a major metropolis and commercial center in Illinois.

1832 – 1839 A Time of Growth

Galena compared to Chicago

In 1840, Chicago surpassed Galena in population, but not in commerce or quality of life. Galena was situated in a picturesque landscape that continues to awe visitors to this day. Chicago, on the other hand, was planted in a swamp.

Note the contrasting factors between these two frontier towns:

Year	Galena	Chicago
1826	50	2
1828	450	60
1829	450	100
1833	1,000	325
1839	3,000	2,800
1840	3,500*	4,470*

Galena was established long before Chicago and had a larger population until 1840.

- Galena was booming commercially and was a destination that was considered to be "*truly romantic,*" due to the beauty of the landscape.

- In contrast, the geography of Chicago was frowned upon by most. It was surrounded by swamp for miles around. In fact, the first buildings in Chicago were built directly on the swampy ground; hence, it was impossible to construct cellars or sewers. It wasn't until the late 1850's that the streets were raised by covering them with dredgings from the river, as well as any other available material. Buildings were jacked up and foundations placed beneath them (note illustration on page 83). By 1858 Chicago had risen a few feet above the mud. [9]

- Chicago was an unhealthy city in its early years. It's residents were afraid of pestilence and disease. They had good reason. A number of cholera epidemics affected the town in its early years and most of those who caught it died. Disease thrived in this frontier town where there was no sewer system, where residents drank water from shallow wells or the lakeshore and the Chicago River was used as the city's sewer. [10]

*1840 Galena Population is estimated,
Chicago's 1840 population is documented.

IS CHICAGO A SWAMP?

A New Orleans View of It—Chicago Dirt and What Will She Do With it?
New Orleans Times Aug 24.

She is Chicago and it is dirt.

Chicago is positively the dirtiest city extant in any civilized or Christian country. A clean level lies behind her, without a rise, to the foot of the Rocky Mountains. A broad, clean inland sea lies in front of her, or her people would have died with pestilence ten times over. She used to be scourged with cholera regularly in the old days, and her frightened citizens fled by thousands to Milwaukee and the towns down the lake. It was hoped that by sewering the place and getting lake water to drink, it might be made healthy if not clean. But the enormous death-rate of the last half year-double to treble that of New Orleans—is causing doubt upon this subject.

There is a well-built and comparatively clean centre in Chicago, but the city sweeps off, on all sides but the front, to a swamp. They call it a prairie there. In Louisiana they call is a swamp. The outskirts of the city are built up with shanties, squatted in this swamp, or stuck upon posts to keep them out of it. Coming in on nearly all the railroads, notably the Michigan Southern or the Northwestern, the traveler passes through miles of these shanties, scarcely superior to the cabins on a rack-rented estate in Ireland, where naked babies and pigs tumble promiscuously. Chicago's face is fair enough, but like Milton's monster, she ends "foul in many a scaly fold." She is the draggle tail of cities.

Chicago Daily Tribune (Chicago, Illinois)
August 28, 1881

- Michigan Avenue was a muddy path filled with horse manure, and the Chicago River had become a convenient way for farmers to dispose of dead cows and hogs. It's no wonder that the town faced another cholera epidemic. [10]

As several historians note in books about Chicago, the Chicago River was the city's sewer, and by 1860, it was a smelly, sluggish stream of filth, so nauseating, that city and state officials decided to reverse the river. They would send sewage south instead of allowing it to continue flowing into Lake Michigan, the source of Chicago's drinking water.[11]

With the above mentioned details of life in early Chicago are compared to that of Galena, it is of little wonder that one of Galena's early and wealthiest residents, Captain Hezekiah Gear, replied to some of Chicago's capitalists the way he did. When encouraged to invest in Chicago, he replied: *Gentlemen, I'll never put a cent of my money in that mud hole.* [12]

Hospitality in Galena

Another factor that certainly added to the popularity of Galena was the hospitality, generosity, honesty and kindness shown to newcomers in this region. "During the early mining days at Galena, men from the South and East congregated to work the mines, and these men as a class, possessed and practiced many of the noblest traits of manhood. As an illustration of their innate integrity of character, it is perhaps only necessary to state that locks and keys were unknown in the country and all places of abode were always left unfastened and open to the reception of all, who received a cordial welcome and a free invitation to partake of every hospitality the 'dug-out' or shanty afforded. Debts were contracted without reserve at the first interview with a newcomer and he seldom ever failed to meet his promise of payment." [13]

"Most noticeable of characteristics common alike to the pioneers of the prairie and the woodland was that of boundless hospitality. The new settler was received kindly and given substantial aid by those who had been in the country longer; his cabin was quickly built and often in addition to assistance thus received, it was not improbable that the friendly neighbors would furnish the new settler with some livestock if he had none. One would give poultry; another, a hog; a third, a calf and so on until there would be quite a drove of stock upon the clearing. No matter how poor the new settler might be, if he did not show a propensity to dispute over trifles or to complain of the disadvantages of the new country, and criticize the manners and habits of the people, and cite the superiority of things in the place from whence he came, he would be received with blunt frankness and unaffected hospitality. His reception was just as much of the opposite character should he presume to cast reflections upon conditions existing in his new home." [14]

With the river, the area's resources and the fine virtues of its residents, the town of Galena continued to develop and was about to enter its golden years, the 1840's and 1850's.

Raising Business Blocks.

THE SUBSCRIBER WOULD ANNOUNCE that he is ready to make contracts for RAISING BUSINESS BLOCKS TO GRADE, and all other operations pertaining to the removal or raising of Buildings of wood, brick or stone, of any size, to any desired height or to any distance.

A long residence in this city, enables him to refer with confidence to many of our best citizens, for all indersements as to character and reliability.

May be found at the of J. S. Wright, Esq., No. 51 Clark street, between the hours of 9 A. M. and 4 P. M., daily.
JAMES HOLLINGWORTH.

Chicago, Jan. 29th, 1857.—3w-194

January 29, 1857 The *Chicago Tribune*

The Raising of Chicago.

During the 1850's and 1860's, engineers carried out a piecemeal raising of the level of central Chicago. Streets, sidewalks and buildings were either built up or physically raised up by jacks. This was because Chicago was so flat that there was no naturally occurring drainage and stagnant water had become a breeding ground for disease, culminating in a Cholera epidemic in 1854 that wiped out 6% of the population.

One of the biggest "raisings" was "The Row on Lake Street" pictured above. By 1860, confidence was sufficiently high that a group of no fewer than six engineers took on one of the most impressive locations in the city and hoisted it up complete and in one go. They lifted half a city block on Lake Street, between Clark Street and LaSalle Street, a solid masonry row of shops and offices 320 feet (98 m) long, comprising brick and stone buildings, some four stories high, some five, having a footprint taking up almost 1 acre (4,000 m^2) of space, and an estimated total weight including hanging sidewalks of thirty-five thousand tons. Businesses operating out of these premises were not closed down for the lifting; as the buildings were being raised, people came, went, shopped and worked in them as if nothing out of the ordinary were happening. In five days the entire assembly was elevated 4 feet 8 inches (1.42 m) clear in the air by a team consisting of six hundred men using six thousand jackscrews, ready for new foundation walls to be built underneath. The spectacle drew crowds of thousands, who were on the final day permitted to walk at the old ground level, among the jacks. *Source—Chaz. Hutton and Wikipedia*

26th Congress [SENATE] [349]
1st Session

DOCUMENT

Showing the statistics of the city of Galena, Illinois.

APRIL 1, 1840
Referred to the Committee on Commerce, and ordered to be printed.

Memorandum of the growth, progress, and present state of the city of Galena, Illinois.

In 1826, there were 4 log cabins, population about	-	50
In 1828, there were 80 buildings, population about	-	450
In 1830, there were 80 buildings, population about	-	300
In 1832, there were 110 buildings, population about	-	900
In 1837, there were 400 buildings, population about	-	2,400
In 1839, there were 550 buildings, population about	-	3,000

Arrivals and departures of steamboats

In 1835,	-	-	153
In 1836,	-	-	182
In 1837,	-	-	359
In 1838,	-	-	307
In 1839,	-	-	272 (very low stage of water)

Lead shipped.

In 1835,	-	-	11 millions of pounds
In 1836,	-	-	13 millions of pounds
In 1837,	-	-	15 millions of pounds
In 1838,	-	-	14 millions of pounds
In 1839,	-	-	10 millions of pounds

From 1836 to 1840, about $50,000 have been expended by the authorities of the town, in improvements on the wharves and streets. This is independent of the disbursements by the county of Jo Daviess, for the court-house and jail.

There are at present, the following public buildings.

A court-house and jail, of stone; 4 churches, 3 of stone and brick, And 1 of wood.

And the following public institutions.

A chamber of commerce, a mechanic's institute, and a lyceum.
Besides a branch of the State Bank of Illinois is located here, and a land office.

THOS. MELVILL,
Secretary Chamber of Commerce

GALENA, *February* 29, 1840

Note.—According to a recent assessment for taxes, the ratable property of the town of Galena is valued at between $1,500,000 and $1,700,000.

Chapter 7

Galena's Golden Years

The 1840's and 1850's were Galena's "Golden Years." At the time, there was little doubt that Galena was and would continue to be a major metropolis and commercial center in Illinois.

In 1826, Galena was just a trading post, a small hamlet of four log cabins with a population of 50 people. By 1839, this outpost at the furthest edge of the frontier, had grown to more than 550 buildings with over 3,000 residents. This was considered a major population center in 1839. In fact, only three cities in the entire country had a population of over 100,000 people at the time.

Galena was a roaring city in the 1840's, which have been referred to as Galena's "most colorful years."[1] The population in town, as well as the surrounding area and farms was growing. Lead production was on the increase. The buildings all along Main Street were fully stocked with merchandise to be distributed throughout the Northwest. Bargemen raced for the limited dock space; sometimes settling a dead heat by a knockdown and drag-out brawl on the wharf in which everything and anything could happen from knee lifting to eye gouging. Blood and whiskey flowed freely along the waterfront and in the mining camps. Welsh miners introduced a new type of "fighting" that they used to settle disputes in the area. It was called the "Stone Duel." Participants assumed positions behind pre-arranged stone piles and proceeded to bombard each other until one of the opponents was dead or unconscious.[2]

The rough and tumble life of the mining region and the waterfront was only one aspect of life in Galena.

> Galena is the grand emporium of northwestern Illinois. It is situated in the midst of the mineral region, and may be truly styled the City of Lead. It contains 100 stores, 20 groceries, 2 printing offices, with taverns and storehouses, a bank, courthouse and jail.— The city has a rough, ugly appearance, being built on the steep stony banks of Fever River, or rather on "seven hills." The distance to the Mississippi, by way of Fever River is seven miles; but the nearest point directly west is 2-1/2 miles. The river is small, but the Mississippi sets back, which renders it navigable for steamboats nearly or quite the whole year. Galena is the county seat of Jo Davies County. Its latitude is 42 degrees and 23 minutes.

Huron Reflector (Norwalk, Ohio) Oct. 19, 1841

General A. L. Chetlain wrote in his autobiography titled "Recollections of Seventy Years":

Galena was the most important commercial metropolis in the Northwest. Its trade, which became a major industry in the 1830's, continued to increase steadily as the country developed. In 1856, statistics show that Galena did a larger wholesale business than Chicago. Lines of fine steamboats plied between St. Louis and Galena, bringing in merchandise and general supplies and taking back lead and farming products. A line of first-class steamboats ran between Galena and St. Paul. The supplies for new settlers were almost all obtained in Galena. Those men who were engaged in the wholesale trade became very wealthy and built large houses on Quality Hill. Additionally, during the early 1840's, Galena became a functioning incorporated town.

On May 29, 1841 the first city government of Galena was organized. Galena was a city—officially. A census was conducted and revealed that there were 650 houses with a population of 2,225.[3] By 1850, it had grown to 6,000. Within eight years, the population increased 233% to 14,000 people in 1858.

As the town grew, so did the lead mining in the surrounding area. In 1845, 65,000,000 pounds of lead were produced in the entire country, with Galena producing 54,500,000 pounds, 84% of the lead. At this time the city led the entire world in the mining of lead and was exporting it internationally to countries as far away as China.

Agriculture increased in the region surrounding Galena. Farmers would bring their crops to market at Galena. When the Market House was eventually

The Market House, located at the intersection of Commerce and Perry Streets, was erected in 1845 and served Galena as the center for farmers and merchants to sell their produce to customers. The *Galena Jeffersonian* of May 30, 1846 stated: "Whatever the season affords, will be displayed for sale, and buyers can easily find what they wish."

Pig lead being weighed on scales in preparation for transport on the train. Each "pig" weighed an average of 70 lbs. The largest quantity of pigs shipped was in 1845 with 778,408 pigs (54.5 million pounds) shipping out of Galena.   Photo c.1860

By the 1840's, weekly transportation by stagecoach in Galena provided access to Chicago, Rockford, Madison, as well as many other destinations. The cost in 1840 to travel from Galena to Chicago was $13. The arrival of the stage was an important event in Galena. Upon its arrival, the stores would suspend business and the merchants would gather around the American House hotel to see the stage come in, carrying fifteen to twenty passengers, and the usual allotment of forty pounds of baggage to each passenger, and twenty-five cents per pound for overweight.[12]

built in 1845, it became a center for produce that teamed with activity.

Large granaries were built near the waterfront. This was an ideal location because of the sharp slope of the land from Bench Street down to Main Street. Wagons would unload their grain into the third floor of the granary on Bench Street where it was processed on the second floor and then sent down to the Main Street level to be loaded onto boats waiting at the waterfront.

Business, transportation and communication continued to develop in the region. On June 17, 1840, the public was informed by notice that ... *the mail stage from Chicago to Galena via Rockford, by Frink, Walker & Co., proprietors, would, through the summer and fall, be run "through in one day" to Rockford, three times a week, fare $5. J. D. Winters was the proprietor of the line. The fare from Rockford to Galena was $8 and from Chicago to Galena, $13.*[4]

In January 1842, stagecoaches began running from Galena to Madison, Wisconsin via Mineral Point and Platteville, with intentions to add Milwaukee and Janesville. [5]

Up until 1842 the only way to gain access across the Fever (Galena) River was by ferry boat, as there were no bridges constructed up until this date. Francis Bouthillier, one of the original settlers of Galena, owned and operated the ferry. He eventually sold this enterprise to Colonel A. G. S. Wight, who ran it until about 1842, when he, by subscription, secured the erection of a wooden bridge at Bouthillier Street. Another bridge was built at Franklin Street by John L. Slaymaker & Co.

Neither bridge lasted very long, being carried away by an ice flood. Thus began the building of bridges as the principle means of crossing the river.

The winters and ice made travel difficult in Galena and its surrounding area. Two Galenians attempted to invent a new and improved means of winter transport. J. D. Carson and Jonathan Haines built a steam powered ice sleigh in the fall of 1835. It was designed to run between Galena and Dubuque. *It was covered, provided with doors, windows, seats, stoves, etc., and was as comfortable as the saloon of a steamboat. It was run on the ice on Fever river, but the steam engine was too small. Unfortunately, it didn't have sufficient power, and was pronounced a failure.* [6]

The 1850's brought change to Galena. With the beginning of the 1849 California Gold Rush, waves of immigrants from around the world (referred to as the "forty-niners"), invaded the Gold Country of California. Many in Galena left lead mining and ventured out west to seek their fortunes. The effect of the exodus was not permanent as many who left were disappointed in California and returned to Galena and the lead mines. In fact, about 300,000 people went to California during the gold rush. About half of this number traveled by water, the other half by land. Hundreds of wagon trains went westward and many came through Galena. Galena actually enjoyed a small boom equipping and supplying these wagon trains.

Because of the California Gold Rush, little building was done in Galena in 1850 and 1851. In 1852 the Illinois Central Railroad announced plans to extend its line from Chicago all the way to Galena. This was one of the factors leading to a new influx of people moving into Galena. This led to an acute housing shortage in 1852.

The first train steamed into Galena in November 1854. The city had been anxiously awaiting this day, hoping that this would energize Galena's industry and commerce. Throughout 1853 newspapers had carried daily accounts of the Galena & Chicago Union Railroad's efforts to reach Galena.

Homes and hotels were in high demand due to this shortage and this called for new construction. In 1855 one of the largest and most elegant hotels in the west opened its doors, The DeSoto House. Boasting 200 rooms and five floors, the DeSoto was and continues to be one of Galena's "Crown Jewels".

The number of people moving West in the middle 1850's is exemplified by the reports of Galena having "600 to 700 arrivals daily" with all boats and trains having their "full squeeze of passengers." [7]

Many came without money. Some were adventurers who had the where-with-all to start off fresh in a new and wild country. There were others who attempted to attach themselves to those more fortunate. There were others living in and around Galena who were less fortunate; some were poor, sick, or disabled.

As far back as 1838, provisions had been made for

> In the poor-houses and county jails of this State, I have not found, at the period of my visits, many insane persons; but I have seen many in private dwellings, in "cabins," in "dens," and wandering at large; often, very often bearing the marks of rude assault, and the effects of exposure to storms and frost. In the poor-house at Galena, the master showed me through a small apartment occupied by poor patients ill of fever, of consumption, and others confined merely through accidents, broken limbs, &c. Passing into the adjacent apartment, also small, I perceived a *man-cage* constructed on one side, with strong perpendicular bars, and inclosing a space about six feet by three. "There, Madam," said the keeper with emotion, "there is the only place I have for keeping the furiously insane, when they are sent to the poor-house—a place not fit for a dog—a place where they become daily worse; and where their cries, vociferations, and blasphemies, with other offenses, drive all peace and quiet from the place. The sick have no respite, and the family at large no rest. We want, madam, a hospital in our State, and the people ought to know it.

Alton Weekly Telegraph (Alton, Illinois)
Saturday, November 29, 1845

those less fortunate. On September 6, 1838, the following order was made: ...*For the purpose of affording relief to the sick and helpless individuals now in this county, the commissioners have this day contracted with Isham Hardin to furnish, on his part, house room in the dwelling now occupied by him for such persons as shall be directed or sent by the direction of a committee hereinafter mentioned, at the expense of the county.* [8]

This arrangement, although well intentioned, seemed to be lacking. The *Alton Telegraph* newspaper, ran an article in 1845 on the Poor Houses of Illinois. It stated that ...*often the insane are found wandering at large, often bearing the marks of rude assault.* Referring to the Galena Poor House, ...*there exists a "man-cage" enclosing a space of 3' x 6' that is for the "furiously insane".* The keeper of the Poor House stated that ... *it is not fit for a dog.*

By the late 1840's the arrangement for assisting those who were poor, sick or disabled was reviewed and a new provision was established. A total of 151.5 acres of land was purchased and a large building was erected in 1850. This was to be a permanent home for the poor in the county.

The "Poor House" farm was the site of the first and only legal execution that ever took place in Jo Daviess County. On January 19, 1855, John I. Taylor was hung for the murder of his wife. The execution was witnessed by as many as five thousand people. A terrible twist to the event is that one of the principal witnesses, and the only important one against Taylor, confessed on his death-bed that he was the one who killed Mrs. Taylor and that Taylor was innocent. [9]

Galena experienced a number of changes in the late 1850's. The production of lead had decreased since 1845. However, manufacturing was increasing in many other areas and this assisted in bringing the population of Galena to a peak of 14,000 in 1858.

In 1858 Galena had numerous stage lines radiating from the city. Even though lead production was on the decline, there were more than 34 million pounds produced by the Galena mines, indicating that lead was still a major component of the Galena economy.

Galena also boasted two daily newspapers in 1858. Its schools were educating 1,500 children. There were more than a dozen mills built on streams near the city, plus brick and lime kilns; seven breweries; three soap and candle factories; three leather finishing houses; wagon shops; pottery plants; lumber yards; two grist mills; two iron foundries; two plow factories; two furniture factories and two carriage factories. There were also two lead furnaces that smelted 15,000 pounds of lead daily. [11]

The 1850's marked the peak of Galena's population and commercial growth. The city had made its indelible mark on the preceding decades.

Changes were still to come but beautiful and historic Galena was here to stay.

The "Poor House" farm was built in 1850 and was located just south and east of Galena. It provided housing for the poor, sick or disabled individuals that were destitute and had no means of providing for themselves. The Poor House farm included 151.5 acres of land that the "inmates" (as the residents were called) worked, thus providing a means for producing food for themselves, as well as a large surplus that would go to market.

Galena in 1856

Galena, looking south, southwest
c. 1890

Chapter 8

A Small Town's Impact On the Civil War

The War Between the States was the cruelest and bloodiest stain on the history of this country.

In 1861 there were thirty-four states in the Union and the total population of the country, based upon the 1860 census, was 31,183,582. The total number of slaves in the U. S. numbered 3,950,528, or 13% of the entire population.

The topic of slavery had been a source of debate and friction since the birth of our nation. In 1786, George Washington stated, *"There is not a man living who wishes more sincerely than I do, to see a plan adopted for the abolition of it [slavery]."*[1]

On April 12, 1861, this 3.67 Inch bore Blakely cannon fired the opening shots at Fort Sumter that started the Civil War. Grant Park in Galena, Illinois has been its permanent home since 1896.

The boiling point was finally reached on April 12, 1861. At 4:30 A.M. on that fateful morning, Confederate artillery batteries opened fire upon the Federal garrison occupying Fort Sumter in Charleston, South Carolina. The Confederate artillery included a 3.67 inch bore English-made Blakely rifled cannon that hurled twelve pound iron projectiles to breach the walls of the fortress, 1200 yards distant. This cannon fired the opening shots that started the Civil War. It is noteworthy that this cannon overlooking Galena since 1896, is located in Grant Park.

Galena is the perfect resting place for this piece of history. Perhaps no other town in the Union the size of Galena could even come close to having the impact that this city had on the war.

On April 13, 1861, Major Anderson surrendered Fort Sumter's federal garrison to the rebel forces. Within forty eight hours, on April 15, President Lincoln called for 75,000 state militiamen as three month volunteers to suppress the insurrection of the seceded states.

Immediately, Galenians answered the call.. On the following evening, its citizens converged on the courthouse for a meeting to consider action. Numerous officials spoke, however, John Rawlin's words were most impactful. He stated: *I have been a Democrat all my life, but this is no longer a question of politics. It is simply Union or disunion, country or no country. I have favored every honorable compromise, but the day for compromise is past. Only one course is left for us. We will stand by the flag of our country and appeal to the God of Battles...* [2]

During the meeting it was resolved that Galena would answer Lincoln's request and form two companies of volunteers. Ulysses Grant, a lifelong Democrat himself, was in the audience. He was impressed with Rawlins' statements. Two days later he agreed to place his military experience at the service of the local volunteers to assist in preparation and training, but his intention, as a former Federal officer and West Point graduate, was to seek an active commission.

On April 21st, in the midst of training and equipping the volunteers, Grant wrote to his father regarding his sentiments and decision to serve: *Whatever may have been my political opinions before, I have but one sentiment now. That is, we have a Government, and laws and a flag, and they must all be sustained. There are but two parties now, traitors and patriots, and I want hereafter to be ranked with the latter, and I trust, the stronger party.* [3]

Grant's expressions mirrored those of the vast majority of the citizens of Galena. They were determined to support the Union and their government.

On Thursday, April 25, the first company of 103 volunteers (the Jo Daviess Guards), equipped and in full uniform consisting of a blue frock coat and dark gray pants with blue cords, (made locally for the volunteers) were escorted to the train depot in preparation for their departure to Springfield. Upwards of 5,000 friends, family and concerned citizens were there to see them off.

While this first company was being organized, uniformed and sent out to join in freedom's battle against treason and slavery, others were forming. In the Galena papers of April 20, there appeared the following call :

Attention, Company! All those that are willing to volunteer, and are in favor of the Union, the enforcement of the laws, protection to our flag, and of responding to the call of the President of the United States, in suppressing rebellion, repressing invasions, dispersing mobs, and in re-capturing and protecting government forts, property, etc., to form a company tor that purpose, and will hold themselves in readiness subject to a call by the Governor, are requested to enroll their names at my office. Said company, when formed, may elect its own officers.

B. B. Howard

Within a matter of weeks, the second company of volunteers were equipped, trained and in uniform. When they left Galena for the war on June 13th, they received the same encouragement and support from the town as the first. They were led by Captain Bushrod B. Howard, a veteran of the Mexican War. Captain Howard's Company was named the Anti-Beaureguards.

We have an eyewitness account of their departure at the Galena depot in the person of Julia Grant, wife of Ulysses. She wrote in her autobiography: *The Captain of this company was a Democrat and enthusiastically loyal. I do not think his wife was in sympathy with him. I was standing with my children in the station house near the south window, and, turning, saw Captain Howard stride in and stop within a few feet of his wife and two little boys and her mother, all of whom were standing near the middle of the room. Folding his arms, he looked sorrowfully at her. She returned his look but did not move. The mother said in a low voice, 'Speak Helen, meet him,' but she did not move. The two little boys running up to him, he stooped and, clasping them in his arms, said; 'God bless and keep you, my darlings,' and turning, he strode out to his company, already seated in the cars, and rolled away.* [4]

This would be the last time that Helen, her sons and many other families of Galena would see their fathers, brothers, uncles and sons who left on this train. On September 17, 1861, a train accident occurred at Beaver Creek bridge, twelve miles west of Mitchell, Indiana, one hundred and forty miles west of Cincinnati. The train was transporting the 19th Illinois Infantry Regiment of which the Anti-Beaureguards were a part. Captain Howard and many others were killed in this accident. According to the newspaper article printed on the following page, there is little doubt that the bridge was tampered with, and was an act of sabotage.

The pain and anguish that Galena experienced was being felt in every hamlet, village and city in the country. There were more U.S. casualties during the Civil War than all WWI, WWII, the Korean and Vietnam wars combined! (620,000 deaths, not including the scores of those wounded and maimed for life.)

If the names of the Civil War dead were arranged like the names on the Vietnam Memorial, it would stretch over 10 times the wall's length. Two percent of the population died, the equivalent of 6 million men today.

As previously stated, the population of the country was 31,183,582 in 1860. Between the North and the South, 3,000,000 soldiers fought in this war. That's 10% of the total population. One in ten people, then alive in this country, fought on the battlefield!

Civil War	620,000
WWII	318,000
WWI	115,000
Vietnam	56,227
Korean War	33,000

522,227

Ulysses S. Grant

When the Civil War began in 1861, Ulysses S. Grant was a clerk in his father's leather store in Galena, earning $600 per year. He was thirty-nine years old. He and his family had just moved to Galena from St Louis the previous year. At the start of the war, after declining service with the volunteers, Grant took charge of the Jo Daviess Guards and drilled its officers and men in rudimentary formations on the lawn of the Washburne residence. After this training, they left on the train and headed for Springfield along with Congressman Washburne. He went along to guide them through the confusion at the state capital, and Grant had come along as well. However, Grant's demeanor in contrast to those of the volunteers is a "scene memorable to American military history....there came trudging along Mr. Grant, battered suitcase in hand, appearing as disreputable as usual in his civilian garb, setting out to implore the authorities for a commission." [5,6]

More than a month passed with no reply from the Secretary of War. Grant's application for a federal position seemed to have fallen on deaf ears. Nor had the Governor of Illinois thought to find Grant a suitable job. In despair, Grant hunted for a commission in Ohio.[4] But then, things changed. He received a telegram from the Illinois Governor, Richard Yates.

Cleveland Morning Leader.

E. Cowles & Co., Publishers. Office No. 142 Superior Street. Terms:

VOL. XV.   CLEVELAND, FRIDAY MORNING, SEPTEMBER 20, 1861.   NO. 221.

The Great Railroad Tragedy

From the Cincinnati papers we take the following additional particulars of the late fearful accident upon the Ohio and Mississippi Road:

The accident occurred at bridge No. 48, about twelve miles west of Mitchell, Indiana, and one hundred forty-three from this city. The train, composed of eight cars, was moving at the rate of twenty-five or thirty miles an hour, and the engine and one car had just cleared the bridge when the structure gave way. Car no. 3 did not become detached from the car in front, but stood on an angle of about forty-five degrees, the forward end leaning against the abutment and the hind end resting in the water. No. 4, containing nearly all of Company I, which suffered so terribly in the disaster, went to the bottom, No. 5 falling upon it, and literally crushing it to atoms. No. 6 also went down, while No. 7 remained in a position corresponding to that of No. 3, the hind end leaning against the abutment. Those in No. 7 and 8 escaped without injury. The rear car contained a portion of the baggage and the hospital stores of the regiment.

The scene which followed the catastrophe in indescribable. Those fortunate enough to escape without injury were almost paralyzed with horror, and knew not what to do for their companions, whose shrieks and moans rent the air. The engineer, more thoughtful than some of the rest, suddenly remembered that the express train going west was nearly due, at that point, and fearful that it might come along suddenly and leap into the yawning chasm, adding, if possible, to the terrors of the scene, he detached his engine, and running with the speed of the wind to Huron, three miles further west, arrived just in time to have the coming train advised of the accident by telegraph at the next station above.

A surgeon at Huron at once returned with him to the scene of the disaster. Two more boarded the express train at Mitchell, while a special train with three others left Vincennes as soon as possible. These all reached the spot within a few hours. Those who left the city on the special train at midnight did not arrive till after daylight. There was still, however, plenty for them to do.

The wreck had not yet been cleared away, and many of the wounded were still firmly wedged among the ruins. The utmost activity, of course, prevailed, but the victim were not all removed till the day was well advanced. The agonies of that terrible night no pen can paint.

Before daylight eighteen bodies were recovered, in addition to rescuing all the living. Lieutenant Whotten was caught by both legs between two platforms, and it required three-fourths of an hour to chop and saw him out, every blow of the axe causing intense agony. A colored servant caught in a similar though less painful situation, was two hours undergoing the operation of rescue. A brakeman, with an arm and leg broken, crawled from under the bottom car to a place of safety. The water in Beaver Creek, over where the bridge passes, was about three feet deep.

Fortunately, both the regimental Surgeons, their hospital steward, and Lieut. Kellot, also physicians, were in the forward car and escaped without injury. Companies I and G were the greatest sufferers — the latter entire company, except Lieut. Bridges and two corporals, were more or less injured. The Colonel, who is an old Russian campaigner, Lieut. Karlett and Fife Major Moore, were accompanied by their wives. These ladies not only rendered great assistance in dressing the wounded, but even tore their under garments off their persons to make bandages.

Capt. B.B. Howard, for many years postmaster of Galena, and a fine soldier of the Mexican war, was completely crushed, not a whole bone being left. After finding the body of their Captain, his company, or the few who were left, covered it with green bushes. An old German, himself badly hurt, sat at the head of the corpse telling of Captain Howard's virtues to all that could listen. One poor fellow named Clark, saw his brother drown, he standing by, unable to help. So far as the officers can judge, 40 to 45 is about the number lost.

Of the cause of the disaster we are somewhat loath to speak. Not a soldier on the train, with whom we have conversed, save one, has any doubts that the bolts had been tampered with, and such, also, is the opinion of many railroad men and the inhabitants thereabouts. Certain it is, the bolts look as if they had been filed. There are some secession sympathizers thereabouts, with whom the company had trouble in times past. Until within two weeks, the bridges have all been watched.

He offered Grant a regimental command, the 21st Illinois Infantry, which Grant had mustered into service in Mattoon one month earlier.

U. S. Grant rose to the occasion and demonstrated his strength of character, decisiveness of action and ability to lead. His first operations were in Missouri.

On July 31, President Lincoln promoted Grant to Brigadier General of Volunteers, following the recommendations of a caucus of Illinois congressmen, including Washburne. Four weeks later, on September 1, he was placed in command of the district of Southeast Missouri.

On November 7, he fought his first battle with the enemy at Belmont, Missouri. This victory was indecisive for either side.

In 1862 he began the campaign by capturing Forts Henry and Donelson, taking 14,623 prisoners. Grant demanded an unconditional surrender.

The surrender of Donelson destroyed the entire Confederate line in the middle theatre of war. It confirmed the loss of Kentucky and presented an imminent threat to Tennessee. As the first major Union victory of the war, it touched off great celebrations in the North, in the course of which Grant's words provoked as much enthusiasm as the victory itself. The happy coincidence of the phrase with his initials, earned him the nickname, "Unconditional Surrender Grant."

General Grant's next battle was at Shiloh, where he defeated Generals Beauregard and Johnston. Shiloh was the severest battle fought up to that time. Grant stated: *"I saw an open field, in our possession on the second day, over which the Confederates had made repeated charges the day before, so covered with dead that it would have been possible to walk across the clearing, in any direction, stepping on dead bodies, without a foot touching the ground."* [7]

In November, 1862, Grant began his campaign to capture Vicksburg, Mississippi. He eventually drove the enemy into the city, to which he laid siege. The Confederates capitulated on July 4, 1863, surrendering 31,600 men and 172 cannons which at that time was the largest capture of men and material ever made in war. Galena's own Washburne Lead Mine Regiment, the 45th Illinois Infantry, earned the honor of raising their flag over the captured city. [8]

U.S. Grant at his headquarters in Cold Harbor, Virginia - June, 1864

The Battle of Chattanooga took place in November, 1863. Union forces drove the enemy from Missionary Ridge and Lookout Mountain. Years later, Grant was asked if the Confederates had failed at Chattanooga because they believed their position impregnable. With a twinkle in his eye, Grant replied, *Well, it was impregnable.*

Grant was appointed Lieutenant General by Congress on March 12, 1864, and given the chief command of the Union armies.[9]

His subsequent Eastern campaign included the battles of the Wilderness, Spotsylvania, Cold Harbor, the siege of Petersburg and the eventual fall of Richmond.

At Petersburg, Grant exerted relentless pressure on the overextended Confederate lines. By August, Grant could see the end. ...*The rebels have now in their ranks their last man. The little boys and old men are guarding prisoners, guarding railroad bridges and forming a good part of their garrisons for entrenched positions. A man lost by them can not be replaced.* [10]

By early April, 1865, General Grant compelled Lee to evacuate Petersburg, and followed up his success by bringing about the Confederate Commander-in-Chief's surrender at the Appomattox Court House on the 9th.

Describing that day, Grant expressed: *I felt like anything rather than rejoicing at the downfall of a foe who had fought so long and valiantly, and had suffered so much for a cause, though that cause was, I believe, one of the worst for which a people ever fought, and one for which there was the least excuse.* [11]

The two generals met in the parlor of the McLean House, Lee in an immaculate new uniform, Grant informally dressed with only shoulder straps to show rank. *We soon fell into conversation about old army times . . . Our conversation grew so pleasant that I almost forgot the object of our meeting.* Finally, Grant wrote a letter embodying his terms and Lee wrote one accepting them. Peace had come to a united nation. [12]

Peace in Union by Thomas Nast, depicts Lee's surrender at Appomattox. The original 9' x 12' oil on canvass is on display at the Galena Illinois Historical Museum

June, 1864, at City Point, Virginia with General Grant seated at the left.

Galena's 9 Generals

We have just detailed General U.S. Grant's campaigns and the events that elevated him from a non-commissioned ex-West Point graduate to the position of General of the Army of the United States. Without a doubt, this in itself "popped the buttons" off the chests of many Galenians. However, there is much more about which Galena had reason to hold her head high and feel a great measure of pride.

There were four additional Galenians who rose to the rank of General during the Civil War. Four others were brevetted as Generals after the close of the war. Each played a major role in the preservation of the Union and the victory over the Confederacy.

Galena's Nine Generals

Ulysses S. Grant

Commissioned Generals during the Civil War

John Rawlins

Augustus Chetlain

John Eugene Smith

Jasper Maltby

Brevetted Generals after the Civil War

John Duer

Ely Parker

William Rowley

John Corson Smith

During the war, a reporter remarked to Grant that his name had been mentioned in connection with the presidency. The General laughingly replied that, "*if he ever ran for office, he hoped that it would be for Mayor of Galena. Then he might have a sidewalk built from his house to the railroad depot.*" Upon his return to Galena, the citizens proudly announced: "General, the Side-walk is built."

On August 18, 1865, the citizens of Galena greeted the return of its victorious General, U. S. Grant, with a grand celebration. A "grand triumphal arch" spanned Main Street by the DeSoto Hotel, and a holiday atmosphere prevailed with a jubilant procession, speeches and evening fireworks.

Chapter 9

An Historical Time Capsule

Galena has over 900 buildings still standing that were built in the 1800's. 85 percent of its buildings are included on the Historic Register of Historic Places. Nestled among the steep hills of the Galena River, Galena is the oldest city in Northern Illinois.

Main Street presents a nearly unbroken line of 140 buildings from the 1800's. There is much more to see beyond business district. The homes, churches and historic public buildings coalesce to make Galena the *timeless treasure* she has become.

This chapter is divided into four sections:
a. Business District
b. Public Buildings
c. Residences
d. Churches

The Business District starts on Main Street as you enter the town and is arranged so that you can walk along Main Street, heading north, and see each building in order as highlighted in the book.

Please note that although each of the buildings listed is special, every building in Galena is special. Because of available photos and history, some have been selected and others have not.

Without a doubt, every building standing, with over one hundred years of history within its walls, could easily be a book in itself. If only the walls could speak!

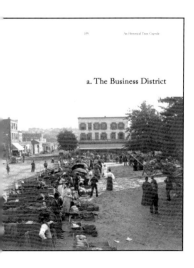
a. The Business District

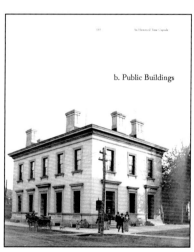
b. Public Buildings

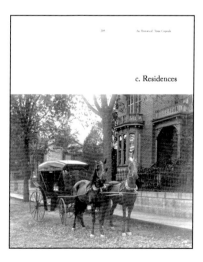
c. Residences

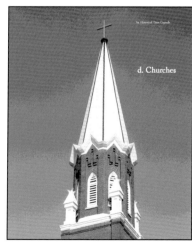
d. Churches

The public buildings are remarkable, intact and stand as they did in the 1800's. The majority of the structures are serving the purpose for which they were originally built to this day.

The homes of Galena are as one writer stated; "An Architectural Legacy."[1] Homes dating back to 1826 still stand in Galena. The section titled, "Residential" will provide an overview of the homes that settlers from all walks of life built, which at the time, were located at the farthest reaches of civilization in the United States.

The final section focuses on the churches of Galena. By 1878, Galena had twelve churches that provided the spiritual foundation of the community. Five of these churches are located on Bench Street and others are on terraced bluffs. Already in the 1800s, visitor's remarked that Galena could well be termed "the City of Churches".

Each section presents detailed photographs of *then and now*. Great care has been taken to provide the reader with the exact view as it looks today, compared to the image that a photographer may have taken, perhaps 150 years ago.

Each photo is really a "Moment Frozen In Time."

Overview of Galena looking north with the Spring Street Bridge (Rte. 20) in the foreground. c.1910

An Historical Time Capsule

a. Business District

Galena, Illinois

Main Street looking north from Washington Street
East Side—c.1880

Main Street—629 South

Two brothers, Nicholas and Thomas Casserly, established a grocery store at 629 South Main, in 1868. Originally from Ottawa, Canada, they moved to Galena in 1851 with their parents, three brothers and two sisters. Their grocery/liquor store was located at the corner of Spring (Rte 20) and Main. (These buildings no longer exist.)

Main Street—507 South

> The Galena Shoe Company, manufacturers of men's, boys' and youths', women's, misses' and children's medium McKay and turned shoes, are nicely situated at one end of the town, and are having their usual good run of business. The factory is 100x25, four stories, employing forty hands, with a capacity of 250 pairs per day, which go to retailers through the West and Northwest. Six salesmen are employed, and are sending in orders in good numbers, which indicate the usual busy run.

Article above taken from the trade journal,
"The Boot and Shoe Recorder,"
Boston, Mass.
December, 1898.

The Galena Shoe Company
c. 1890.

Galena, Illinois

Main Street—401 South

Coldwell Bankers Realty currently occupies 403 South Main. The original structure (below) had already begun to deteriorate in the 1800's. Without any prior knowledge of this original wooden structure, the current owner, Terry Heim, stated that his grandfather built the current 'stone' building in the 1950's. The current face of the building recently was redone. It is uncanny that this building (by coincidence) bears such a resemblance to the original wooden structure that occupied the location more than 100 years ago.

Main Street—230 South—The DeSoto House

Ground was broken for the DeSoto House on June 28, 1853. The intention was that the DeSoto House would be the largest and most luxurious hotel around. It definitely lived up to these plans. When the doors opened nearly two years later on April 9, 1855, the huge five-story building comprised of 1,800,000 bricks, became one of Galena's jewels and marks of prosperity.

The cost to build the DeSoto was $85,000 in 1855. By today's valuation, the cost would have been over $2,300,000.00.

Billed at the time as "the largest hotel in the West," the DeSoto had 225 guest rooms and numerous public rooms.

The first floor of the hotel included the main entrance and office of the hotel. There was also a washroom, coat room, gentlemen's reading room, carving room and the dining hall that was 100 feet long by 34 feet wide and could seat 300 people. The first floor also contained three stores and a railroad office.

The second floor included the ladies' parlors. These were beautifully furnished with velvet carpets, rosewood furniture, gilt mirrors, marble-top tables, satin damask curtains, and a double round seven-octave carved rosewood "piano forte." There were also two private parlors furnished in a similar style. The second floor also had two sitting rooms toward the back named the Green Room and the Blue Room, predominantly reflecting the colors that were emphasized in each room.

The guest suites complete with parlors and bedrooms, were located on the third and fourth floors with smaller single rooms on the fifth.

The basement housed a massive kitchen that included among its equipment, a Patent Roaster, capable of roasting meat for 500 people at a time! There was also a cook stove that was said to be "large enough to supply the entire town." The Green Street side of the basement contained several commercial

This rare photo of Galena was taken from the east bank of the Galena River directly across from Green Street. The DeSoto House has all five stories in this photo, dating this photo to pre-1880. The Green Street Bridge is also intact. Although taken nearly 140 years ago, the silting in of the Galena River was already a very real dilemma. Note the low level of the river.

Prospect Street is also in clear view. The original high school built in 1860, but destroyed by fire in 1904, is in view to the left. The elevation of Main Street is 601 feet, Bench Street is 637 feet and Prospect is 730 feet above sea level.

Photo of Grant's return to Galena after the family's world tour that concluded in November, 1879. His wife, Julia Dent Grant, wrote in her personal memoirs (Pg. 312) of this occasion. She stated: *After leaving Burlington….Then on to Galena, dear Galena where we were at home again in reality. The return here was like our return after the war. The entire town was decorated as on the previous occasion, and everything was done that could be done to welcome back their citizen, General Grant."*

Note the five story DeSoto House in the photo. The following year, the two upper floors would be removed.

Galena, Illinois

establishments including a saloon, barber shop and the office of the Mississippi Telegraph Company.

The history of the DeSoto House could fill volumes. Some of its more memorable events include the July 23, 1856, speech Abraham Lincoln delivered from the balcony in support of John Fremont, the Republican Presidential candidate of that year.

Two years later, on July 25, 1858, Stephen A. Douglas, the Democratic Party nominee for President in the 1860 election, spoke from the same balcony.

On August 18, 1865, Ulysses S. Grant, Commanding General of the Union Army and Galena's most famous citizen returned home. 25,000 people were on hand to welcome him home. Bands, parades, and

Fully decorated 3-story DeSoto House. Note the mature Centennial Elms along side the hotel. These were planted in 1876, marking the 100 year birthday of the country. The passengers in the beautifully decorated carriage are O. C. Kraehmer with his wife, Clara. The Kraehmers were life-long residents of Galena and very successful business owners. c.1895

BILL OF FARE

August 27, 1858

ROAST (STEER) BEEF, Suet Pudding	40c
PORTERHOUSE STEAK, Cepes	45c
PORK CHOPS, Apple Dumpling	25c
BAKED WILD TURKEY, Corn Bread Stuffing	30c
FRIED HAM, Red Eye Gravy, Sweets	25c
POT CHICKEN AND DUMPLINGS	20c
SADDLE OF VENISON, Chutney Sauce	55c
FRIED CATFISH, Corn Fritter and Sorghum	25c
NATIVE BEAR STEAK, Elderberry Jelly	55c
BEEF STEAK AND KIDNEY PIE	30c
BOILED HAM with Mustard Greens and Soppin Bread	20c

Cream of Yellow Corn Soup

Cabbage Salad in Sour Cream

Boiled Potatoes and Peas   Fresh baked bread, home churned butter

Apple Pan Dowdy, Warm Spiced Cream

Washington layer cake   Persimmon pudding

Charlotte russe

Coffee   Tea

BEVERAGE LIST

IMPORTED CHAMPAGNE—(large bottle)	$1.50
CIDER, APPLE OR CHERRY—(mug)	.05
BEER—(mug)	.05
DRY RED WINE	.05
HOMEMADE WINE	.03
SASSPARILLA	.05
CORN WHISKEY	
WHISKEY—(1 finger)	
(2 finger)	

The "Bill of Fare" predated menus in the early 1800's. This DeSoto House "Bill of Fare" is dated August 27, 1858, and offered quite s selection for the time period.

cannon salutes preceded a Grand Reception Ball that was held at the DeSoto for some 2,000 people.

Grant later used rooms 209 and 211 of the hotel as his presidential campaign headquarters.

During the 1870's, the fourth and fifth floors were closed off. There were reports that bats and birds were inhabiting these floors. In 1880, Captain Asa Haile, the man that had originally directed the construction of the hotel 25 years earlier was back on the scene. Using screw jacks, the entire roof of the DeSoto was lifted off of the building. The fourth and fifth floors were completely removed and then, the roof was lowered onto the third floor where it sits until this day, 135 years later.

In 1883, the bar was moved to its present location on the Green Street side of the hotel, and a small bowling alley was added.

In May of 1892, a new balcony was put on the front

The DeSoto House, c. 1890

of the hotel. Then in 1894, further renovations took place, which included a stable where the present hotel parking garage is located.

For nearly a century to 1983, the hotel went through many renovations as well as a number of owners. All had visions of grandeur, but inadequate financial resources. The real cost of doing business eventually put an end to their dreams.

In 1993, Daniel Kelley, became the sole owner of the property. The DeSoto has been under his watchful care, now for more than two decades.

Today, in 2015, the history-filled DeSoto House is the oldest operating hotel in Illinois. Guests can come and stay at this elegant Victorian hotel that was advertised in 1855 as the "Largest Hotel in the West."

In 1883, the bar was moved to its present location on the Green Street side of the hotel (shown here)

Panoramic view of the DeSoto House and Main Street looking northeast from Green Street. c.1910.

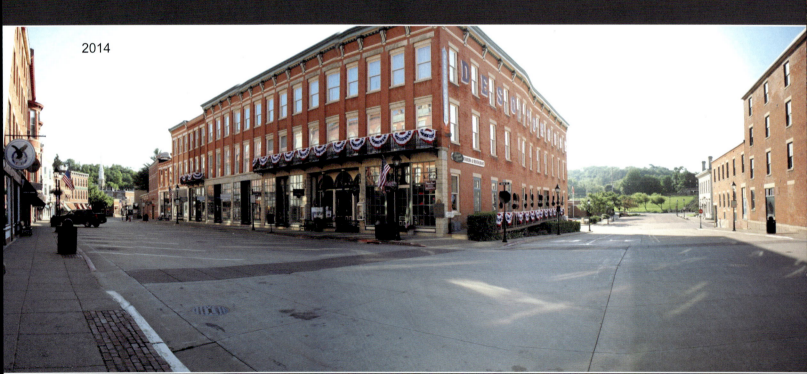
2014

Upper Photo highlights the ornate staircase and the front desk. Produced by the Brunswick-Balke-Collender Company that began in 1845, this "Bar" has serviced the front desk, tavern and a restaurant throughout the DeSoto's history. Now it is once again in use in the lobby.

Left - The "General's Restaurant" named in honor of Galena's nine Civil War Generals.

The Courtyard Restaurant in the center of the hotel. When originally built in 1855, this was an "Open Air" courtyard.

Main Street—222 South

The *Galena Gazette* newspaper has been in continuous publication since November 29, 1834.* Newspapers were political tools at this time. The Whigs, (later known as the Republican Party) were determined to establish their own newspaper and thus have a voice against the Democratic paper, the *Galenian*. Twelve prominent individuals invested $100 each; sent to St. Louis for material, and Sylvester M. Bartlett and Charles E. Loring came from that city to run the paper.

Initially named the *Northwestern Gazette* and *Galena Advertiser*, the first issue was released with the editorial reference: *"it gives the news of the day and sustains the Whig cause."* The battle lines were drawn between the papers.

At one point, Bartlett's editorial attacks on Martin Van Buren were so bitter and abusive that he feared for his life. He kept a loaded pistol on his desk in readiness. His apprehension was not unfounded; the political quarrels verbally being fought between Bartlett and John Turney, the editor of the *Galena Democrat*, escalated to "mortal combat."

Bartlett was challenged to a duel by Turney and Bartlett accepted, probably to the surprise of Turney. In the nick of time, friends intervened, the duel was compromised and bloodshed was prevented. Evidently one shot was fired, but this was accidently.

The *Galena Gazette* is the second oldest** business in continuous operation in Galena, being founded in 1834. The Gazette is also the fourth oldest newspaper in continuous publication in the State of Illinois.

* The Gazette was not the first paper published in Galena, the first being the *Miner's Journal*, first published on July 28, 1828.

** The Clingman Pharmacy, dating back to 1832, is not only the oldest business in continuous operation in Galena but is the oldest continuously operating pharmacy in Illinois. The name has been changed a number of times.

The Gazette at 105 Main, now 222 South Main. c.1889

Above: The Gazette in 2015, located at 716 S. Bench St.

Left: Current photo of 105 Main, now 222 South Main. Located on the DeSoto House block.

Galena, Illinois

Main Street - 219 South

Frank Kempter was a manufacturer of sheet iron pumps for miners; as well as tin, copper, and sheet iron ware. He dealt in wood or coal burning parlor and cooking stoves and sold crockery, glassware, lamps and house furnishing goods. Located at 112 Main Street, his residence was over the store with the entrance on Bench Street. Kempter was born in New Bavaria, Germany on January 10, 1834. He came to Galena in 1852. He went into business for himself in 1858. (112 Main was changed to 219 S. Main in or around 1900.)

Main Street—130 South

In the early 1900's, O. C. Kraehmer had a highly successful music store in Galena located at 130 S. Main. It provided high-quality instruments for the public including pianos and organs. The store also sold Edison's new invention called a "phonograph".

> O. C. Kraehmer, the enterprising piano man of Galena, Ill., has just ordered a full carload of Hobart M. Cable pianos from headquarters. He expects to place several carloads in his locality during the holidays and speaks very highly of the Hobart M. Cable pianos.

O.C Kraehmer ordered a (train) carload of Hobart M. Cable Pianos in 1901. This was so uncommon his order was published in the Music Trade Review. (1901)

His wife, Clara Kraehmer *(in photo)* ran the O.C. Kraehmer Music Co. Store

Main Street—122 South

In 1841, Ulysses S. Grant's father, Jesse R. Grant and Eli A. Collins opened the first leather and saddlery store west of Buffalo. It was here in Galena, located in a small frame building on the lot where the DeSoto House now stands. The business was named E. A. Collins and Company.

The business prospered until 1853, when Jesse Grant ended his partnership with Collins and opened a competing store in the stone Dowling Building at the corner on Main and Diagonal Streets. He put his oldest son Simpson in charge. (Note 1854 Advertisement just below). While managing the leather store in the Dowling building, Simpson became very ill and was unable to maintain the business. His brother Orville, came to Galena to assist with its operation.

Advertisement found in the 1854 Galena Directory

In 1858, the business moved out of the Dowling Building and into the Coatsworth Building at 145 Main Street. Today this is 122 South Main.

W. T. Medary, a close friend of Simpson Grant, travelled with Simpson up to Minnesota with the hope that his health might be restored, but this failed. Simpson died on September 13, 1861.

In April, 1860, Ulysses S. Grant came to Galena to work for his father in the store located in the Coatsworth Building. He stayed there for approximately one year until he quit his job to offer his services to the Union Army. In 1864, Orville Grant formed a partnership with C. R. Perkins and moved to 173 Main Street. (Note photo on following page. The building address of 173 Main Street was changed in or around 1900 to 103 North Main.)

Details above taken from autobiography of John Sloan Collins, son of Eli A. Collins

J. R. Grant Leather Store Receipt from 1861 signed by Jesse R. Grant, while located in the Coatsworth building. (122 South Main today)

An Historical Time Capsule

Left:
In 1858, the J. R. Grant Leather, Saddlery Hardware Co. moved into the Coatsworth building. This is the location Ulysses S. Grant worked at, until the outbreak of the Civil War.

Below:
In 1864, Jesse R. Grant formed a partnership with C. R. Perkins and moved their Leather and Saddlery and Hardware business into this building located at 173 Main Street. (103 North Main today)

103 North Main

Galena, Illinois

Main Street—106 & 109 South

The photos on this page and the following, are of O. C. Kraehmer's Jeweler and Optician store at its original location at 106 South Main.

In 1917, Kraehmer moved across the street to 109 South Main (Note page 128). The jewelry store was on the ground floor and the music store was upstairs. The Kraehmer store was operated by various generations of the family with Dorothy Kraehmer O'Neil and her husband David, being the last generation. In 1978, the "baton" was passed on to Lisa Hesselbacher who owned and operated this store for many years until her death in 2005.

The jewelry store is now gone, but the display cases remain in place, as they have stood for nearly a century. Hesselbacher's husband, Orville, owns and

Today, Chef Ivo & Son's award winning Gourmet Food Store at 106 South Main

Exterior of 106 South Main. C. 1900

An Historical Time Capsule

Chef Ivo's interior as of 2015

maintains the store which is available for rental.

It's amazing to walk into 109 South Main Street today, and see and touch the same counters and cases as those shown in the photos on the following pages. The final owners of the display cases, Hesselbacher Jewelers, took great care to maintain the distinct century-old atmosphere of the store.

Many people feel that coming to Galena is like stepping back in time. This store is laid out almost exactly as the original Kraehmer store was, nearly 100 years ago. The counters and cases are in pristine condition, the original cash register, Jeweler's desk and cashier cage are all in place to this day, adding to the ambiance of this store.

Interior of 106 South Main.

Main Street—106 & 109 South

In the early 1900's, O. C. Kraehmer published a catalogue touting his quality merchandise. This became a great tool that could be used throughout the country to advertize his business in Galena.

The publication included items priced from as little as $1.00 on up. Solid gold, diamond jewelry including rings, pins, necklaces and bracelets as well as broaches, cuff links and tie clips were listed.

It also advertised a huge selection of time pieces, including pocket watches. Other items included fine quality, rich cut glass items ranging from bowls to lamps, silverware, French ivory hand-held mirrors and hair brushes.

A number of pages from the book and the cover are displayed on the following page.

O. C. Kraehmer Jewelry was originally located at 106 South Main. In 1917, the Kraehmer's moved their (Jewelry & Music) stores to 109 South Main. The cabinets are still in place at 109 as they have been since 1917.

Interior of 109 South Main in the early 1900's

An Historical Time Capsule

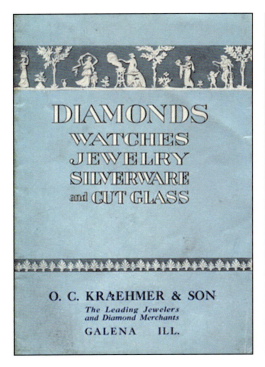

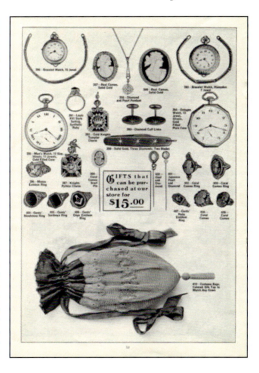

The O. C. Kraehmer Jewelry cashier cage is still in the 109 S. Main St. store as well as the early 1900's cash register and jeweler's desk.

Main Street—115 North

John Cloran and his son, John Jr., owned and operated the Cloran Grocery Store. As seen in the photo below, canned goods were in the window, Ivory Soap was advertised above the door, and there was a sign on the lower left wall advertising "Gold Dust." The Clorans operated this store until 1917. The Cloran store was originally at 185 Main. It was changed to 115 North Main in or around 1900.

The C. A. Asmus Store dealt in stoves and ranges. It also sold complete home heating systems, a new modern invention of the time.

Photo c. 1894

203 N Main—John Meusel Hardware Store

John A. Meusel was born in Bavaria, Germany in 1828 and came to Galena on May 24, 1850. He was a manufacturer of copper, tin and sheet iron work and a dealer of stoves, hardware, glassware and house furnishing goods. His store was located at 203 North Main. When he died in 1904, his son, Benjamin Franklin Meusel took over the store.

The photo below shows Benjamin F. Meusel and his daughter, Clara in the store in 1914.

Evidently, there were three Meusel brothers in Galena. Abram, born in 1855; Benjamin Franklin, born in 1864, and Albert, born in 1867. Each brother had their own hardware store. Albert Meusel on the next page, was Benjamin's brother.

208 N. Main

The Albert Meusel Store photo below dates back to around 1900. Note the variety of products in the photo, ranging from stoves and lamps, to bird cages, metal tubs and glassware.

The storefront has not changed over the past one hundred years. The doors and the woodwork in the current photo (right) are identical to those of the early photo.

Main Street—210-212 North

This 1888 Italianate commercial building housed one of Galena's many 19th century cigar manufacturers. It was home to the Standard Cigar Factory. Tobacco was a cash crop for some county farmers until the 1890's.

The Cigar Factory interior

Main Street—213 North

This stone building was built in 1837 by John Dowling. By June of 1837, the second floor of the building was being used as the Circuit Court. The court eventually moved to the first floor where it continued to function as the Jo Daviess County Courthouse until the completion of the Courthouse located at 330 Bench Street in 1844.

On October 31, 1838, Mr. McKenzie and Joseph Jefferson opened a theatre in "Mr. Dowling's large room" on the second floor. Their first performance was *"Wives as They Were and Maids as They Are,"* which was first performed in 1797 at the Theatre Royal Covent Garden in London. "Tickets were $1, to be had at the bars of the Eagle Saloon and the Galena Hotel." [6]

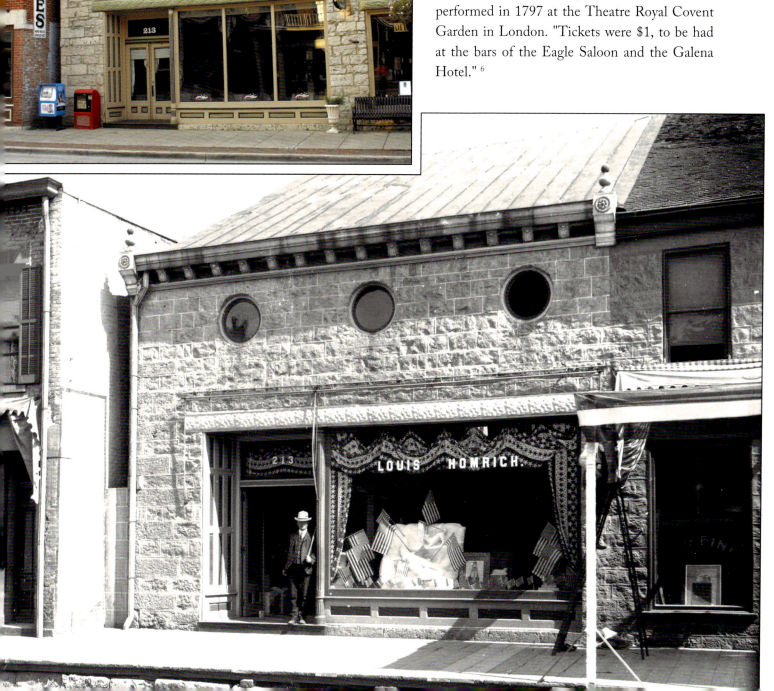

Corner of Diagonal St. and Main

Frank Knoebber & Son Shoe Repair was located on the corner of Main and Diagonal Streets. Knoebber came to Galena from Germany in the early 1880's. His residence was on Franklin Street. In 1933 Frank and his wife were still alive and living in Galena, where they celebrated their Golden Anniversary. The photo to the right is of Frank and his son, c.1900. The lower photo depicts a much older Frank.

Commerce Street—106 South

In the 1800's livery stables were thriving businesses in towns where horses, teams, wagons, buggies and carriages were available for hire. People could also pay a daily, weekly, or monthly fee to have someone board their horses. Often, liveries were in close proximity to hotels or boarding houses, so travelers could have easy access to their horses and buggies.

The livery was much more than a "hotel for horses" or a place to keep your carriage safe while traveling through towns. People who didn't own a horse could rent one at the livery. Buggies, wagons and sleighs could be rented as well.

The Comstock and Hunkins Livery Stable was located on Commerce Street, a short distance from the Galena River and less than a block away from the DeSoto House. With its ideal location, the livery became a very active and successful business in Galena.

245 N. Commerce Street

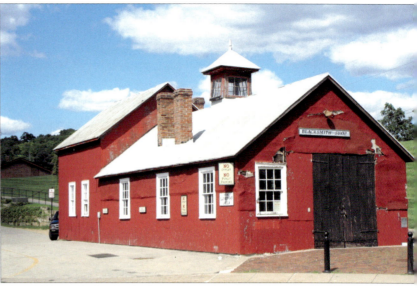

Constructed in 1897 by Louis Readel, this blacksmith shop is the only remaining shop of its type in Galena. When the horse and buggy was the primary mode of transportation, there were 20 to 40 individuals claiming their occupation as "blacksmith" in Galena. In the 1858-59 City Directory at the time when Galena had a population of 14,000, there were approximately 35 blacksmiths listed.

Willard Richardson had grown up on a farm that had a forge. He started learning the trade at 19 years of age in Hazel Green in 1912 where he earned $1.25 a day. He started working in this (Galena) shop in 1921 and by the end of the decade, he purchased the shop.

Left to Right: Fred Kloth, Louis Readel—the original owner and blacksmith, Adolph Wandell and William Strickland. c.1910

There were two blacksmiths who worked in the front part of the shop, while harness and woodwork was done in the back. Wagon wheels were a major product of the wood working shop.

Electricity was brought to Main Street, Galena in the early 1900's. The blacksmith shop began using electricity in 1910. Its system of pulleys, shafts and belts to run the equipment are still intact to this day.

Willard Richardson shoed his last horse in 1951 and stopped active work in 1969.

The City of Galena purchased the shop in 2002 when it became necessary to realign the street. The shop was moved 100 feet to its current location. The Galena-Jo Daviess County Historical Society was then awarded a Public Museum Capital Grant through the Illinois State Museum for the restoration of the structure.

The forges were rebuilt brick by brick, exactly as they had been at the turn of the century. In fact, the entire shop was kept exactly as it had been for the past 80 years of use.

Willard Richardson's original tools are on display in the shop. While the shop is a museum, the forges are totally operable, and blacksmiths are regularly on duty working the trade.

Blacksmiths Bryan Ackerman (left) and Rich Tickner working at the forges. (2015)

Galena, Illinois

The 118 year old forge and anvil blacksmith shop is in operation today, much as it was when it originally opened in 1897.

Note the Canedy-Otto Blower that historian-blacksmith, Rich Tickner, is operating in the photo to the right. This is the same blower that has been used in this shop for over one hundred years.

The "ad" on the following page is the original advertisement by Canedy-Otto in 1902, promoting their product. This "ad" was printed in the October 1902 issue of the *American Blacksmith* magazine.

Blacksmiths Bryan Ackerman and Rich Tickner working at the blacksmith shop using the same tools, equipment and procedures that blacksmiths used back in the 1800's.

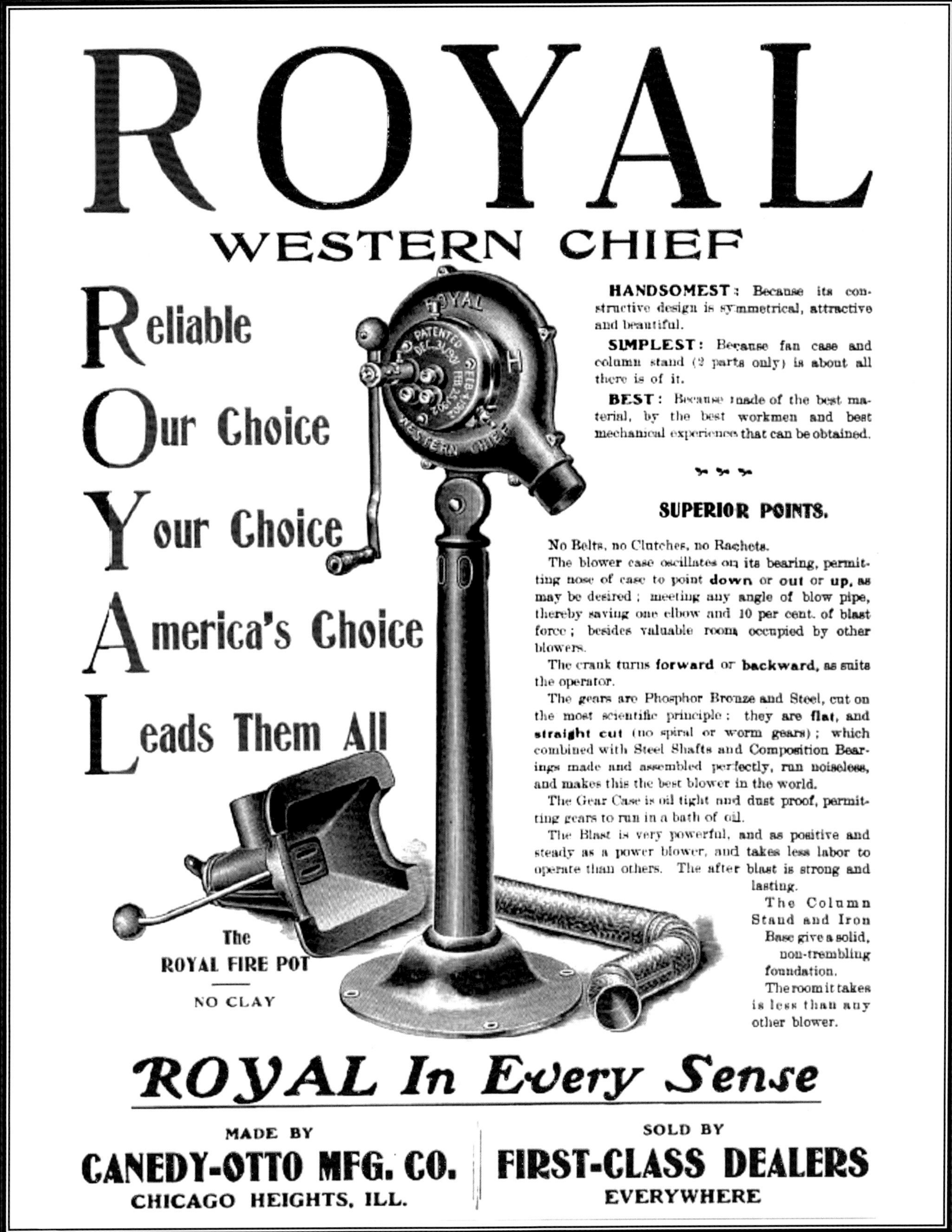

ROYAL
WESTERN CHIEF

Reliable
Our Choice
Your Choice
America's Choice
Leads Them All

HANDSOMEST: Because its constructive design is symmetrical, attractive and beautiful.

SIMPLEST: Because fan case and column stand (2 parts only) is about all there is of it.

BEST: Because made of the best material, by the best workmen and best mechanical experiences that can be obtained.

SUPERIOR POINTS.

No Belts, no Clutches, no Rachets.

The blower case oscillates on its bearing, permitting nose of case to point **down** or **out** or **up**, as may be desired; meeting any angle of blow pipe, thereby saving one elbow and 10 per cent. of blast force; besides valuable room occupied by other blowers.

The crank turns **forward** or **backward**, as suits the operator.

The gears are Phosphor Bronze and Steel, cut on the most scientific principle; they are **flat**, and **straight cut** (no spiral or worm gears); which combined with Steel Shafts and Composition Bearings made and assembled perfectly, run noiseless, and makes this the best blower in the world.

The Gear Case is oil tight and dust proof, permitting gears to run in a bath of oil.

The Blast is very powerful, and as positive and steady as a power blower, and takes less labor to operate than others. The after blast is strong and lasting.

The Column Stand and Iron Base give a solid, non-trembling foundation.

The room it takes is less than any other blower.

The **ROYAL FIRE POT**
— NO CLAY

ROYAL In Every Sense

MADE BY
CANEDY-OTTO MFG. CO.
CHICAGO HEIGHTS, ILL.

SOLD BY
FIRST-CLASS DEALERS
EVERYWHERE

Original advertisement by Canedy-Otto in 1902 promoting their product. This "ad" was printed in the October 1902 issue of the *American Blacksmith* magazine.

Westwick Foundry—Field Street

John Westwick was born in Yorkshire, England on March 30, 1822. He came to Galena in May of 1852, where he started a foundry and machine shop, originally located on Claude Street near Meeker Street. Some time later, he moved his operation to Field Street.

In 1898 the John Westwick & Son Foundry doubled in size. The photo below was taken during this expansion.

John Westwick & Son have been established here thirty years in the foundry and machine business. Their specialties are steam engines and boilers and castings. They do general repairing. Their trade extends northwest as far as Wyoming Territory. The concern has been successful from the start.

The Inter Ocean Newspaper, Chicago, Wed, Dec. 29, 1886

John Westwick & Son Foundry on Field Street looking north to Shot Tower Hill. c.1898.

By 1854 the John Westwick & Son Foundry was established in Galena. They soon became famous for the manufacture of what was known as the Vasco-Westwick warm air furnace.

In 1909 they opened a Chicago branch at 150 W. Lake Street, with V. A. Smith, an engineer and heating expert, as full partner and manager.

Eventually, Smith started his own company. By 1915 Smith and Westwick dissolved their partnership, with Westwick retaining the foundry in Galena and Smith purchasing the Chicago branch, merging it in February, 1916, with the V. A. Smith Company.

The Westwick Foundry in Galena supplied the furnaces to the V. A. Smith Company. The business continued to grow and the furnaces were in such demand that the foundry in Galena had difficulty in meeting the demands of the sales. In 1916 more than 1,200 furnaces were sold in 10 months alone.

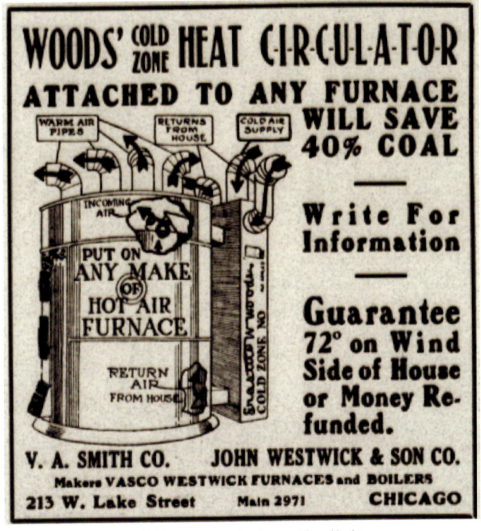

1916 newspaper advertisement found in the
Chicago Eagle, 11-11-1916, Page 12

Galena, Illinois

343 Franklin Street

The Bader Grocery Store single story building was built in 1844. The photo below was taken around 1880. Michael Bader (born 07-31-1842, died 11-25-1910) owned the grocery store, manufactured vinegar and was also a carpet weaver.

In the late 1800's a second floor was added to the building. (Note photo to the left) The building no longer exists.

Right:
Sullivan & Caille, Galena Undertakers hearse c. 1903

Below:
The J. P. Vincent & Sons Monuments Company delivery wagon c. 1910

Frank Einsweiler's First Foundry

Frank Einsweiler Sr. began working in the foundry business in the late 1800's at the John Westwick Foundry on Claude and Meeker Street. In 1900 he began his own operation in a rock building at the corner of Gear and Bench Street, which is now the *Galena Gazette* property.

Einsweiler would bake the cores in his wife's cookstove oven, then pour the castings outside in the wood shed. In 1902 the Galena Iron Works purchased his business, merged it into theirs, and made him superintendent. He stayed in this position until 1912, when he decided to establish his own company again.

He started the Leadmine Foundry Company in a brick building at the corner of Hill and Water Street. It was located at the rear of the current Leadmine Foundry (Lemfco) location at 100 S. Commerce Street. Because lead mining was booming in this area, the first castings he made were lead mining equipment products. Other early products included sleigh shoes (iron runners for sleighs), window sash weights, iron wheels for the oar cars at the mines, and water and oil pump castings. Eventually he began making the stoves, called "Leadmine" and a model on higher legs which was called "Kitchen Queens." He also produced tank stoves that hooked up to water heaters, and "pot-bellied" stoves, which were called "Cold Chasers." These were sold to Montgomery Ward, Spiegel and Sears & Roebuck.

Lemfco and the Einsweiler family (now on the 4th generation) celebrated 100 years in business in 2012.

Building in the foreground is Frank Einsweiler's Foundry located at the corner of Gear and Bench Streets. c.1900 (The present location of the *Galena Gazette*)

An Historical Time Capsule

Galena's Breweries

Back in the 1800's, there was as many as eight breweries in Galena at one time. The two shown on these pages include the Fulton Brewery and the Galena Brewing Company.

Mathias Meller Jr. was the owner of the Fulton Brewery that was located on the corner of Spring and Prospect Streets. Born in Germany on April 9, 1827, he came to Galena in 1849. Along with his father, Meller was engaged in the brewery and bakery business before leaving Germany.

In 1860 he purchased the Fulton Brewery and continued in the business until 1885, with good financial results. He then rented the brewery and retired from the business.

According to newspapers from 1886, the Fulton Brewery was completely destroyed by fire in that year. Eventually, the plant was rebuilt and continued to produce beer for years to come.

One of the most famous beers produced here was "Red Stripe Beer". It is claimed that the recipe was handed down from the Fulton Brewery.

When prohibition began in 1920, the owners of the brewery sold the recipe for "Red Stripe" to two

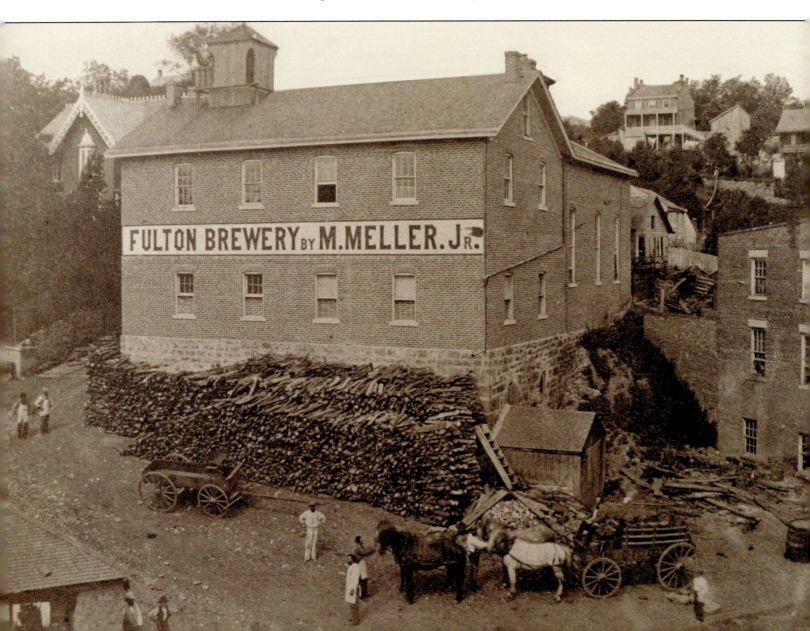

An Historical Time Capsule

British men who took it to Jamaica. Later, Red Stripe Beer became very popular among U.S. soldiers stationed there during WW II.

After Prohibition ended in 1933, the Galena Brewing Company applied for a federal permit to again manufacture beer. The permit was granted in early 1934, and the brewery began manufacturing "Red Stripe" in kegs and "New Life" bottled beer according to a formula they had recently purchased from Louis Eulberg, one of the brewers who had manufactured beer in this plant prior to prohibition. It is noteworthy that the Eulberg family had brewed beer in Galena since the 1850's. In 1886, they were producing 400 barrels of beer per month.

Intersection of Main & Green Streets

An Historical Time Capsule

2014

Main Street from Franklin

2014

Main Street north, from Washington

2014

Franklin Street, Main to Bench

2014

Galena, Illinois 160

Corner of Main and Perry

c. 1864

An Historical Time Capsule

Corner of Main and Diagonal Street 2014

Main Street—Lower West Side
2014

Galena, Illinois

Kerry's Spreader Day Parade
December 12, 1911

b. Public Buildings

County Court House

In December of 1838, John Slaymaker and Samuel Mazzuchelli were appointed engineers to oversee the architectural work required in the building of a new courthouse located at 330 N. Bench Street for Jo Daviess County. Although construction began early in 1839, it would take five years to complete, due to shortages of materials, labor and finances. Overruns increased the final price to nearly twice that of the cost projected. [1,2]

County Courthouse c. 1890

Courthouse with new addition c. 1902

The original structure had a beautiful Greek Revival portico with four large columns. These were removed in 1900 when a three-story brick addition with mansard roof was added including a "Second Empire" front and a beautiful and ornate cupola. By the end of December in 1900, the new addition, which rose 90 feet to the top of the tower, was ready for occupancy.

The cupola deteriorated badly over the years and in 1930, a severe storm toppled it to the ground. It was never replaced. The years 1970, 1976 and 2000 saw the rear additions to the building that are used for public safety facilities. [3]

The building is used to this day for its original purpose and also houses the majority of the Jo Daviess County Administrative offices.

County Courthouse addition under construction in 1900

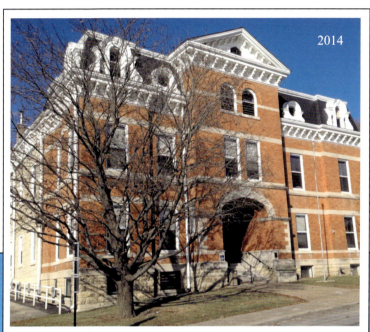
2014

2014

Feehan Hall
(Annunciation School)

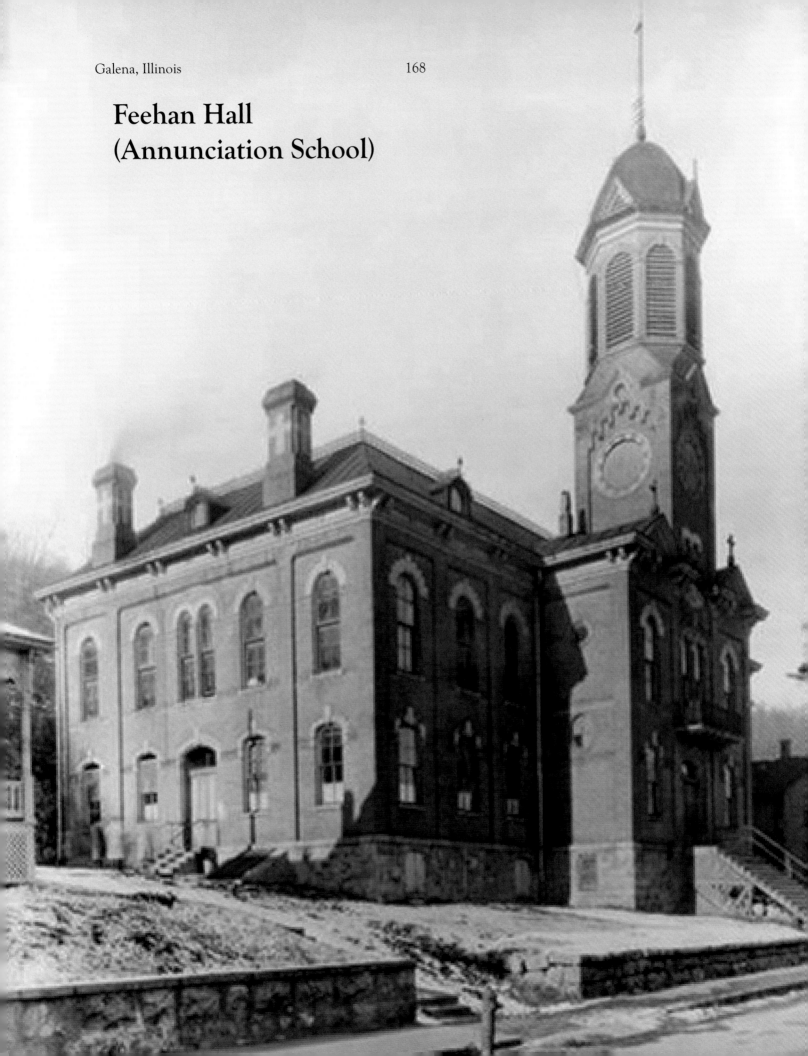

On March 12, 1886 Catholic priest, Father Meehan, purchased lots 13 and 14 on Bench Street for the purpose of building a Catholic school. Excavation for the new school building began on the Feast of the Annunciation, March 25, 1886. One week later, work began on the foundation of the school. One week after that the plans for the school were finally revealed. It would be a two-story building with a bell tower and a town clock.

The new school, named Feehan Hall, had its grand opening on December 24, 1886. The Dominican Sisters were in charge of the school. Measuring 100 feet by 54 feet, the school was equally divided into four classrooms. It was considered one of the finest of its kind in the Archdiocese of Chicago.

Electricity was in its infancy at the time Feehan Hall was constructed. Therefore, electricity was not yet an option for either Galena or Feehan Hall. Main Street in Galena didn't have electricity until the early 1900's. The school remained without electric light until renovations in 1929, which included the removal of the stoves from the classrooms and the installation of a steam plant that included radiators for all the rooms in the school downstairs as well as the hall upstairs.

The hall was well appointed and could be used for even the most formal parties. There was even a "dumb waiter" (a small elevator for carrying food and dishes between the floors of the building) installed enabling the entire space to be utilized as a vast banquet hall.

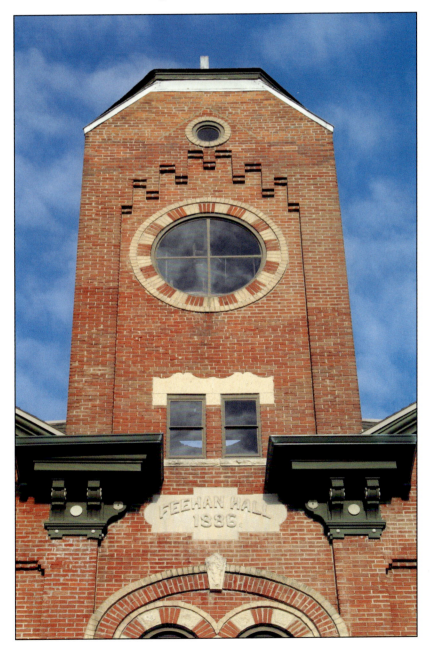

By the late 1960's Feehan Hall began a new life as the home of the Galena Art and Recreation Center. This non-profit organization continues to own and operate this historic structure to this day.

GALENA'S NEW SCHOOL EDIFICE

GALENA, Ill., July 4. –*Special Telegram*– The corner-stone of Feehan Hall, the new and handsome school edifice just completed in this city, thanks to the enterprise and persistence of Father Meehan, the popular curate of St. Michael's Church, is to be laid with imposing ceremonies in September next, on a day not yet fixed upon. Archbishop Feehan, in honor of whom the building has been named, has accepted the invitation to visit Galena and conduct the ceremony. He will be assisted by many priests of the diocese. Feehan Hall is the largest and finest structure, architecturally, in the city, and will cost, when fully completed, as it nearly is, not far from $40,000, the aggregate of which sum has been raised entirely in Galena by private subscription, the giving of private entertainments, and other means planned and carried out by Father Meehan. The school is to be under the charge of the Dominican Order of Sisters.

The *Daily Inter Ocean*, Chicago
July 5, 1887

ARCHBISHOP FEEHAN HONORED

Citizens of Galena Tender Him a Brilliant Reception

GALENA, Ill., June 12- [Special] - The Rt. Rev. P. A. Feehan, D. D., Archbishop of Chicago, who is paying this city an official visit, was tendered a public reception this evening at Feehan Hall, which was named in his honor. Among those present were the Mayor and City Council, members of the clergy, and many visitors from abroad. An interesting program, consisting of vocal and instrumental music and literary exercises, was rendered by pupils of Annunciation School, connected with Feehan Hall, after which an eloquent and appropriate address was delivered by the Archbishop. The reception closed with a great display of fireworks and a band concert. Tomorrow Archbishop Feehan will conduct the ceremony attending the laying of the cornerstone of the large and magnificent Annunciation School building recently completed in this city and built by St. Michael's Catholic Church parish.

An early postcard of Feehan Hall with the cupola still in tact.
c.1910

The *Chicago Tribune*
June 13, 1888

Galena, Illinois

Galena Fair Grounds

The Galena Fairgrounds were located just north of town on Field Street. Today this is named Galena Recreation Park. For more than one hundred years, residents of Galena have used this beautiful property for recreational and sporting activities. As shown in these early 1900's photos, horse racing was a major event in Galena.

Recreation Park, 2015

Galena Fairgrounds c. 1905

The Washburne Lead Mine Regiment, was organized by Galena resident John E. Smith, who was commissioned Colonel of Volunteers on July 31, 1861. The regiment, during its organization, rendezvoused here at the Galena Fair Grounds and the camp was named Camp Washburne, in honor of E. B. Washburne, member of Congress from the Galena District. The seven companies that trained here also received their uniforms and weapons at Camp Washburne. They were armed with the best weapon of the time, the short Enfield rifle. On November 22, 1861, Camp Washburne was broken up and the regiment was mustered into service as the Forty-fifth Infantry.

Another historic note: The Chicago Cubs played Galena's local baseball team here on June 15, 1909. The Cubs won. The final score was 6 - 2. There were 3,000 fans on hand.

Galena Fairgrounds c. 1920

Galena Fairgrounds c.1911

Galena Fairgrounds 09-29-1911

Galena, Illinois

Fire Station No 1.

A meeting was held at the Court House on August 25, 1835, to consider the question of procuring fire engines and forming a fire company. By the following evening the committee reported that the sum of $1,557 had been subscribed, and that they thought that the further sum of $215 could be secured, making $1,772, which the committee thought would be sufficient to procure an engine of the first class. [4]

The committee purchased two of the largest fire engines built by Selye Manufacturing of Rochester, New York. They were warranted to throw water from 100 to 150 feet, according to size. The engines included drag-ropes, suction hose, wrenches, axe, torches, pilot, etc. The large engines required a team of twenty men to operate and could discharge 200 gallons of water per minute. Each engine cost $700; hose and extras, made up the sum paid. [5]

The Galena Fire Department is the oldest fire department in Illinois.

It celebrated its 185th anniversary on February 1, 2015.

An Historical Time Capsule

The Old Fire Station No. 1 is one of the oldest fire houses of its type in Illinois, and may in fact be the oldest. Also significant is the fact that one of Galena's fire engines or pumpers from the 1850's is still housed in the structure. The large glass panels allow Galena to showcase this 1850's pumper year round. The photo to the left and also on pg. 177 was taken through the window at about 11:00 p.m.

"Old Reliable", shown in the photo on the previous page, is one of the original two fire engines (Pumpers) purchased for Galena, arriving in September 1836. The two fire engines were named the Cataract and the Neptune. This Fire Station, No. 1, was home to one of these. [6]

Fire Station No. 1 has changed very little since its early days dating back to 1851, the year it was constructed.

Today, the large wooden doors have been replaced with doors with large glass panels.

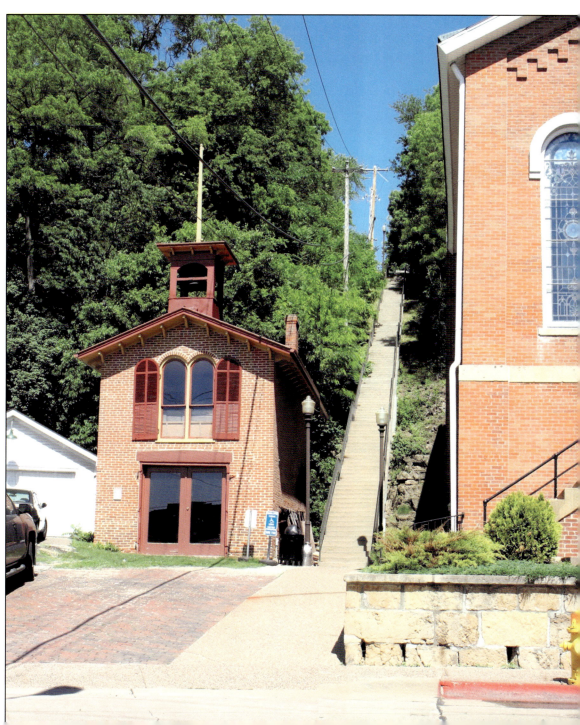

1853 Agnew Fire Engine (Pumper)

Bench Street at the Intersection of Franklin Street   c. 1900

The Fire Companies were reorganized in the early 1850's and the companies purchased two first-class engines, costing $1,600 each. They were built by the John Agnew Fire Engine Manufactory in Philadelphia. They also purchased 1,000 feet of double-riveted leather hose, manufactured by its inventor and manufacturer, Adam Dialogue of Pennsylvania. [7]

Galena's 1850's John Agnew Fire engine

An Historical Time Capsule

Galena Resident G. H. Mars, a tailor whose shop was located at 127 Main,[8] served as Galena's agent and went to Philadelphia and made these purchases. The engines arrived in Galena on January 5, 1855.[9]

This fire engine currently on display in Fire House No. 1, is one of the two fire engines purchased in 1855 for Galena, built by John Agnew. It has been completely restored and is truly a prized "Jewel of Galena".

Liberty Company No.1, c. 1890

The 1850's John Agnew Fire engine has been completely restored and is on display at it's home, Galena Firehouse No. 1. on Bench Street.

Spring Street Hose Co. No. 5

Located on Spring Street (U.S. 20), the high tower at Hose Company No. 5 was used to hang the leather hoses so that they could properly drain and dry. This building is no longer standing.

Galena Chief Long in Service

Fire Chief W. H. Hirst, of the Galena department, has just entered upon his twenty-fifth year of service. He joined the volunteer fire department here in 1901, at the age of 18, when hand carts were in use. Hose was carried on carts with two large wheels. A short time later carts were equipped so that they could be drawn by horses. While horses were kept by the city for this purpose, draymen, or liverymen with teams near the five fire houses would unhitch their teams at the sound of a fire alarm and pull the trucks to the blaze.

In 1915, it was decided to motorize the equipment and Hirst, then chief of the department, led the modernization movement. Volunteer firemen under the leadership of Chief Hirst raised a large portion of the funds at bazaars and carnivals to purchase new equipment.

Members of the five companies here are all volunteers and each company has a waiting list of those seeking membership.

Chief Hirst has three sons following in his footsteps. Al Hirst is assistant foreman of Spring Street Hose company No. 5; Osborne Hirst is assistant foreman of Leadmine Hose company No. 3; and Earl Hirst is a member of Spring street hose company.

Freeport Journal Standard
05-17-1933, Page 15

The Galena Fire Department holds the title of being the oldest fire department in Illinois, serving since the 1830's.

On November 8, 1836, the first fire company of Galena was organized with a roll of sixty-six members. This company was called the "Galena Fire Association No. 1." At their next recorded meeting, the association was named the "Cataract Engine Company No. 1." [10]

The Old Fire Station No. 1 was the first of five fire houses that were ultimately built for the various fire companies around town. One fire house was located behind the County Court House, next to the Old City Cemetery; Hose Company No. 5 (shown on the previous page) on lower Spring Street (Route 20); another at the Market House and the final one was located on the east side.

The individual fire companies were put under the direction of one chief in 1875. The various companies were reorganized in 1935, resulting in the Galena Fire Department. The individual fire stations were closed soon thereafter. The present station next to Turner Hall was dedicated in 1940.

Above—The current Galena Fire station that was dedicated in 1940.

One of Galena's five fire stations was located at the Market House (shown here) on Commerce Street as of 1879. It was closed in 1938.

Galena, Illinois

1860 Galena High School

The construction of the Galena High School began in the summer of 1860. Oliver Marble was hired to superintend the completion of the building and reported it finished on December 8, 1860. It was a large, brick structure of three stories on Prospect Street. The contractor, D. Farr, received $11,219.35 and a bill of $1,712.92 was allowed for furniture. When the school opened, seventeen teachers were hired. The school principal, A. F. Townsend, was paid $60 per month. [11]

Miss Gardner's Kindergarten Class—1900

Fire destroyed the school in April, 1904. According to reports, the fire began when the school was in session and filled with 600 students. The students and faculty escaped with no fatalities, but the entire structure was destroyed.

The small primary school building next door (small photo on previous page) was untouched by the fire. However, it was torn down to make way for the new high school that would be built the following year. According to local lore, when it was torn down, a determined Mrs. Kilburg went on a mission. Longing for a home, she ventured over to the school ruins on Prospect Street and began piling bricks into a market basket, perhaps five or ten at a time. She then carried them nearly 1/4 of a mile to Dodge Street. After making countless trips back and forth from the school to Dodge Street, she had accumulated enough brick to build her home. The home, made of the school house brick, still stands at 119 S. Dodge to this day.

119 South Dodge Street

> Fire destroyed the Galena high school building. The 600 pupils escaped in safety. This building was erected in 1860, and in it the Campbells, Kohlsaats, the younger Washburnes and others who have become noted in the business history of Chicago secured their early schooling.

The *Daily Herald*, Chicago IL.
April 22, 1904

Galena, Illinois

1906 Galena High School

This magnificent structure was built in 1905 to replace the high school that was destroyed by fire the prior year. This new building served as Galena's High School, then Middle School, from 1906 to 1980.

After the school was closed, the building and grounds were sold and converted into condominiums. Located at 411 S. Prospect Street, this historic red brick building continues to dominate Galena's skyline as it has for the past 110 years.

The current steps from Bench Street to Prospect Street.

The Old High School Steps

An Historical Time Capsule

Galena, Illinois

Grant Park

Above: Entrance to Grant Park—The wooden eagle came from Captain Daniel Harris' steamship the *Grey Eagle*. This was the fastest steamer on the Mississippi until its wreck in 1861.[12] The wooden eagle was carved out of a single piece of oak. The naval cannon in the photo center is a "magnificent trophy of war" captured by United States forces from the Spanish cruiser Vizcaya at the famous Battle of Santiago Bay. This battle was the concluding engagement of the Spanish-American War, in which U. S. successes on land and sea resulted in final victory over the Spaniards. The campaign took place during June and July, 1898. Less than one year later, this 19 foot long "monster gun" weighing nearly 5 tons was shipped to Galena by rail. The weapon was dedicated in Grant Park as part of the city's annual Grant Birthday Celebration on April 27, 1899. It was dedicated to "be a display of public valor and virtue in all coming time." Photo c.1900

. . . A little more than one year ago Herman H. Kohlsaat, whose successful career in the metropolis of the West had made his name familiar and honored in the city which he left as a poor boy hardly twenty years ago, made public his intention of giving to the home of Grant a bronze memorial of the hero . . . The announcement was formally made at a special meeting of the city council, at which it was voted to buy the property bounded by Johnson, Jackson, and Second Streets on three sides and by the river on the fourth to be converted into a public park, and therein to erect the statue. This was the beginning from which grew beautiful Grant Park, the pride of Galena today, rich in natural beauty and in all that art can do to increase its charms.

The Establishment of Grant Park
Galena Weekly Gazette, June 4, 1891

Naval cannon captured in 1898 during the Spanish-American War

An Historical Time Capsule

Left: The fountain was presented by the Ladies Auxiliary of Galena; dedicated May 1891.

Above: Grant's bronze statue was dedicated in 1891. The band stand—gazebo was constructed in 1900.

Above: On April 27, 1896, this Blakely Cannon was formally presented to the Grant Park Commission in Galena. This historic cannon is the first rifled cannon to be fired in combat on the American continent. This occurred on April 12, 1861 at Fort Sumter.

Right: The Soldier's Monument was installed here at Grant Park upon its opening in 1891. It has inscribed upon it, the names of the Galenians who served during the Civil War.

Marine Hospital

In 1856 an Act of Congress appropriated money for the construction of a Marine Hospital in Galena. Work began in June of 1857 and was completed in the fall of 1859. The cost was $43,430.00. [14]

The nation's Marine Hospital system was created to care for ailing men of the seafaring business. Ely S. Parker was appointed superintendent of construction. Parker, a full-blooded Seneca Indian, later served on Ulysses S. Grant's staff. [15]

The structure was all brick with walls two feet thick. Ceilings were of brick and I-beam construction. This served as a method of fireproofing, but it also helped to keep the temperature constant. In addition, the floors are able to support tremendous weight.

The second floor originally contained two large wards, the apothecary shop and two full baths. The main floor had a parlor, bedroom, office, sitting room and a full bath. The basement had a kitchen, laundry room, fruit and vegetable storage room, furnace room, dining room, closets and a full bath. Cisterns with a capacity of 30,000 gallons were constructed for a water supply. An elaborate sewer system was added, complete with tunnel and branch system. The whole building was heated by a hot air furnace, along with numerous fireplaces and wood stoves. The hospital was eventually closed in 1865 because it was too costly to operate. Patient costs were $3 a week, physician fees ran $1.75 a week, and medicine costs ran $0.70 (cents) a week. [16]

German English Normal school c.1880

In later years, the hospital was home to the German English Normal school, the Nash Sanitarium, and the Nash Medical company from 1912-1933. It also has had many private owners through the years. This is one of the few remaining Marine hospitals left in the country.

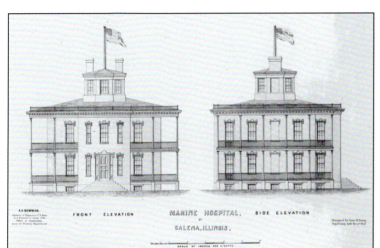

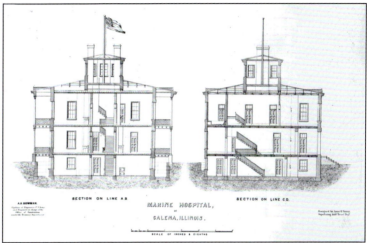

Market House

The Old Market House, constructed in 1845-1846, was the focal point of community life during Galena's heyday. The Greek Revival building sheltered vendors and shoppers, who gathered in the heart of the river city's business district until 1910. [17]

A plan for financing and constructing a public market house was first proposed in 1838. The city purchased four city blocks from the federal government, which owned the lots as part of the United States Lead Mine District. Construction funds did not become available until 1845, when the city sold $5 shares of stock to raise the $2,500 needed for the market house construction. [18]

The Market House was designed by Galena city alderman Thomas Blish and built by H. J. Stouffer. The new structure dominated market square, which was raised nine feet before construction of the 2-1/2 story building commenced in 1845. The city took ownership in January 1846 and officially opened it in July.

The new Market House was greeted with considerable enthusiasm. "*Buyers and sellers would congregate there,*" wrote Galena's semi-weekly newspaper, *The Jeffersonian*, "*and the competition would lower prices.*" Galenians would no longer be compelled to "*traverse half the city to make some paltry purchase,*" and new shops were expected to spring up around the square.

A market master supervised the Market House, that had a first floor divided into twelve stalls and rented

The Market House c.1890

for $50 a year. He was "to enforce order and decorum, and decide all disputes in the market between the buyer and seller. . . be present during market hours, and ring a bell announcing the opening and closing of the market." He was also to "have the market house and market place thoroughly cleansed and swept in the morning of each day; and in the winter season to have the ice and snow swept from the footways and steps . . . " For his effort in 1847 the market master received an annual salary of $250, with additional income from operating the hay scales. [19]

The Market House was also a multipurpose municipal building. Its second floor housed the surveyor's office and the city council chamber. Two jail cells were built in the basement in 1846, but a decade later it was nothing more than a "miserable hole."

In 1879, the Neptune Fire Company began to store their fire engine and equipment in the south side of the building. The city marshal moved into an office in the south wing in 1883, and six years later a two story addition was added to the rear of the building. The first floor of the addition housed a new jail cell, and city records were stored on the second floor. [20]

City markets ended about 1910, and floods accelerated the old building's deterioration. In 1938 the city council and fire department moved to new quarters, leaving the Market House vacant. The Market House was transferred to the State of Illinois in 1947. Following its restoration in 1954 the old Market House once again became the keystone in a town known for its architecture. [21]

Looking south, the Market House is to the left just behind the tree, Commerce Street is to the right and the market square in front is in full session. c. 1900

Galena, Illinois

Post Office / Customs House

The present Post Office was initiated by Congressman Washburne and appropriated for by Congress on August 18, 1856, after Galena outgrew its original main street store which was established in 1826. Construction of the Post Office/Customs House began in 1857. [22] The footings and foundation were laid in the fall, and pigs of lead approximately the weight of the completed building were placed on the foundation and left until the following spring when construction continued. [23]

The best quality limestone was quarried and shipped up the Mississippi from Nauvoo, Illinois, located about 180 miles south.

The *Weekly Northwestern Gazette* of August 9, 1859 reported, *the building is so substantial it will last 1,000 years with only two forces capable of destroying it, one being an earthquake and the other a mob.*

Two men played major roles in the construction of the Post Office. The first was the Supervising Architect for the Office of Construction of the Treasury Department, Ammi B. Young. Some of Young's works include the Treasury Building in D. C. and the Territorial Capitol Building of New Mexico. He also had created what many at the time considered as the leading design for the US Capitol, but

Ammi B. Young

Ely S. Parker

eventually lost. The other was Ely S. Parker, who held the title of Construction Superintendent. Ammi B. Young had a grandiose vision for the Post Office, including many of today's features. These include the mahogany counters in the lobby and the high solid oak doors on the second floor.

The Post Office has been used for many functions during its 157 year history. The second floor, which housed the Customs House, has been used for many social gatherings, including a party thrown for a soldier on November 16, 1861. Also, the second floor was used as the Public Library (until the present day library building was built in 1902) and the GAR Memorial Hall, a meeting place for Civil War veterans. Galena was the nation's first Post Office to be designated by the Smithsonian as "A Great American Post Office." [24] For this distinction a Post Office must meet two of the following three criteria:

1. Outstanding architectural features.
2. Historical significance to the community.
3. Outstanding service to the community.

Galena's Post Office met all three.

Today it is the oldest continually owned and operated Post Office in America.

Galena, Illinois

1857 Railroad Depot

In the early 1800's, railroads were in their infancy. John Stevens built the first test track and ran a locomotive around it at his summer home estate in 1825. [25]

The first operating steam locomotive in the United States was the "Stourbridge Lion". It was also one of the first locomotives to operate outside of Britain. It took its name from the lion's face painted on the front, and Stourbridge in England, where it was manufactured in 1828. [26]

The Stourbridge Lion's first run on 08-8-1829, as depicted by Clyde Osmer DeLand c.1916

The Galena Railroad Depot c.1890's

At this early date in Galena, steamship traffic was the major resource for revenue and commercial activities and one of the leading factors responsible for the fame and growth of the city.

As the railroad continued to progress and spread across the states, it would be only a matter of time before a railroad connection to Chicago, Illinois or other cities became a reality.

Progress in this direction began with the Galena and Chicago Union Railroad Company in 1836, but a number of years would pass before any track was laid. In 1852 the Galena & Chicago Union Railroad reached as far as Rockford and the following year, Freeport. When the railroad finally did arrive at Galena in 1854, it was a branch of the Illinois Central, extending from Freeport. [27]

The *Galena Daily Advertiser* kept the residents of Galena abreast to the development of the railroad in Jo Daviess County. *The Galena Daily Advertiser* of November 28, 1853 stated, *The work on the Galena branch of the Illinois Central Railroad is being*

pushed forward rapidly. In about sixty days, twenty-four miles of track southwest of Freeport will be completed, leaving but twenty to twenty-five miles to Galena unfinished. This twenty-five miles is very hard work and will not be finished for some time.

The *Galena Daily Advertiser* of October 28, 1854 proudly reported, *a train of cars from Freeport ran over the Illinois Central Road into Galena for the first time. This event was hailed with the liveliest satisfaction. It is the realization of what has so long been hoped for.*

Quoting from the *Chicago Tribune,* dated the 26th of October, 1854, The *Alton Evening Telegraph* ran an article titled, *Galena and Chicago United*. It stated, *By a telegraphic dispatch received here on last night, we learn that the last rail, on the Illinois*

The building to the left of the Train Depot was built in 1899 by a man named Otto Sallman. His intent was to have a restaurant. An article in the *Galena Daily Gazette* dated October 20, 1899 states, "Otto Sallman's Restaurant Handsomely Equipped" "The lower floor is divided up into a sample room, buffet, ladies' waiting room and a restaurant with a kitchen attached from which will be served lunches and meals at all hours." Due to financial difficulties, sadly, Otto was never able to open his much acclaimed establishment. Otto lived upstairs and rented the downstairs in 1900 to the Chicago & Northwestern Railroad.

Central Railroad, between this city and Galena, was laid down yesterday, at Scale's Mound, and the communications is now perfect between this city and Galena. The regular trains through, will commence running on Monday next, the 30th inst., making the connection in about nine hours. The first regular train will leave Galena, on Monday morning next, at nine o'clock.

In early November of 1854, a celebration was given at Galena in honor of the completion of the railroad there. The work westward continued.

The arrival of the Illinois Central Railroad opened up a good part of the county for the transportation of people and goods. Many towns and communities grew and prospered because of it. This progress continued with the addition of more railroads in later years.

In 1857 the impressive two story red brick Italianate depot was built by the Illinois Central Railroad Company. Costing $8,000 to build, it included both ladies' and gentlemen's parlors, as well as a baggage room.

Galena Water Works - 720 Park Avenue

Built in 1886-7 by the Galena Water Company, this Italianate style water works plant included an artesian well 1,520 feet deep. Powered by two duplex pumps built by the Smedley Steam Pump Company located in Dubuque, Iowa, the water works was capable of flowing between 1,800 and 2,000 gallons per minute. 70 Ludlow hydrants were installed throughout Galena and six miles of cast-iron pipe.

The Galena Water Company had a 30 year contract on the franchise. In 1917, the City of Galena purchased the Galena Water Works plant, using the earnings to go toward improvements of the plant and extensions of the service.

The building foundation is lime stone. Exterior walls are brick. The building has a front-gable roof clad in asphalt shingles. Windows are original wood 1/1 double or single-hung, segmental arch. Doors are original or historic wood glazed, paneled with fanlight.

Today, the building is used as the administrative office of the Galena/Jo Daviess County Convention & Visitors Bureau.

St Mary's Hospital—418 Franklin Street

St. Mary's German Catholic Church was organized in 1851 under the name St. Joseph's Catholic Church. The original wooden church was built in 1852. In 1860, the old church was sold and moved to a different location and the present brick church was built—St. Mary's.

In or about 1854, a two story frame school house was built next to the church at what is today 418 Franklin Street. This building was used until 1865, when it was replaced by the current (shown here) two story brick structure with a basement. This continued to be a German school house for some time.

In 1902 this building became St Mary's Hospital. It was a public hospital and had eleven beds. Henry T. Godfrey was the practicing physician and the sisters of St. Mary's were in charge.

Today it is a private residence.

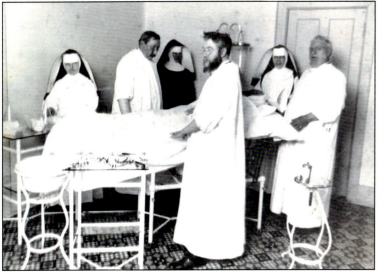

Above: Doctors Gunn, Wirich and Godfrey in the St, Mary's Hospital upstairs operating room, assisted by the nuns during an operation. c.1906

Right:
St Mary's Hospital
c.1906

Galena, Illinois

Turner Hall

Laying the Turner Hall Cornerstone
June 1874

Laying the Turner Hall Cornerstone in June, 1874

The Galena Gazette in June 1874 wrote: "The day broke on a city alive with strangers from the surrounding villages, called thither to witness the pageantry and ceremony attending the laying of the corner-stone. Main Street was almost impassable. The hotels were crowded to their utmost capacity, and still each incoming train brought more. At half past 10 o'clock a.m., a signal from Liberty's bell tower announced the time for morning the line, and a general rush was made for Bench Street where were quartered the different societies and companies, resplendent in gold lace and elegant attire, while over their heads floated silken banners bearing the insignias of the respective Orders. Although the sky was overcast with threatening clouds and the sun but occasionally lent its aid in enhancing the grandeur of the scene, it was such as to inspire the utmost enthusiasm on the part of the beholder, and not a little pride among the participators."

The processional moved all through town and finally arrived at the future site of Turner Hall where an address was given by its President of the Day, Frederick Stahl. His address included the following:

Our city needs a public hall of sufficient capacity to accommodate a large audience, both for the purposes of amusement and instruction. This building, which is now being erected, appears to be well suited to meet the present and future wants of our city. It will present no stately columns, no beautiful statuary, no lofty dome to attract the wonder and admiration of the beholder; but it will be simple in style, durable in structure, simple in its dimensions and in harmony with the means and wants of the community. May I not add, that when finished, it will present to the mind a fitting emblem of the character of the sturdy men who are now engaged in its erection."

Preparations were then made for laying the cornerstone by depositing therein a zinc box, hermetically sealed, containing the following objects: a list of the members of the Turner Society, copies of the subscription list and private donations for the Hall, the constitution and by-laws of the Turner Society, The *Galena Daily Gazette* of June 12 and 13, 1874, the Volksfreund; several envelopes containing donated valuables; a book of poems; a collection of coins, and the bylaws of several Galena organizations. And so the cornerstone sits yet today.

NEW TURNER HALL
GALENA, ILL.

COMPLETED JANUARY, 1875.

SEATING CAPACITY, 1,000.

Solid stone building, with hall on first floor, and necessary dressing rooms and other conveniences.

Seated with chairs

Usual price of admission, 50 cents. Reserved seats, 75 cents.

First Class Scenery of seven complete sets.

Size of stage, 46x22. Drop curtain, 24 feet. Height of ceiling, 25 feet.

Hall lighted with gas, with 60 lights on stage.

Hall licensed and provided with first-class Piano.

Population of Galena, 9,000.

For terms and further particulars, apply to

.... MANAGER.

AGENT.

Photographed by J. E. JAMES, W. BARNER.

Galena, Illinois 202

The photo below shows Turner Hall just after completion in 1875. The photo was taken from the roof of the building directly in front of the Turner Hall on Main Street.

The August 2, 1879, advertisement to the right was for a Gymnastic Exhibition and Ball. Galena has always been and continues to be a town filled with activities.

Turner Hall upon completion c.1875

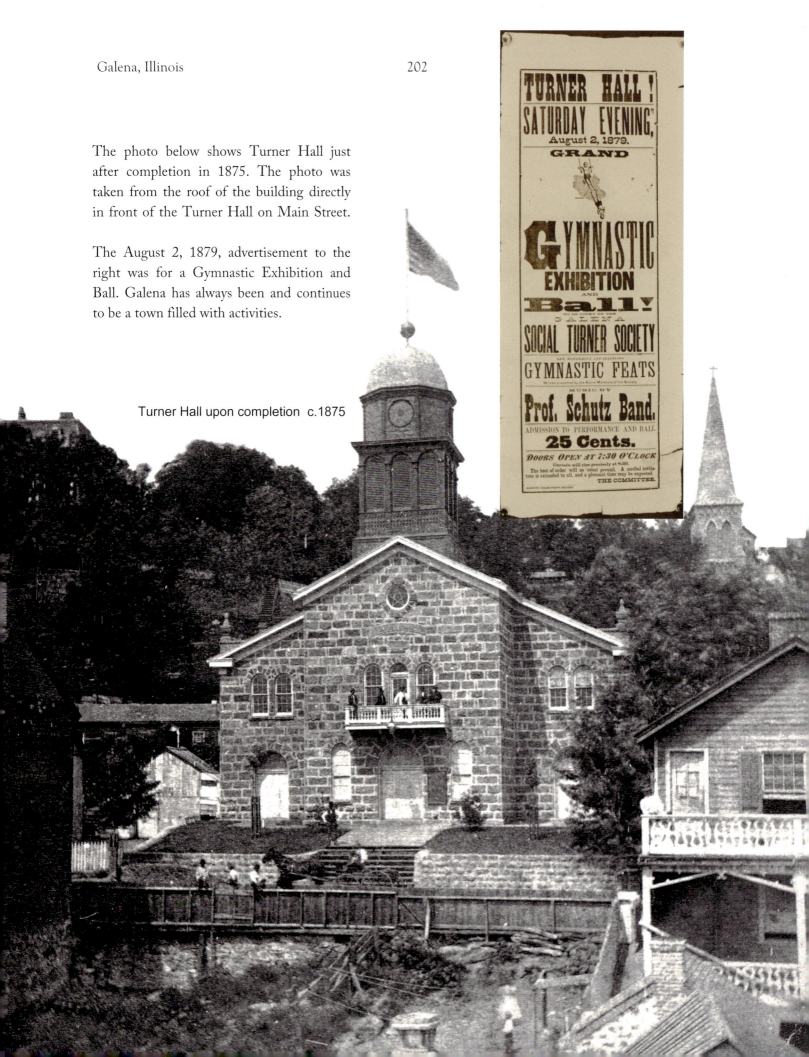

The Turner Opera Hall was used for many types of events. Perhaps the saddest event was the death of Ulysses S. Grant. On July 23, 1885, General U. S. Grant died as a result of throat cancer. The news of his death reached Galena at 7:20 A.M., July 23rd, via the Western Union Telegraph at Dubuque. The first bell to alert the public of the news was that of the First Presbyterian Church and was tolled by Dr. G. Newhall.

The first flag to be flown at half-mast was run up by William H. Blewitt of the DeSoto House. Within short order scarcely a building in the city was without somber drapery of some kind, in respect for the distinguished dead. The feeling in Galena was one of unbounded sorrow over the calamity which had befallen the country. General Grant was greatly beloved in Galena, and this sentiment was not confined by any means to his personal friends, but extended to all classes of people.

Perhaps one of the greatest testaments to the depth of Galena's sorrow was displayed at the Turner Opera Hall. The entire hall was draped in mourning for General Grant (Note photo below). Here the public could come to mourn the death of their fallen hero.

The Turner Opera Hall continued to be a center of amusement, entertainment and education on into the 1920's.

On July 1, 1926, the Old Turner Opera House was gutted by fire. The loss was considered nearly total or over $12,000. This was a huge sum of money at that time.

Over the fall and winter of 1926, the rebuilding of Turner Hall progressed rapidly and was duly reported in the *Galena Weekly Gazette*. In October it was reported that, *the rebuilt Turner Hall would have separate restrooms for men and women.* In mid December, it was reported that, *two boxes are arranged at either side of the stage, each box accommodating parties of 8, that in the basement, in addition to the heating plant, will be shower baths and a dressing room, and that the hall would open the first part of January.*

Finally on December 30, it was announced that the Hall would re-open on January 7, 1927 with the world famous production of "No No Nanette," the "round the world musical comedy sensation" with a notable cast of stars and a gorgeous garden of girls. Tickets for the grand event were $2 plus war tax. The *Gazette's* headline after the event was "Eagle Auditorium Opening Most Successful Event 'No, No, Nanette' Super Fine." They noted the marble floored lobby and stated it was "just a step from the old antiquated Turner Hall to this dreamland of an opera house," just a step and $75,000. [30]

The entertainment continued through the 1920's including a show that would now be called community

Turner Hall Interior c.1890's.

theatre, but was then referred to as a show using "home talent". "The Girl from Babylon" was a huge hit. In 1930, Cliff Floto and his Alaskans, "A Cold Name but a Red Hot Band" appeared. March 9, 1930 was the first day of roller skating at the hall. Skating took place on Sunday afternoons and Sunday, Tuesday and Thursday evenings for 30 cents. The hall continued to host events including, a Progress Exposition in 1935, showing "exhibits of the latest models in automobiles, radios, refrigerators, electric and gas stoves and household appliances." [31]

To this day, Turner Hall is regularly booked on weekends for weddings, plays, concerts and many other types of special events. The rental cost of the Hall has intentionally been kept low to make it easily accessible to the citizens of Galena.

Turner Hall has always been an important part of Galena and continues to be a significant feature in the lives of the citizens of Galena and the surrounding area.

Aftermath of the fire of 1926

Galena, Illinois

Left
The Turner Opera Hall, 2014

Below
The Turner Opera Hall, 1950's

An Historical Time Capsule

c. Residences

Ulysses S. Grant's Original Home in Galena
121 South High Street

John Robinson, a Galena resident that built a number of Galena rental properties in the 1850's, built this home in 1859. Shortly thereafter, "In April, 1860," to quote from Hamlin Garland's *Life of Grant*, "Men stood on the levee, watching the Steamer 'Itasca' while she nosed her way up the tortuous current of the Galena River; as she swung up on the wharf, attention was attracted to a passenger on the deck wearing a blue cape overcoat. As the boat struck the landing, this man rose and gathered a number of chairs together, evidently part of his household furniture. 'Who is that?' asked the man of a friend on the river bank. 'That is Capt. Grant, Jesse Grant's oldest son; he was in the Mexican War—he is moving here from St. Louis,' was the reply." [1]

"Capt. Grant took a couple of chairs in each hand and walked ashore with them. His wife, a small alert woman, followed him with her little flock (four children, Frederick, Ulysses, Jesse and daughter, Nellie). The carrying of the chairs ashore signified that Ulysses Simpson Grant had become a resident of Galena." [2]

Grant's wife Julia, stated in her personal memoirs, *We took passage by steamer for Galena. After a journey of four or five days, we arrived at Galena, a charming, bustling town nestled in the rich ore-laden hills of northern Illinois.*

We were quartered with Captain Grant's brothers for two or three days. The Captain had already secured a nice little brick house of seven rooms, which was nestled high up on the hill on the west side of the town in the best neighborhood and with a lovely view. [3] The rent was $100 per year. [4]

The Grants lived in this home until the outbreak of the Civil War, the first shots being fired at Fort Sumter on April 12, 1861. By April 30th U.S. Grant was already in Springfield at Camp Yates, acting as a drill officer. [5]

Although Ulysses S. Grant left for the war, his wife and children remained here in this home in Galena until, urged by her husband, Julia left with her children and joined him at headquarters in early November of 1861.

Today, this is a private residence.

Galena, Illinois

Grant's Home - 500 Bouthillier St

The brick house, which was designed by William Dennison, had been constructed in 1860 for former City Clerk Alexander J. Jackson. Thomas B. Hughlett, on behalf of a small group of local Republicans, purchased the house for $2,500 in June 1865 and presented it to Grant two months later. The house is typical of the Italianate style, which is characterized by well defined rectilinear shapes, projecting eaves supported by brackets, low pitched roof, and balustraded balconies over covered porches. [6]

Following his election as president in 1868, Grant visited only occasionally. In 1873 Grant commented that *although it is probable I will never live much time among you, but in the future be only a visitor as I am at present... I hope to retain my residence here . . . I expect to cast my vote here always.* The house was maintained by caretakers in anticipation of the President's visits, the local newspaper reporting that it was *in excellent order and ready for occupation at any time*, adding that *visitors are always admitted.* [7]

Grant made his final visits to his Galena home in 1880. At that time he found that several changes had been made: *a new sidewalk laid in front of the premises, the outbuildings repaired, the trees handsomely trimmed, a new and commodious wash house built and other improvements made.* [8]

In 1904 Grant's children gave the house to the City of Galena with the understanding that the property was to be kept as a memorial

This photo composite dating back to 1879 includes: 1. Ulysses S. Grant Portrait, 2. Home at 500 Bouthilliar, 3. Grant Leather Store on Main Street, 4. Grant Home at 121 South High Street.

to the late General Ulysses S. Grant, and for no other purpose.[9] However, maintaining the Grant home proved too costly for the city and the Grant Home Association, so in 1931 the city deeded the house to the State of Illinois.

A thorough restoration project was undertaken in 1955. Considerable research was done in order to return the house to its 1868 appearance. Fortunately, much of the furniture used by Grant and his family remained in the house. Restoration returned the home to its appearance as pictured in the November 14, 1868, issue of *Frank Leslie's Illustrated Newspaper*.

The Grant Home was designated a National Historic Landmark on December 19, 1960 and added to the National Register of Historic Places on October 15, 1966.

The painting on the wall depicts U. S. Grant being commissioned to Lieutenant General by Elihu Washburne and Abraham Lincoln.

The fireplace is original.

The large book on the table is Julia Dent Grant's Family Bible.

Ninety per cent of all furniture in the house is original.

Below:
The chair to the right was U. S. Grant's favorite.

The Red Vases on mantle were gifts Grant received from the King of Bulgaria during his world tour in 1878.

Above:
Grant Dining room with painting of Julia Dent Grant above the fireplace.

The china setting on the table is from Nellie Grant's wedding at the White House in 1874. This was the first White House wedding in 32 years.

The Silver setting is also from the White House, in use while Grant was in office.

Right:
The kitchen in the Grant home still has the original dry sink.

Nelson Stillman Home -513 Bouthillier St

The Stillman Mansion was built in 1858 by Nelson Stillman, a dry goods merchant and sugar dealer. Stillman was born in Connecticut in 1815. He came to Galena when he was 23 years old and is credited with starting the first public school in Galena. [10]

He became a very wealthy man while here in Galena. The mansion had 22 rooms. This is a very large home. When you consider the fact that the city charged tax on each interior door in a house, this made for a significant tax that he had to pay. [11]

Stillman had a small family including a wife and two children. The children lived on the third floor with a nanny.

In time, Stillman's estate came to include 20 acres of farm land and mineral land known as Barrows Place, which adjoined the city on the east; two brick stores, several city lots and also an interest in the DeSoto House.

Nelson Stillman became gravely ill in August 1871 and died at the age of 56. Upon his death, his wishes were that his properties and assets were to be sold.

Over the years, there has been a number of people that have owned this mansion. In the 1930's it was converted to a nursing home, first called the Bronell Nursing Home and thereafter Sunny Hill Nursing Home. In 1970 it came under new ownership and was converted into a restaurant. [12]

Dave and Bernadine Anderson fell in love with this mansion, purchased the property in 2000 and transformed it into the stunning *Bernadine's Stillman Inn,* Bed and Breakfast.

An Historical Time Capsule

The Belvedere -1008 Park Avenue

The 22 room mansion named the Belvedere (in Italian "Belvedere" means beautiful) was built by Joseph Russell Jones in 1857. It is one of the most lavish mansions in Galena. What is truly amazing is that the man who originally had this beautiful home built, J. Russell Jones, had nothing when he first arrived in Galena back in 1842. Here is his story:

Joseph Russell Jones was born in Conneaut, Ohio, Feb. 17, 1823. His father died in 1825. Although his mother left for Pecatonica (Rockton) Illinois and eventually remarried, Joseph remained in Conneaut, and was raised by his uncle, Judge Dart, his mother's brother. [13]

By the age of 13 in 1836, Jones was working as a clerk in a general store in Conneaut, where he remained until August 1838. He left Conneaut and joined his mother's family at Rockton, Illinois.

Joseph Russell Jones

He didn't stay for long with his family in Rockton. Shortly after moving to Rockton at the age of 15, he set sail aboard the schooner, the "J. C. King" bound for Chicago, a one year old city (in 1840) at the foot of Lake Michigan boasting 4,000 citizens. He remained in Chicago for just about two years, before he again became restless. At the age of 17 (in 1842), he made the move to a more refined city located further west and considered the Metropolis of the West, Galena.

When he arrived in Galena, he had just one dollar in his pocket. With that dollar, he purchased a hat. The events that followed allow us to perceive the type of personality and work ethic that this young man possessed. The very first day of his arrival, he got a job at the grocery company of Christy and Bolvinth. Within a few months, he changed companies and had a better job working for Benjamin H. Campbell, Wholesale Grocers. He wasn't afraid to take on any task and within a short time, was recognized as one of the company's most valued employees. Within eight years (1850) he became a partner in the mercantile firm of Benjamin H. Campbell. He was just 27 years old!

From 1846 at the young age of 23, he was the secretary and treasurer of the Galena and Minnesota Packet company. He maintained this position up till 1861. Jones served as a representative in the Illinois legislature in 1860; U.S. marshal for the northern district of Illinois, 1861-69; U.S. minister to Belgium, 1869-75; declined the cabinet appointment of secretary of the interior in 1875, and was collector of the Port of Chicago, 1875-76. [14]

Jones developed close relationships and friendships with many powerful men over the years, including his neighbor, Elihu Washburne, Ulysses S. Grant and even Abraham Lincoln. Abraham valued Jones insight to such a degree that when Grant was first talked of (running) for the presidency, Lincoln telegraphed to Mr. Jones asking if he could tell him whether Grant wanted to be president. [15]

Certainly not, said Mr. Jones, who at once reported to Lincoln. *He would not take the office if it was offered to him. So far from being a candidate himself, I know him to be earnestly in favor of your reelection.* [16]

Mr. Lincoln's countenance relaxed and he said, *My friend, you don't know how gratifying this is to me.* Adding reflectively: *No man can ever tell how deep that presidential grub gnaws till he has had it himself.* [17]

Joseph Russell Jones resided with his family in the Belvedere mansion that he had built until 1861, when he and his wife, Elizabeth Ann, and children moved to Chicago. He organized the Chicago West Division Railway company in 1863 and was its president for twenty-five years, retiring from business in 1888.

Today, this beautiful mansion is open to the public for tours and is filled with treasures from throughout the world. The Belvedere is the most often visited Italianate mansion in Galena.

A rare photo of the Belvedere dating back to c.1890.

Galena, Illinois

The Belvedere

An Historical Time Capsule

Top Left—The Gold Bedroom: damask draperies, gilded Victorian mirrors, crystal chandelier and silk bedding

Middle Left—The formal dining room

Middle Right—Veranda interior

Lower Photo—View of south side of the Belvedere with enclosed veranda.

Ryan Mansion -11373 West US Hwy 20

Located at the intersection of Oldenburg Lane and U.S. 20, the James M. Ryan Mansion, built in 1876, is Galena's largest historic mansion with well over 9,000 square feet of luxury details. The gorgeous 24-room mansion has ruby glass windows oriented to the summer solstice, 12 fireplaces, and 9 servant's bells. [18]

Built by James M. Ryan Jr., this man's brief biography is of interest. His parents, James and Margaret Ryan were born in Ireland, where they were reared and married. After they married they sailed for America, originally settling in Maryland.

Within a few years they moved to Ohio. James Jr. was born near the city of Zanesville, Ohio on October 8, 1828.

In April of 1846, when James Jr. was 17 years of age, the Ryan family moved to Galena, Illinois. This was at the time when Galena was a large metropolis with nearly 14,000 residents, a major city in 1846.

James Sr. died two years later at the age of 51. His son James Jr. continued to run the family's farm with fair success.

One of the conspicuous industrial establishments of Galena is the packing, curing, and smoking establishment of James M. Ryan, provision dealer. One hundred and twenty hands are employed here during the season. The buildings utilized cover a large area, and present a busy scene during the slaughtering season. The main packing building is 220x130 feet. The smoke-house has a capacity of 200,000 pounds of meat.

The Inter Ocean Newspaper, Chicago Wed. Dec. 29, 1886

He soon established a wholesale and retail grocery business in partnership with his brother, called William & J. M. Ryan. They continued together until August 1868, when the partnership was dissolved and James became sole proprietor. [19]

Prior to the dissolution of the business, both brothers had abandoned the wholesale grocery trade and taken up pork-packing. James Jr. eventually turned his full attention to this latter industry and began to reap excellent profits. He owned slaughter houses which processed up to 1,000 hogs per day, and soon became known as the leader in this business in Northern Illinois - outside of Chicago. James Jr. owned and farmed over 600 acres just outside of Galena, which comprised a very valuable piece of property, and there he made this home. [20]

Built around 1902, this beautiful 9000 square foot mansion has 24 rooms and 12 marble fire places. It is the largest home in Galena and is one of Galena's premier bed and breakfast lodging establishments.

Cloran Mansion -1237 Franklin Street

John Cloran emigrated to Northern Illinois as a young man and initially settled in East Galena in the summer of 1849. Later he sold his property to the Illinois Central Railroad Company, and in 1853 crossed the river and relocated his store to 185 South Main. He purchased the grocery stock of James M Ryan and his brother William, but a year later, the store and stock were destroyed by fire. [21]

Cloran was a forward thinking man who took a philosophical view of life, and realized that no business enterprise could expect to exist without losses. Within a short time he reopened his business in a new brick building at the same location on Main Street.

He grew his city properties to include three business houses and two residential dwellings, while outside the city limits he had a farm of 140 acres including his home, pictured here. [22]

Cloran wasn't given life's fortunes on a silver platter. He started "at the foot of the ladder" and climbed his way up by being industrious, economical, having

perseverance and sound common sense.

Born in Ireland around 1815, he came to the United States with his brother in May 1841. [23] John served the Union during the Civil War enlisting Sept. 2, 1861.

John Cloran's name appeared in a newspaper from Belvidere, Illinois, the *Belvidere Standard*, dated January 07, 1879. This event demonstrates that although Galena was a beautiful city to live in, not all lived according to the "golden rule."

The article reads, *John Cloran, a grocer of Galena, barely escaped being shot dead by T. D. Kelly of the same place. Cloran had just sued Kelly for a bill of groceries, and had just received judgment. Shortly afterward, Kelly entered the store at the back door, shot gun in hand and approaching Cloran unseen, fired one barrel at his head, fortunately just grazing his ear.*

Felt Manor -125 S. Prospect Street

Lucius Sawyer Felt built this beautiful mansion in 1848. He was born in Plattsburgh, New York on Nov. 9, 1815. He married Katherine E. Sullivan in Plattsburgh, Oct. 14, 1845. Felt left his home in New York State in 1837, and after spending a short time in Wisconsin and Iowa, he settled in Galena, where he engaged in the mercantile business. The L. S. Felt Company was located in the four story brick building on Main Street that later became known as the Coatsworth Building. Felt was in business until his death on August 5, 1876. [24]

Felt was a dry goods merchant, an estate manager, a director of the Merchants National Bank, and one of the incorporators of the Galena Gas Light Company in 1853.

In 1875 he remodeled his Greek Revival home into an elegant and impressive Second Empire mansion, complete with a mansard roof.

The beautiful estate is a bed and breakfast today and still has the original brick carriage house, original ice house and an 8,000 gallon underground cistern.

The remarkable limestone steps and wrought iron railings in the front of the Felt residence were built by Felt in the 1860's and christened "Felt's Folly" by a local wag.[26] It is reported that these steps cost $40,000 to construct. That is equivalent to nearly 1.5 million dollars today, in 2015.

HALLETT - FELT
Special Telegram to The Inter Ocean.

Galena, Ill., Feb. 9.— The residence of Mrs. L. S. Felt in this city was the scene this evening of one of the most brilliant weddings that has ever occurred in Jo Daviess County. The high contracting parties were the Hon. Moses Hallett, Judge of the United States District Court at Denver, Col., and Miss Kittie L. Felt, eldest daughter of the late L. S. Felt, Esq. The Rev. A. C. Smith, of the South Presbyterian Church performed the ceremony. Between 300 and 400 guests attended the reception, including the following from Chicago: Mr. and Mrs. W. A. Montgomery, Mr. and Mrs. Addison Philleo, Mrs. James Root, Mrs. J. H. Long, and Mr. and Mrs. Neef. The bride was the recipient of many rich presents. Judge Hallett and bride left on the 10:58 train this evening foe a two month tour of the South. Denver will be their permanent home.

This residence was the scene of one of the "most brilliant weddings" that had ever occurred in Galena.
Inter Ocean, Chicago 02-10-1882, Page 3

PRESIDENT GRANT.

Visit to Farmington, Connecticut.

Nellie Grant at School-Journey from Hartford to New York and Enthusiastic Reception at All the Stopping Places-Arrival in New York and Programme of Future Movements.

President Grant, accompanied by Mrs. Grant and Mr. L. S. Felt, arrived in the city at ten minutes past five yesterday afternoon, having left Hartford, Conn. in the one P. M. train. A special drawing room car - as has been the case during all his Eastern trip - was placed on the train for the exclu-

The Felts were close friends with President Grant and his wife.
New York Herald, NY NY 09-30-1870, Page 3

Loveland Estate -301 S. Prospect Street

Daniel Frazer Loveland was born on Sept. 10, 1817 in Westport, New York. He was 29 years old when he traveled west from Westport in March of 1846. He went by way of the Hudson River to New York, from there to Philadelphia and Baltimore by rail. Once there, he crossed the mountains to Pittsburgh by stage, went down the Ohio River to Cairo and up the Mississippi to Galena, and then on to La Crosse, Wisconsin, arriving there in April, 1846. Along the Ohio River the peach trees were in bloom. At La Crosse the snow was one foot deep. He was in the lumber business there for four months but returned to Galena and engaged in merchandising. [27]

His wife Eleanor came to Galena when she was a small child with her family. Daniel and Eleanor met in Galena and were married on Feb. 8, 1854. They had two children, Jennie and William. William died at three months of age, whereas Jennie survived into adulthood. [28]

Daniel and Eleanor built this impressive Italianate mansion in 1870.

The Lovelands maintained and updated the mansion with the most modern of conveniences available at the time. In the July 5, 1888 the *Freeport Journal* Newspaper, Freeport, IL. reported, *The Bartlett Hardware Company of Freeport has just completed a contract for steam heating and plumbing in the residence of D. F. Loveland, Galena.*

WONDERLY—LOVELAND
Special Telegram to the Inter Ocean

Galena, Ill. Nov. 17.-Dr. T. G. Wonderly, one of our most well known and highly esteemed citizens, and Miss Jennie Loveland, daughter of D. F. Loveland, Esq., were united in marriage this evening in the presence of a large number of guests, including friends from Platteville, Dubuque, Chicago, and other cities. The ceremony was performed at 7:30 o'clock, at the elegant residence of the Loveland family, by the Rev. W. W. Steel, rector of Grace Episcopal Church. The Misses Kittie Howard, of Galena, and Bessie Duerr, of Monticello, Iowa, officiated as the brides attendants, and Messrs. W. W. Wagdin, J. S. Baume, John Dowling, and C. S. Merrick as ushers. The bride was the recipient of a small fortune in the way of presents. The groom and his accomplished bride took the night train for Chicago.

Jennie Loveland and Dr. T.G. Wonderly were married in this home on Nov. 17, 1881.
Inter Ocean, Chicago, 11-18-1881

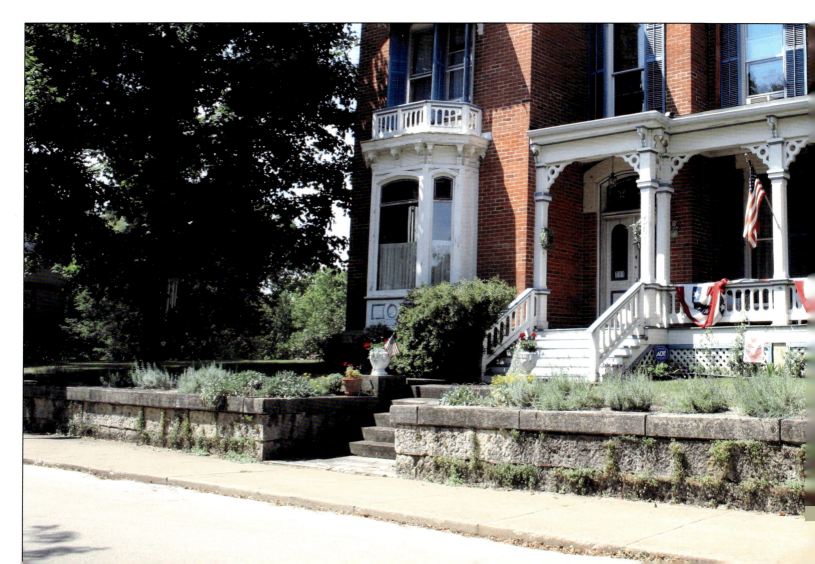

Habich Residence -113 S. High Street

Fred C Habich and Catherine Riede were married on January 08, 1891 and resided in this home along with their children. Habich was the last official market and weigh master in Galena and also operated a barge line on the Galena River. He died in 1950 at 83 years of age. [29]

Xavier Kammerer Residence -516 Green St.

Xavier Kammerer built this stone home in 1852. He was a stone mason and also Galena's Street Commissioner in the early 1870's. Xavier and his wife had at least four sons. His son, William F. Kammerer, was born in this house in 1865.

In 1886 William headed for Montana where three of his brothers had preceded him. He went to Virginia City, and by the next year he was an employee and stockholder of the Alder Gulch Consolidated Mining Company. He married and gained the reputation of being "liberal, honest and true." But his life was to end tragically. Near Ruby, Montana, on a January day in 1908, Willie Kammerer was employed as the second shift "flume man" on a dredge boat. While unwinding a winch, he lost control of the handle which struck him in the head, killing him instantly. He was buried in the Virginia City Cemetery.

A twist of fate is connected with this home and the person that owns the home today at the time of writing (2015), namely Scott Wolfe.

A few years ago Wolfe and his wife Nancy were on vacation in the Rocky Mountains and happened upon Virginia City, Montana. "Scanning the horizon," Wolfe spotted the Virginia City Cemetery in the distance. He ventured over to read some of the tombstones. The very first stone that Scott encountered read: WILLIAM F. KAMMERER, DIED JAN. 9, 1908, AGED 43 YEARS. [30]

What were the chances of traveling well over 1300 miles and by happenstance, coming across the tombstone of a man that died over 100 years ago and was born in the house that you currently live in?

John Fiddick Mansion - 213 S Prospect St

John Fiddick had this beautiful home built in 1859. He was born in Cornwall, England on February 22, 1826, and came to Galena at the age of 15 in 1841. His mother had died when he was just two years old, and his father died shortly after. He went to live with his paternal grandfather, Thomas Fiddick, who was a miner. When his grandfather died, John traveled from England by himself to Galena and began working as a clerk in his uncle's (William Fiddick) store. [31]

His uncle had come to Galena six years earlier, arriving Nov. 2, 1835. He started into the Mercantile business in 1839.

John Fiddick married Mary Bastiau in February, 1850. Shortly thereafter, he left for California, swept up by the prospect of the California Gold Rush. Not having success, he returned to Galena in 1852 and started a firm named the W. & J. Fiddick Company. with his uncle. [32]

By 1869 his uncle, having become quite wealthy, retired from the business. William's son and John's 23-year old cousin Richard, now became his partner. The company name was changed to J. & R. H. Fiddick, Dealers in Dry Goods, Carpets, Boots and Shoes, Furs and Feathers. Their store was located at 156 & 158 Main Street. This partnership lasted until

1883. Richard withdrew his interests from the store and started "The People's Bank." John thus became the sole proprietor of the company. [33]

John Fiddick was a practical and successful businessman. Although he came to Galena with little means, he rapidly rose in wealth and became a well respected person in Galena.

John lived until March 16, 1918. He was 92 years old when he died.

This majestic home on Prospect Street is a testimony to the fact that life's obstacles can be overcome. John Fiddick was put into a position early on where he was responsible for his own resources. He certainly overcame this seeming handicap.

The John V. Hellman Mansion -318 Hill St

John V. Hellman (b. 1849) was one of six children. He was raised in Galena. His father's (John A. Hellman) home was located on Prospect Street. He joined his father's grocery business in 1882. Originally, his father had entered into the grocery business with a partner, John Burrichter. Some twelve years later, the partnership was dissolved and each partner went into business for himself. The ad on the following page was in the *1854 Galena Directory*. [34, 35]

On September 12, 1872, John V. married 18 year old Wenona Harris, the daughter of Captain Daniel Smith Harris. Captain Harris was one of Galena's most important steamboat magnates. John and Wenona had three daughters, Pauline, Irene, and Eleanor. He built this home in 1895 for his family.

With their roots firmly planted in Galena and John V. a success in his own right, the Hellman family lived in late Victorian splendor in their nine room home. The third floor was originally built as a ballroom where the Hellman family entertained guests.

The home retains its original stained glass windows, original woodwork, five fireplaces and sliding pocket doors. The original dining room set was recently brought back to the home. [36]

Today, this remarkable home is a bed and breakfast. It is named the Hellman Guest House Bed and Breakfast.

John V. Hellman c.1919

Advertisement found in the *1854 Galena Directory*

The Dowling House -216 Diagonal Street

Galena's oldest home was built by John Dowling and his son Nicholas upon their arrival in Galena from Dublin, Ireland, via St. Louis, in 1826.

They promptly got to work and constructed the building shown here out of native limestone. Today, the Dowling House has the distinction of being the oldest standing stone structure in the state of Illinois. Note that, although by today's standards this is a small home without the frills that we're accustomed to, when this structure was built, this would have been a home of high prestige and an example of wealth. Many lived in shacks or one room log cabins with dirt floors.

Dowling established a trading post on the first floor, selling goods to workers in the area's lead mines, while he and his son Nicholas lived on the second floor. Their residence and trading post was the center of the social and commercial life in this early frontier community.

The Dowlings were able to branch out into a more substantial building for their trading post in 1831. They built a stone structure on Main Street across from their own home. It had a large hall on the second floor, a room for a school in the basement, and was called "Dowling's Stone Store."

A MELANCHOLY DEATH. — The national Intelligencer mentions the death of an old gentleman named John Dowling, from Galena, Ill., which took place under peculiarly melancholy circumstances. He arrived in Washington and took lodgings at Brown's hotel on Tuesday evening, 28th ult. The next morning he said, at the bar, that he had lost a check of $500 on the Metropolis Bank. He locked his room, and went out with the key in his pocket; and, as he did not return, the proprietors of the hotel became fearful some accident had befallen him. — They went in quest of him, and on Monday heard that an old man had died the day before at the Asylum, (or Poor-house.) Mr. Morse, the bar-keeper, had the coffin opened, and found that it was Mr. Dowling. He learned that the day he left the hotel, he was found in the evening near the Navy Yard, and that some person there kept him all night, and the next day sent him to the poor-house. He was evidently of deranged mind. When his room was broken open, his baggage and papers were found there, and amongst his papers the $500 check which he supposed he had lost. He gave no evidence of being deranged when he left the hotel. He was interred on Monday evening in the Catholic burial ground attached to St. Patrick's Church.

The Sun (Baltimore, Maryland)
Thursday, March 9, 1843

John Dowling was very active with the affairs of Galena and was even elected onto the Board of Trustees in 1838.

His son Nicholas eventually became one of the richest and most influential men in Galena's history.

John Dowling died on Monday March 5, 1843 while in Washington. The unusual circumstances can be read in the news article reprinted to the left. As you read this, keep in mind that the average skilled worker earned less that $1 per day in 1843. [37]

The Dowling House has been preserved and is open to the public.

The Dowling House -216 Diagonal Street

The Dowling House looks today as it would have when John and his son Nicholas lived and worked here.

The upstairs living quarters (photos on this page) is furnished in the simple style of the time. All the furnishings date from the early 1800's. This would have been considered a mansion in 1826. The sink in the kitchen is the original. A butter churn stands in the kitchen.

The downstairs trading post (photos on previous page) contain objects Dowling might have offered for sale in his store, such as oil lamps, candle molds, and other artifacts, all dating back 150 to 200 years. Among the most prized exhibit is a fine collection of Galena Pottery, made from 1841 to 1847 of local clay and glazed with lead.

c. 1939

2014

Washburne Residence - 908 Third Street

Elihu B. Washburne (1816-1887)

The Elihu B. Washburne House at 908 Third Street in Galena was constructed in 1843 in the popular Greek Revival style and enlarged sixteen years later to its present size. [38]

Galena was a thriving commercial center for a profitable lead-mining region when Elihu Washburne arrived in 1840. A recent graduate of Harvard Law School and a Whig, Washburne knew that there was work to be found in Galena, where most of the lawyers were Democrats. Galena residents were, wrote Washburne, a *litigious set* who rarely crossed party lines when employing an attorney. [39]

Washburne opened a law office "in the good part of town," joined the Episcopal Church, became friends with the editor of the local Whig newspaper, and campaigned for Whig candidates. Soon he was employed by Galena's leading Whig lawyer, Charles S. Hempstead, with whom Washburne boarded for several years. There he met Hempstead's niece, Adele Gratiot, whom he married in 1845. The couple had seven children. [40]

Politically active, Washburne served as a delegate to Whig conventions, but by the mid 1850s, he was a member of the newly formed Republican party, which he and his three brothers helped establish. An avid supporter of Abraham Lincoln's unsuccessful bid for the Senate in 1858, Washburne devoted his "whole soul and energies" to Lincoln's campaign for the presidency in 1860. He advised Lincoln before and after the election and kept him abreast of political developments in Illinois and Washington, D. C. [41]

Washburne promoted the military and political career of another Galena resident, Ulysses S. Grant. Following Grant's election as president in 1868, Washburne served briefly as Secretary of State before the President appointed him ambassador to France. Recalled from France when Grant's second term of office ended in 1877, Washburne returned to the states but chose to live in Chicago. From 1884 until his death on October 22, 1887, he served as president of the Chicago Historical Society. He is buried next to his wife in Galena's Greenwood Cemetery. [42, 43]

Elihu Washburne (1816-1887), occupied the house with his family until 1882. Only one other family, the Sheehan family, owned the house until 1968 when it was purchased by the State of Illinois. Today the house is a state historic site managed by the Illinois Historic Preservation Agency. [4]

Election night 1868 in the home of Congressman Elihu B. Washburne.

Local artist Thomas Metcalf, depicts the library of Congressman Elihu B. Washburne's home on election night, November 3, 1868. Elihu Washburne was in the United States House of Representatives from 1853-1869. He was President Grant's Secretary of State and later, Ambassador to France.

This painting of Grant's election night in 1868 includes important details: Western Union set up a special telegraph machine in the library of the Washburne home on election night. The telegraph machine can be seen on the table in the far right of the painting. Congressman Washburne is the second man on the left in the painting, and soon-to-be President Grant is seated in the chair in front of the fireplace, smoking a cigar.

The Chicago History Museum comments on the uniqueness of having a telegraph wired to a home in the 1860's:

For many of us, the telegraphic system, a precursor to e-mail in many ways, is somewhat mysterious, even romantic. We typically imagine a small rectangular sheet of paper with the Western Union logo at the top and a very short, urgent message typed or written out without any punctuation. The Museum's telegram collection of the 1868 election returns, aside from two on official Western Union stationary, are newsprint sheets with messages of all lengths scribbled in pencil. They weren't at all what I expected.

The night of the election, presidential hopeful, Ulysses S. Grant, walked down the road to Elihu Washburne's house. Washburne, a congressman and friend to Abraham Lincoln, was a longtime friend of Grant's and a great supporter of his throughout the Civil War, as well as during his political career. On election night Washburne set up a telegraph machine in his home for returns to be sent directly to General Grant. I assume, therefore, that the Museum's many plain newsprint telegrams are the ones that came to Washburne's residence, as opposed to the town's central telegraph office.

How typical was it to have a telegraph machine in your own house in the 1860's? It was almost entirely unheard of. Although Washburne was quite sophisticated and well-off, even he was pretty taken with the idea that presidential election returns were being wired directly to his very own library. In a letter to his wife at six o'clock on the night of the election, Washburne wrote:

> *You ought to be here this evening for you would enjoy it. The telegraph machinery is all in and I am writing at the table where the instruments are in front of the window that looks out on the porch. The operator is here and we are waiting for the returns to come in. . . . Now we all come out from tea into the library and the telegraph ticks away, but as yet brings no news.*

Apparently, they were on pins and needles as the news streamed in. According to Washburne:

> *The little old library looks like a committee room of ward politicians this morning. . . . It was very exciting receiving returns. After success seemed to be assured, the Lead Mine Band came over and gave some music and we felt pretty foxy. The General staid [sic] till about one o'clock this morning. . . . The General was very cool, yet anxious. What a terrific contest we have had! It has come out right, but what a narrow escape.*

Source—*Man Behind the Grant Telegrams"* by Naomi Blumberg, 11-05-12

Strode Residence -209 S High St.

This residence was originally built by Mary Strode in 1852. In 1869 Richard H. Fiddick, a young man of just 23 years, purchased the house. He had just been married to his bride, Fannie Alden, a few months prior (in 1868). His father William was very successful here in Galena in the mercantile business. Richard followed in his father's steps and expanded into various areas including banking as well as additional mercantile shops, including the "St. Louis Store," a very popular store in Galena for many years. [44][45]

This elegant home was remodeled in 1892 with a three-story square tower and wing with a two-story bay on the north side.

The Richard Seal House -225 S. Prospect St.

In 1871 the Honorable Judge Richard Seal built this charming home. The home was completed in just six weeks at a cost of $4,000. [46]

His wife, Mrs. Alicia Seal, died in 1853 at the age of 42 and never lived at 225 South Prospect St. According to the 1880 census, Judge Seal was living in the home with his "niece and housekeeper," Lucella (Lucy) Goodman. Judge Seal lived in the home until his death in 1888 at the age of 81. He was a resident of Galena for 52 years. [47]

Back in 1853, Seal was elected to and held the office of County Clerk for 22 successive years. He was elected County Judge from 1869 through 1872. Judge Seal was compensated $2.50 for every day he held court. He was a member of the Episcopal Church and also the Odd Fellows.

Galena, Illinois

407 Park Avenue

This home was built in 1879 by Henry C. Telford, a well known architect, contractor and house builder. The mansard roof sets off the classical Second Empire style of this gorgeous home.

Prospect Street c. 1890

An Historical Time Capsule

d. Churches

"City Of Churches"

Religious worship and spiritual interests were extremely important to the early settlers of Galena. In the historical reference, *The History of Jo Daviess County*, published in 1878, it stated: "At the present time, Galena has twelve churches, of which five are situated on Bench Street. Being of tasty, construction and located on terraced bluffs, these edifices are shown to good advantage, and, as a visitor remarked, Galena might well be termed *the City of Churches.*[1]

Seven of the twelve churches that were here in 1878 are still centers for worship in Galena to this day. They are:
First Presbyterian Church - 106 N. Bench Street
First United Methodist Church - 125 S. Bench Street
St. Michaels Catholic Church - 227 S. Bench Street
St. Mary's Catholic Church - 406 Franklin St
Grace Episcopal Church - 107 South Prospect St
St. Matthew Lutheran Church - 127 S. High Street
Westminster United Presbyterian Church - 513 S. Bench St.

The history of each church is unique and some find their roots in Galena's earliest days.

According to the reference previously quoted, "The earliest public worship that can be traced in history was conducted in 1826, by a weather-bound preacher, en route to the East from the Selkirk settlement, north of Minnesota."[2]

Then in 1827, "...lay readings of the Episcopal Church were held by Mr. Gear (one of Galena's earliest settlers) at his house. In the same year, religious meetings were held by Rivers Cormack, a settler who remained many years."[3]

"The first regularly appointed preacher to Galena is a matter of some dispute. Both the Methodist and the Presbyterian societies appointed men of the cloth at about the same time. The two men were the Revs. Aratus Kent (Presbyterian) and John Dew (Methodist). Mr. Kent arrived on the first of April, 1829, and Mr. Dew one week later."[4]

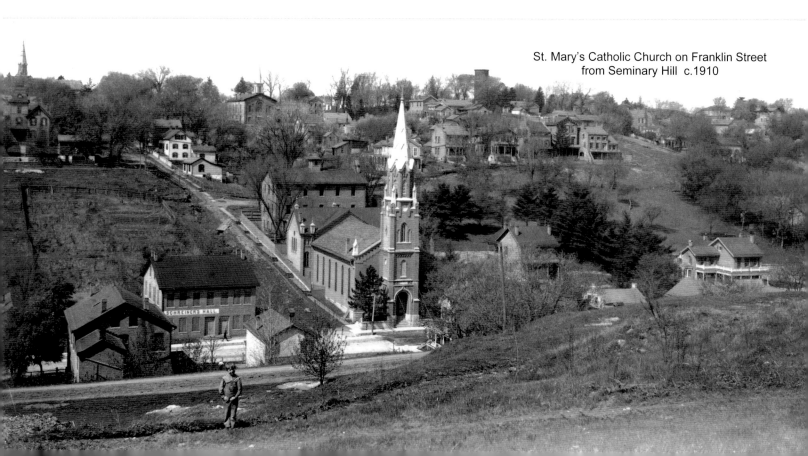

St. Mary's Catholic Church on Franklin Street from Seminary Hill c.1910

First Presbyterian Church

The First Presbyterian congregation is housed in the oldest church building of any Protestant denomination in continuous service in the Old Northwest Territory (which consisted of all or part of six states: Illinois, Indiana, Michigan, Minnesota, Ohio and Wisconsin).

The building was built in 1838, but the congregation really had its start in 1829 when the Reverend Aratus Kent decided to leave his prestigious New York City parish to bring the gospel to what was then this country's western frontier. He wrote to the American Board of Home Missions and asked to be sent to "a place so tough, no one else will take it." They assigned him to Galena. [5]

It took him almost a month to get here from New York, traveling by horseback and steamboat. He arrived on a Sunday morning and immediately went knocking on doors, telling everyone he could find, that he was going to have a worship service that afternoon at 3 o'clock. [6]

He swept out the back room of a saloon on the corner of Bench and Hill Streets (next door to where the church is located today) and about 50 people showed up. At that point, he probably thought that evangelizing the frontier was going to be an easier job than he'd imagined, but those 50 people turned out to be the largest group to attend one of his services in Galena for many years. Apparently, many of them came to that service because worship was such a novelty in Galena. For the next several years, Rev. Kent worked very hard, riding a circuit with a one hundred-mile radius, preaching at dozens of locations and teaching numerous Sunday school classes. Eventually, it all began to pay off in terms of church membership. He was able to found a number of congregations throughout Illinois, Iowa and Wisconsin, including the First Presbyterian Church in Galena, which was officially organized in October 1831. [7]

At that time, there were only six members of the church: two who lived in Galena and four others living as far as 40 miles away. That's a very healthy commitment in the days of horse-and-buggy travel. [8]

First Presbyterian Church at 106 N. Bench Street
c.1890

By 1838, this First Presbyterian congregation had grown to include 100 members. It was then that they decided to build the church building still used today. (Before that time, the congregation had been meeting in the old log court house that was located next door to the present church location on the Franklin Street side.) The building was constructed with limestone quarried in the Galena area. [9]

The pews used to this day are original - from 1838 - except that they used to have doors on the entrances to keep drafts off people's feet as they sat in worship. At that time the only heat in the sanctuary was from two fireplaces in either corner up front, so that in those early days, unlike today, everyone wanted to sit up front in order to be closer to the heat. However, in those days, people couldn't just sit wherever they pleased. Each of the pews was numbered on the back along the aisle side, and every family was assigned to a certain pew for which they had to pay a pew tax. That was the way the church raised money to pay the internal bills of the congregation, such as the pastor's salary, the purchase of candles, etc. The congregation would also take an offering to be used for mission work - those needs which were outside of the immediate congregation. The church still has a receipt for one family's pew tax from the mid-1840's when the tax was $6.00 a year. [10]

The founding pastor, Rev. Kent, was a graduate of Princeton and Yale Universities. When he officially organized this church in 1831, Yale donated the pulpit and the four chairs that are currently in the front of the sanctuary. This was a gift to the fledgling congregation and a means of encouraging the mission located at what was then the country's western frontier. The two chairs on either side of the communion table and the two in the back of the sanctuary came from Rev. Kent's home. No one is sure of their exact age, however, he died in 1869, so they're at least that old. The large chair in the right front was built in the 1860's and was designed to match the style of the chairs behind the pulpit.

View of the First Presbyterian Church at 106 N. Bench Street with Hill Street in the foreground. Probably taken from a business rooftop on Main Street. c.1905.

When the building was built, the windows were made of an opaque yellow glass. The stained glass windows you see today were installed between 1890 and 1910. They all have a dedication plaque near the bottom of the window. A couple of the dedications are to previous pastors, and one is for the Christian Education Society; all the rest are to former members. The windows are made of Belgian stained glass with the colors fired in rather than painted on.

The vestibule section was added in 1851. That addition included the steeple, which stretches 125 feet above the street.

Even though the congregation officially began in 1831, the current pastor - the Rev. Jim McCrea - is only the 20th installed minister to have served the church.

Above: One of many beautiful stained glass windows.

Above: Interior of the First Presbyterian Church on Bench Street, circa 1890, during the Celebration of the annual "Harvest Festival".

2015

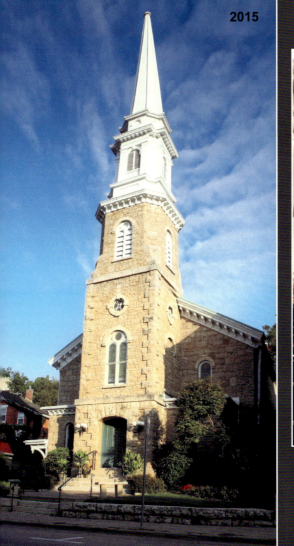

Interior of the First Presbyterian Church in 2015

Galena, Illinois

First United Methodist Church

In 1829 the Rev. John Dew, the first regularly appointed Methodist minister, arrived in Galena. By 1832 a plain frame church was erected on Bench Street, but was lost to fire in 1838. This is the oldest Methodist Church and Methodist Congregation in the State of Illinois. A new building was built in 1841, and by 1856 the congregation had grown so that yet another new brick and stone church needed to be built. The old church was sold, and the present church was built at the corner of Washington and Bench Streets at a cost of $23,000. The present church was dedicated on January 18, 1857. [20]

Ulysses S. Grant came to live in Galena in April 1860 and to work in the family leather store with his brother. During that time, he attended the Galena Methodist Church.

At the end of the war, he returned to Galena and the entire town turned out to welcome him home. The Methodist Church was decked with flags and buntings to welcome and honor him.

When news reached Galena of President Grant's death at Mount McGregor in 1885, the church was draped in mourning and a memorial service was prepared. In front of the pulpit was placed "a stand of pure white flowers, with the initials, U. S. G., in purple flowers." [21]

Quoting further from Wilbur Crummer's book, *General U.S. Grant*, "The pew formerly occupied by the General when there, was covered with the United States flag, tastefully draped. The house was filled with his friends and neighbors, and a feeling of personal loss was felt by all. The services were simple but beautiful. Several of his personal friends spoke feelingly of the great General's life."

The pew General Grant occupied while in Galena is marked with a flag and a plaque till this day.

Other historically significant features are the twelve stained glass windows that adorn the church. These windows date back to 1856, when the new church was built. Members of the congregation at that time donated these windows.

The 1880's Lancaster-Marshall 18 rank pipe organ was built in Moline, Illinois. Pipe organs such as this were built on order, and were made to fit in the specific size available at the church. Once built, experts from the organ company came to the church and spent 20-30 days erecting and finishing this fine instrument. The original pipe organ continues to fill the church with beautiful music although it is more than 130 years old.

U.S. Grant's reception in 1880 after his return from a 2-1/2 year world tour.

The pew that General U.S. Grant and his family occupied while living in Galena is still in use at the First United Methodist Church.

An Historical Time Capsule

Twelve (12) Historic Stained Glass Windows:

When the new church was built in 1856, members of the congregation donated several of the 12 stained glass windows lining the church. Between 1984 and 1987, the fellowship committed to restore ten of the windows. The final two were restored in 1991.

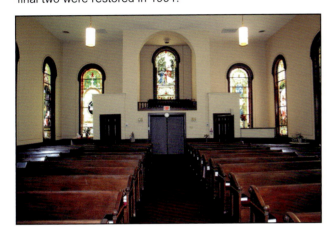

The 18-rank 1880's Moline Pipe Organ behind the altar is still in use until this day.

St. Michael's Catholic Church

St. Michael's parish was formed in 1832 and has the distinction of being the oldest Catholic parish in the Rockford Diocese. In fact, there was a resident pastor in Galena, Father John McMahon, fully a year before Father St. Cyr selected a lot on Lake Street for the first Catholic Church in Chicago. [22]

At the time, Galena was a lead mining town and was known as "one of the roughest places you ever saw or heard of with a good many rough chaps about." The first pastor assigned here in that year was John McMahon who died of cholera within the first year as did the second pastor, Charles Fitzmaurice. The third pastor was Fr. Samuel Mazzuchelli, who saw the need of a church in Galena, and work began in 1835 and was completed in 1842 at a cost of $14,000. [23]

One of the worst fires in Galena's history occurred April 1, 1856. It destroyed more than thirty buildings including St. Michael's Church.

But the faith of the parishioners carried on and work soon began on a new church under the supervision of Fr. Samuel Mazzuchelli. Within one week of the fire, over ten thousand dollars had been subscribed for the construction of a new church. The present church was completed in 1863 and measured 135 feet in length, 60 feet wide with the walls 35 feet high. From the floor, the ceiling rose to a height of 44 feet. The 18 windows in the auditorium measured 20 feet high and 5 feet wide. [24]

In 1871 new altars were installed, Stations of the Cross were hung and the cathedral glass windows were installed. In 1884 the square towers were finished. Renovations to the interior, including pews, painting, lights and kneelers, have continued over the years.

The roof and ceiling of the church are supported by a wooden truss formation that is quite unique to the area, as there are no supporting pillars in the church. The style of the architecture is Romanesque Revival. The openings on all the windows and doors are rounded arches of a medieval style. The numerous semi-circular arches inside the church are supported by Corinthian columns.

Galena, Illinois

View of the interior rear of St. Michael's with the pipe organ originally installed in the 1880's. c.1910

Below: Interior of St. Michael's, c.1925

An Historical Time Capsule

St. Michael's interior c.1932

Below:
Interior of St. Michael's today

St. Mary's Catholic Church

St. Mary's German Catholic Church was established in 1851 under the name of "St. Joseph's Catholic Church," in the old Catholic church. The first church was frame, built in 1852 on the corner of Franklin and High Streets. The first to preach in the church was Father Heimerling, who remained until the present church was built. In 1860 the old church was replaced with the present large brick church that measures 40 by 80 feet in size, that was built at a cost of about $8,000. In 1867 a 32 by 65 foot addition of was built on to the rear of the church at an equal cost. By 1876 the church tower was added. [11]

In 1865 a two story brick German schoolhouse with a basement was built on the same lot. This building stands vacant behind the church today.

St. Mary's Catholic Church

Left: Purchased from St. Michael's in Galena shortly after St. Mary's was established. This frame building originally had been a Baptist Church, but it had been used as a school for St. Michael's. It served as a church for the first 11 years of St. Mary's history from 1850-1861.

It was then sold and was moved across the street from the parish buildings. This first building was to see many more uses made of it, including a barber shop, saloon, blacksmith shop, paint store and wagon shop. [12]

Below: Interior of St. Mary's as of 2015

The altar of St. Mary's as of 2015

Right: St. Mary's Altar, c. 1910

Grace Episcopal

Galena's Grace Church is the oldest Episcopal Church in continuous use in the Diocese of Chicago. Going back to the roots of this church, the first lay service of the Episcopal Church and the first classes of the Sabbath-school took place at the residence of Captain H. H. Gear in Galena in 1827. The church was first organized in October 1834 in a frame building, formerly used as a stable, but repaired for a court house, on the site of the present day DeSoto House. [13, 14]

A chapel was erected in the summer of 1838 on the northeast corner of the block at the junction of Bench Street and Comstock's Alley. It was consecrated in August of that year by the Rt. Rev. Jackson Kemper, who was the first missionary bishop of the church for the Northwest. In the same year (1838) a pipe organ was purchased for the church from the Henry Erben Organ Company in New York, and was the first and only organ in Galena for many years. This organ was shipped from New York to New Orleans and then up the Mississippi. As of 2015 this organ's chords still fill this sanctuary with its beautiful tones. [15]

The Rev. James De Pui succeeded Father Gear in 1847, and was in turn succeeded by Rev. Alfred Sonderback. During the rectorship of Sonderback, the present Grace Church was erected. The corner stone was laid April 5, 1848. [16]

The building, constructed of limestone quarried on the site, was consecrated by the Rt. Rev. Philander Chase, D.D., on the 28th day of April, 1850. [17]

Grace Episcopal is filled with many precious objects. Some of the stained glass windows are of irreplaceable Belgian glass, and a few of them are in Tiffany style. The chapel, altar area and sacristy were added in 1893. Extensive stenciling and historic memorial plaques give Grace Church a unique character.

In 2000 and 2001 the congregation spent $450,000 to completely restore this historic building.

The pipe organ was purchased for the church from the Henry Erben Organ Company of New York in 1838 and is still in use till this day.

Interior of Grace Episcopal Church
C. 1890

Grace Episcopal Church—2015. Note the depth of the chancel above compared to the photo on the previous page. In 1894 the limestone bluff in back of the church was cut back thirty feet and the original chancel wall was demolished. A new chancel twenty-five feet deep and eighteen feet wide was erected.

The steeple was removed in 1903.
Photo circa 1898

Galena, Illinois

St. Matthew Lutheran Church

In 1858 a young pastor from Germany, the Rev. John Klindworth, formally organized St. Matthew Lutheran Church in Galena. Traveling pastors had laid the groundwork. The congregation had no church building for its first seven years, but with the end of the Civil War the present brick church building was finished. Located on High Street between Hill and Washington, the original structure was 32 by 60 feet in size. Cost to build the church was $3,500. [18]

In 1874 the roof of the church was blown off by a tornado, after which it was rebuilt with a 25 foot addition. This was completed in 70 days at a cost of $2,000. The Rev. John Klindworth made national headlines throughout the country in 1892 when he stood behind the decision of the synod and barred individuals belonging to what they termed "Secret Societies." His example demonstrated that he was a man of conviction and stood for what he believed. Note the following article found in the *Brooklyn Daily Eagle* Newspaper, Brooklyn, N.Y., 09-19-1892:

CONDEMNING SECRET SOCIETIES

Galena, Ill., September 19 - The Rev. John Klindworth, who is pastor of a Lutheran church in Galena, and his son, who has charge of a country parish, are causing a sensation by their hostilities to the Grand Army of the Republic and the farmers' alliance. The son refused the sacrament to members of either organization. The father refused John Sass the sacrament because he belonged to the Grand Army and notified him to withdraw from the order or stand suspended from the church. Sass sticks to his brass buttons and stays at home Sundays. The preachers say that the organizations are secret and a ban has been proclaimed by their synod against such bodies.

Right:
View as of 2015

Below:
The Rev. John Klindworth organized St. Matthew Lutheran Church in 1858. He actively served as their minister up until his death in 1907. This photo was taken at the time of his funeral.

Note the gas lights and pot belly stoves.

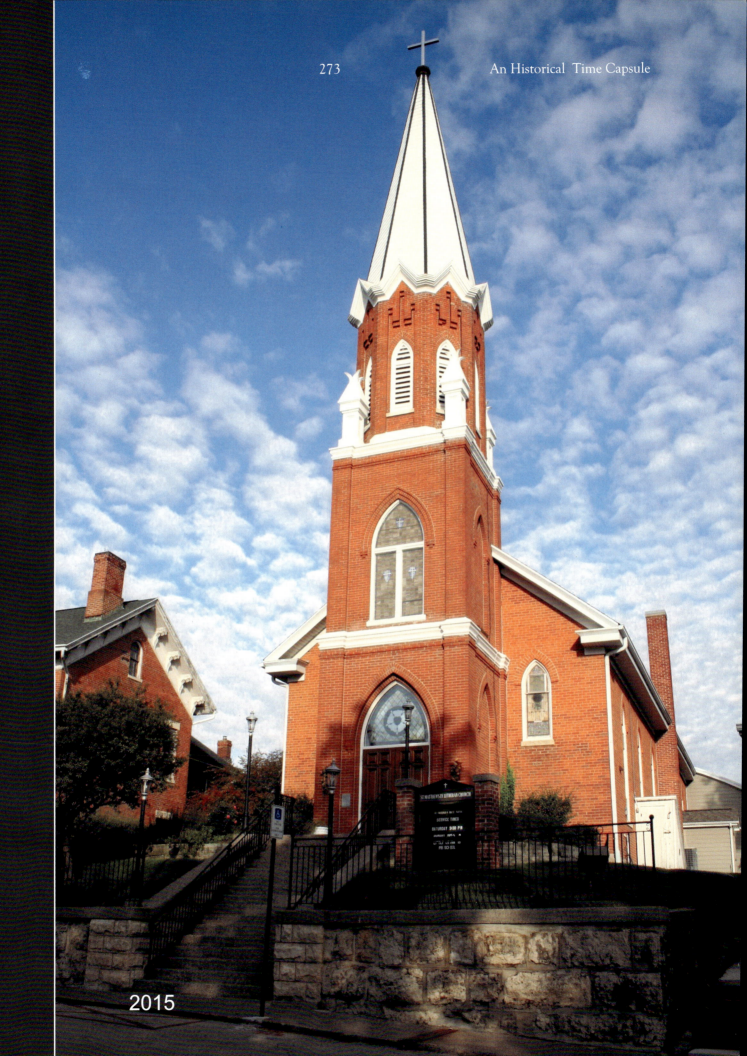

Galena, Illinois

Westminster United Presbyterian Church

The roots of the Westminster Presbyterian Church date back to 1846. In that year a theological controversy known as "Old School" and "New School" resulted in "an amicable parting of the ways" for some members of First Presbyterian Church, who later formed the South Presbyterian Church here in Galena. [25]

For the first two years until the completion of the present church, the congregation worshiped in a building rented from the Baptists. They eventually moved into their unfinished church in 1847. It was completed in 1848 and dedicated on the 10th of September of that year, Rev. John M. Smith of Pittsburgh officiating. [26]

In 1854 a German-speaking congregation established the Presbyterian Church, later to be named the Hill Presbyterian Church, and a church was built on land donated by the South Church. Periodic efforts to unite Galena's three Presbyterian Churches were unsuccessful until 1960, when the Hill and South Presbyterian congregations finally voted to unite and become Westminster United Presbyterian Church. [27]

Extensive renovation and rededication of the sanctuary were completed shortly after the merger. The beautiful stained glass windows were left intact.

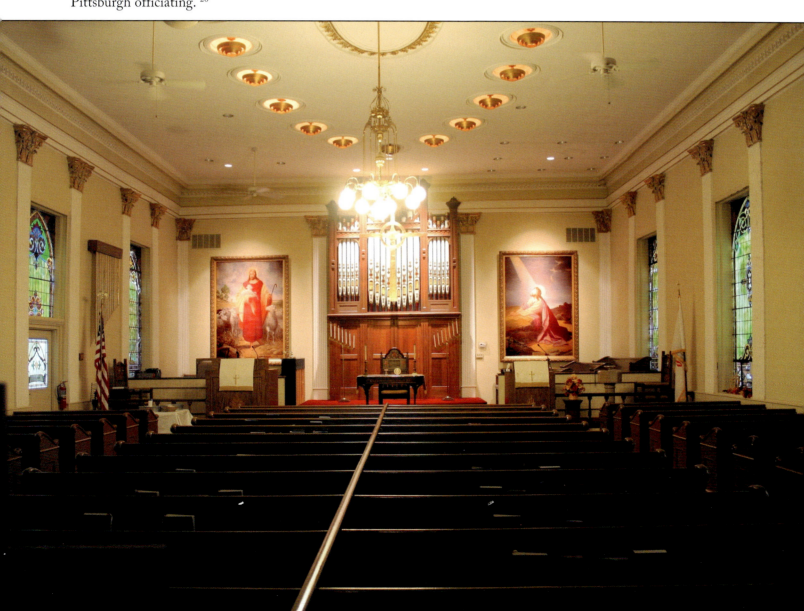

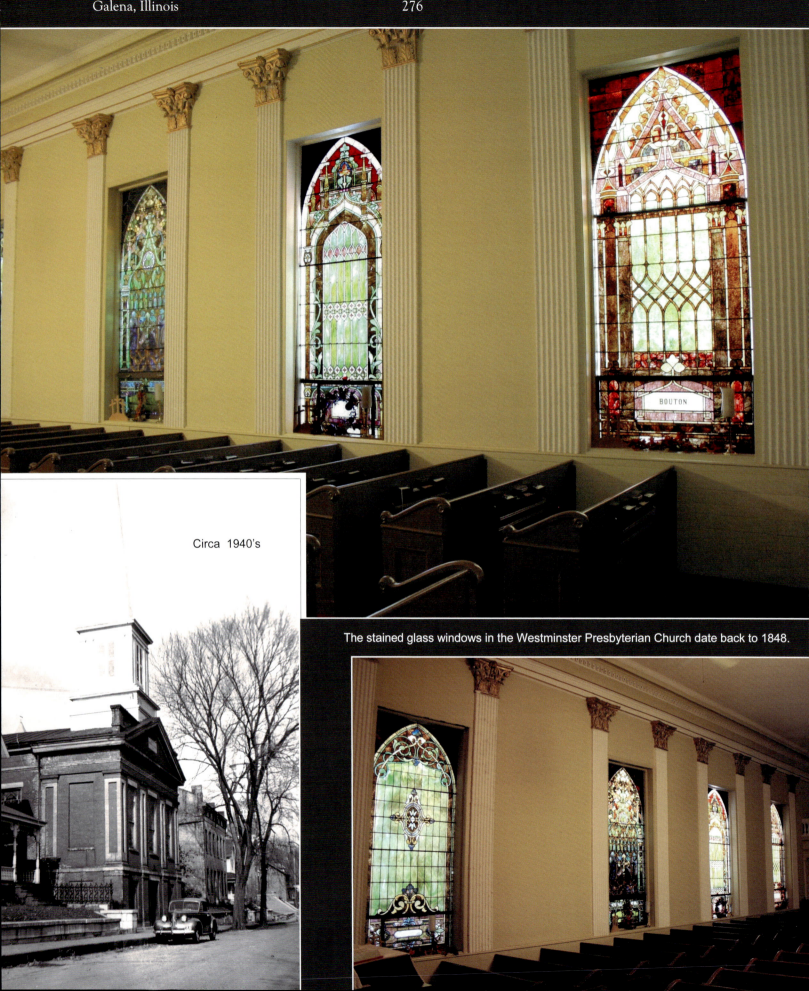

Circa 1940's

The stained glass windows in the Westminster Presbyterian Church date back to 1848.

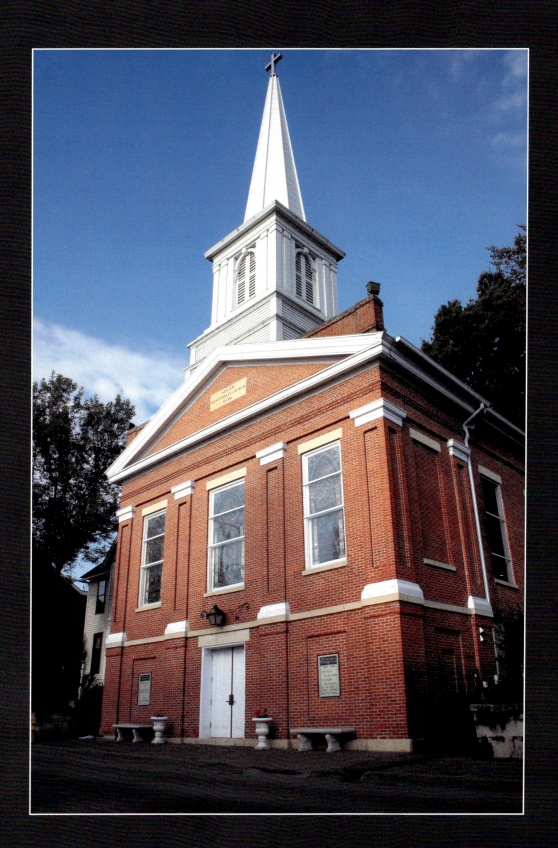

One of Galena's many floods.
c. 1900

Chapter 10

The Floods

The history of Galena would not be complete without a mention of the floods.

The Galena River is part of the Mississippi River system, the largest river system in North America. Originating at Lake Itasca, Minnesota and terminating ninety-five miles below New Orleans, the Mississippi River is 2,320 miles long. Thirty-one U.S. states, stretching from the Continental Divide in the Rocky Mountains in the West to the Appalachian Mountains in the East, drain into the Mississippi River. It is the fifth largest river by volume in the world. [1]

Although the Galena River is a smaller tributary, its effect on Galena is monumental. The Galena River is some fifty-four miles in length, arising south of Benton, Wisconsin and traveling south through Galena before emptying into the Mississippi. Therefore, Galena is the hardest hit by fifty miles of river drainage before the river empties into the Mississippi, four miles downstream.

Today the Galena River pales in comparison to the river that it once was. Some estimates put its width in Galena during the 19th century at 350 feet, with a depth two feet deeper than the main channel of the Mississippi. As many as eighteen steamers were tied up at one time, loading or unloading. [2]

Being built on the banks of the river, Galena experienced numerous destructive floods that paralyzed its commercial district.

The earliest recorded flood was in 1828. A newspaper in Clarion, Ohio recorded that the Fever River (the original name of the Galena River) raised six feet in three days. Evidently the water was so high, that steamboats were floating down Main Street in Galena. [3]

Although there were numerous floods that have occurred over the years, the worst recorded flood was in 1937. The February 22, 1937 *Chicago Tribune* ran an article which stated that up to seven inches of rain had fallen during the evening of Saturday, February 20th, causing unprecedented flooding in towns along rivers and creeks. It stated that *Galena was one of the hardest hit.*

The *Tribune* went on to say: *Galena . . . saw the Galena river rise from a flood stage of 13 feet to 27.5 feet in eight hours.*

A general alarm at 5 a.m. called Galena residents from their beds. About 300 persons were forced to leave their homes. Merchants rushed into the business district and began piling stocks out of reach of the water, at least above the then record flood mark of 1916, but this point soon was passed and large stocks of merchandise were lost. Then the flood fell

Galena, Illinois

almost as rapidly as it came.

Although the waters subsided quickly, the damage in their wake remained. The citizens of Galena were then hit by 30 mile per hour winds that carried blizzard conditions with them. Temperatures fell from the low 40's to the teens causing a quick freeze over the entire area. We can just barely imagine the difficulty of attempting to function in these dire conditions.

Influential men including Galenian Frank Einsweiler and Galena's Congressman, Leo E. Allen began seeking congressional assistance to address this ongoing threat to Galena.

On July 19, 1937, the House of Representatives passed the Galena Flood Control Bill, providing for a survey of the Galena River by the War Department to determine the causes of the flooding in the valley and the means of preventing them. Thus began efforts to finally alleviate the flooding of downtown Galena. On August 10th of the same year, it passed the Senate, and only needed the signature of President Roosevelt in order for it to become law. This success was due to the efforts of Congressman Leo E. Allen of Galena.

The President did sign the bill into law. Of course projects like this take time. The Army Corps of Engineers did their due diligence. In the summer of

**Flood of 1911,
S. W. Corner of Commerce and Perry streets**

1941, they completed their surveys of the river and on August 1, 1941, presented their recommendations to Congress. They estimated that the cost of construction would be $418,000, with annual maintenance costs of $4000.

Within days, Pearl Harbor was bombed and the U.S. entered World War II. The Galena River flooding was placed on the back burner and wouldn't become a topic of conversation until after the war. By 1946, funds and contributions began to come in again for the Galena Flood Control Committee.

Another flood hit Galena on February 27, 1948, sending four to six feet of water down Main Street. Galena firemen used canoes to rescue more than 200 people marooned in apartments above buildings in the low-lying section of the business district.[4]

Finally in 1948, the levee embankment project was underway. It would take parts of four years to finally be completed in 1951, with the twenty foot flood gates firmly in place.

On Feb. 14th, 1911 an ice jam on the Galena river, followed by heavy rain, flooded the city. During the height of the flood, the business section of the city contained three to six feet of water and the citizens paddled about the city in boats.
Belvidere Daily Republican 02-17-1911

Flood of 1911, Corner of Commerce and Hill streets looking north

Galena, Illinois

Galena Flooded

Galena, Ill., Sept. 9.—(AP)—Business streets here were flooded today after a terrific all night rain and the Galena river still was rising at noon.

Freeport Journal Standard—09-09-1927

September, 1927
Main Street looking north, west side of the
100 South Main block.

Historic flood of 1937
Intersection of Hill St. and Main

The flood gates have saved the downtown business district on a number of occasions. In 1993 a late spring season rainfall put the Mississippi and Galena rivers at record flood levels. Almost eight feet of water threatened downtown Galena, but was stopped by the earthen levee and the floodgates.

In 2010 eight inches of rainfall in one night caused the Galena river to swell to twice its usual level. The flood gates were closed. If they weren't in place, it is estimated that six feet of water would have covered Main Street.

The following year, 2011, Galena was hit with more than 10 to 15 inches of rain within a 12-hour period. Again, the Galena River rose to more than twice its normal height and, possibly, its highest recorded level since the flood gates were built. Although there was damage due to the amount of rainfall, the flood gates kept the river from downtown, lessening the damage that would have been even more devastating. However, there was major damage to downtown businesses, the city's trail system and roads. But this was due to the deluge of rain, not the river.

1937 Flood, Main Street looking north, east side of 100 South Main block.

The completed Floodgates and Levee embankment, c.1952

Initial construction of the Galena levee.

ROCK ISLAND DISTRICT.   CORPS OF ENGINEERS, U. S. ARMY.   ROCK ISLAND, ILLINOIS.

Initial construction of right bank levee embankment, Local Protection Project, Galena River, Galena, Illinois. Contractor, M. L. Gaber Construction Company. Contract No. DA-11-117-eng-71, dated 14 September 1949. Funds 21X3113 Flood Control, General.

Looking south, showing open inspection trench from Station 0+50 to Station 4+50.

13 October 1949

Galena, Illinois

The Galena flood gates in January, 2015

Chapter 11

Present Day Galena

Galena . . . You would be hard pressed to find another destination that can compare to its uniqueness, charm, personality and landscape.

In 2011, Galena was rated as one of the top ten "charming small towns" by *TripAdvisor.*

The *Conde Nast Traveler* Readers Choice Survey rated Galena as the 2nd friendliest city in the United States in April of 2013. It's true! Where else can you walk down the street and have people smile and make eye contact with you, or greet you with a kind hello?

Galena is truly like walking back in time. Although just a little more than a three hour drive from Chicago, the pace of life in Galena and the tone of its citizens are laid back, calm and happy.

Being an "outsider" myself, I relish the fact that there is a location which I can visit that is so close to where I live, (near Chicago), where I have the opportunity to absorb this spirit, this energy that emanates from Galena and its citizens.

Evidently, I'm not alone. It is estimated that 1 million to 1.5 million tourists per year visit Galena. There is only one other location in Illinois that receives more tourists, and that, of course, is Chicago.

Although Galena at its peak boasted over 14,000 citizens in 1858, today the population is around 3,400.

If you enjoy history and architecture, Galena is definitely a destination for you. The Galena Historic District takes in a 581-acre section of the city and is listed on the National Register of Historic Places.

The architecture of the structures throughout the historic district include:
Vernacular
Greek Revival
Gothic Revival
Italianate
Queen Anne
Romanesque Revival
and High Victorian Gothic

With its rich historic and architectural heritage, Galena has so much to offer its visitors. Galena's business district is filled with unique shops and art galleries.

The city has an active arts community. At any given hour, you're bound to find a musician strumming a guitar or playing the flute somewhere along Main Street. Family activities abound as well. Note some of the examples on the following pages:

Breathtaking scenery surrounds Galena. Called the "Driftless Area", this land was missed by the glaciers eons ago, thus maintaining its features of deeply carved river valleys and picturesque landscapes.

Photo courtesy of the Galena Jo Daviess County Convention & Visitor's Bureau

Present Day Galena

Trolley Tours are a perfect way to take in the history and architecture of Galena. Tours are narrated by skilled, knowledgeable and entertaining guides that reveal the history behind the majestic and stately structures located throughout Galena.

Throughout the year, there are numerous "special" events. One of the annual highlights in December is "The Night of the Luminaria." It is, without a doubt, one of the most beautiful and romantic visions of the year. From Main Street to the surrounding hills, all of Galena is glowing with over 5000 candle-lit luminaries on streets, steps and sidewalks. This enchanting magical night attracts thousands each year. Whether you drive the streets, walk the sidewalks, take a trolley or enjoy a carriage ride, you'll be amazed at the beauty of Galena as she is bathed in holiday lights.

Photos courtesy of the Galena Jo Daviess County Convention & Visitor's Bureau

Step back in time and visit a bygone era when steamboating and lead mining once ruled the day. Marvel in 19th century architecture or take a guided tour of the local attractions. Learn how faded memories of the past come to life while exploring the historic sites and museums of Galena.

The Old Blacksmith Shop— *245 Commerce St.*

This authentic 1897 Old Blacksmith Shop is open to the public with working forges. The original tools and equipment that were used over one hundred years ago are still on site, and some are still in use today. The workers are historians that will captivate you in the art of blacksmithing as it was done here in Galena.

Other Museums and Historic sites in Galena include:

- The Old Stockade on the Cobblestone Street—*208 Perry St.*
- Ulysses S. Grant Home State Historic Site—*500 Bouthillier St.*
- Old Market House State Historic Site—*123 N. Commerce St.*
- Elihu B. Washburne House State Historic Site—*908 Third St.*

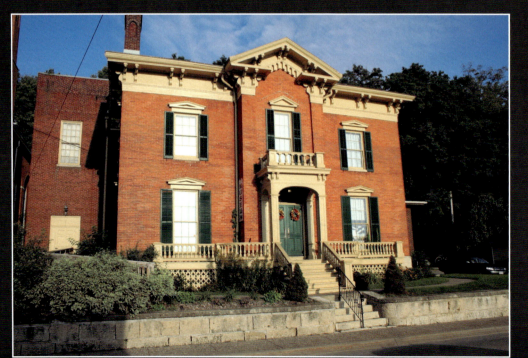

The Galena-Jo Daviess Historical Society Museum, located at *211 South Bench Street*, is a must see for visitors coming to the city. The Museum is filled with treasures that can't be seen anywhere else. Examples of these rare and precious artifacts include the original 9' x 12' painting, *Peace in Union*, by Thomas Nast (1895), depicting Lee's Surrender to Grant at Appomattox in 1865. The flag raised over Vicksburg is also on display. Or, peer down an 1830's lead mine shaft.

The hundreds of unique shops on Main Street attract tens of thousands of people to Galena throughout the year. There are also various special events that fill out the calendar, such as this image of a classic car show.

Photo courtesy of the Galena Jo Daviess County Convention & Visitor's Bureau

Galena is renowned for its local award-winning wineries and vineyards. Indulge in one of Galena's wineries and benefit from learning about the craft of wine making or enjoy specialty wine tastings.

Galena offers amazing dining options including warm and friendly bistros, premium chop and steak houses, cafés, specialty coffee houses and diners.   Enjoy entrees that will satisfy any palate, ranging from American, Greek, Mexican, German, French to Italian.

Photo courtesy of the Eagle Ridge Resort & Spa

The Eagle Ridge Resort & Spa is the premier golf destination in Northern Illinois. With its four impeccably maintained professional courses, the North Course, East Course, South Course and the General, you will enjoy the tranquility of the breathtaking landscape and truly enjoy a relaxing round of golf.

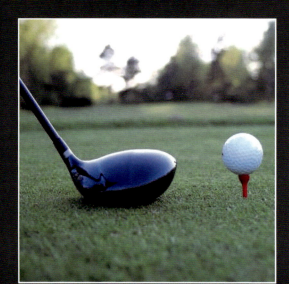

Present Day Galena

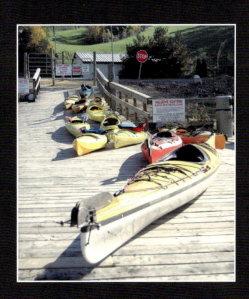

Outdoor activities abound in Galena. Kayaking and canoeing on the Galena River thrill people of all ages. The Galena River is one of the most beautiful rivers in Northern Illinois.

Biking, hiking, and hot air balloon rides are just some of the activities during the spring to fall months. During the winter, outdoor activities include: skiing, snow boarding and snow tubing. Chestnut Mountain is a favorite destination for these activities.

No matter the season, something is always happening in Galena.

When it comes to the arts and entertainment, no matter the season, music is always happening somewhere in Galena.

Photo to the left highlights Scott Rische on mandolin and Jordan Danielson on acoustic guitar.

Photos courtesy of the Galena Jo Daviess County Convention & Visitors Bureau

Galena, Illinois

Aerial photographs courtesy of pilot and photographer
James Schmidt

Credits and References

Chapter One
1. Illinois State Geological Survey. 1999. *Pleistocene glaciations in Illinois.*
2. www.warpaths2peacepipes.com—Alchin, L.K, Native Indian Tribes
3. Cahokia—City of the Sun, Page 12
4. Paleo-Indian and Archaic Archaeology, Part II, Page 108 by: Michael D. Wiant
5. History Of Jo Daviess County—1878, Page 843,844
6. Ibid
7. Sac and Fox Nation of Missouri Website: http://www.sacandfoxks.com
7. Twelve Moons—A Year With the Sauk and Meskwaki, 1817-1818, Tom Willcockson, Elizabeth Carvey pg. 12
8. Life of Blackhawk By Blackhawk, Pg 33
9. Encyclopedia Britannica
10. History Of Jo Daviess County—1878, Page 243
11. Ibid, Page 452
12. Christie Trifone-Simon of JDCF, Quoted in the Galenian Online, http://www.galenianonline.com/SiteImages/SpecialSection/36/p75c2.html

Chapter Two
1. http://en.wikipedia.org/wiki/Hernando_de_Soto
2. History Of Jo Daviess County—1878, Page 21
3. Ibid
4. https://www.illinois.gov/ihpa/Research/Documents/Vol3n2FrenchPeoplePP.pdf
5. History Of Jo Daviess County—1878, Page 117
6. Galena's Old Stockade by May Belle Rouse Page 8,9
7. Ibid
8. Ibid
9. History Of Jo Daviess County—1878, Page 223

Chapter Three
1. History Of Jo Daviess County—1878, Page 226
2. Ibid
3. Ibid
4. History Of Jo Daviess County—1878, Page 227
5. Ibid, Page 228
6. Ibid
7. History Of Jo Daviess County—1878, Page 236
8. Ibid, Page 237
9. Ibid, Page 234
10. Ibid, Page 231
11. Ibid, Page 233
12. http://www.stanford.edu/dept/EHS/prod/general/asbestoslead/leadfactsheet.html
13. http://pubs.usgs.gov/fs/2011/3045/pdf/fs2011-3045.pdf
14. http://minerals.usgs.gov/minerals/pubs/commodity/lead/
15. History Of Jo Daviess County—1878, Page 226
16. http://iagenweb.org/dubuque/bio/Dubuque_Julien.htm
17. Ibid
18. http://www.encyclopediadubuque.org/index.php?title=JULIEN_DUBUQUE_MONUMENT
19. History Of Jo Daviess County—1878, Page 226
20. Ibid
21. Ibid
22. Galena's Old Stockade by May Belle Rouse Page 25
23. History Of Jo Daviess County—1878, Page 237
24. Ibid

Credits and References

Chapter Four
1. History of Jo Daviess County, Page 241
2. Ibid
3. Ibid
4. Ibid
5. History of Jo Daviess County, Page 242
6. Collections of the State Historical Society of Wisconsin, Page 279
7. History of Jo Daviess County, Page 243
8. Ibid
9. Ibid
10. Minnesota: A History of the State, by Theodore Christian Blegen, Page 112
11. The Virginia, By William J. Peterson, page 347
12. The Times-Picayune (New Orleans, Louisiana), Thursday, July 10, 1879
13. Grand Excursions on the Upper Mississippi River, 2004 By Ed Hill
14. University of Wisconsin-La Crosse, Murphy Library, Special Collections—Historic Steamboat Photograghs
15. Steamboat Times, A Pictorial History of the Mississippi Steamboating Era
16. A Raft Pilot's Log, by W. A. Blair, Pg. 24
17. History of Jo Daviess County, Page 242
18. History of Jo Daviess County, Page 248
19. History of Jo Daviess County, Page 265
20. History of Jo Daviess County, Page 245
21. Ibid
22. Ibid
23. History of Jo Daviess County, Page 244
24. Ibid
25. Life of Blackhawk By Blackhawk, Page 33
26. Life of Blackhawk By Blackhawk, Page 38

Chapter Five
1. Life of Blackhawk By Blackhawk, Page 33
2. Ibid,
3. Ibid, Page 40
4. Ibid, Page 41
5. Ibid
6. Legends of American Indian Resistance, Page 61, by: Edward J. Rielly
7. The Black Hawk War of 1832 By James Lewis, Ph.D.
8. History of Jo Daviess County, Page 282
9. Life of Blackhawk By Blackhawk, Page 56
10. History of Jo Daviess County, Page 282
11. History of Jo Daviess County, Page 284
12. Ibid
13. Whitney, Ellen M., ed. *The Black Hawk War, 1831-1832*. (Springfield: Illinois State Historical Soc., 1970), p.393]
14. Ibid
15. Ibid, Page 286
16. History of Jo Daviess County, Page 288
17. Ibid
18. Ibid, Page 293
19. Ibid
20. Ibid, Page 292
21. The Black Hawk War of 1832 By James Lewis, Ph.D.
22. History of Jo Daviess County, Page 584

Credits and References

Chapter Six
1. http://mykindred.com/cloud/TX/Documents/dollar/ - Historical Value of Currency
2. The Evening Post Newspaper, New York, October 9, 1833
3. The Evening Post Newspaper, New York, October 26, 1833
4. The Boston Post, Boston Massachusetts, Tuesday, December 23, 1834
5. History of Jo Daviess County, Page 458
6. Ibid, Page 463
7. 1920's Selye Fire Engine—Courtesy of Heritage of Flames, by Donald J. Cannon
8. Wikipedia—Galena Historic District
9. History of Chicago, Illinois—http://www.u-s-history.com/pages/h2188.html
10. Chicago Tribune, Article—A 150-year War On Fear, Death, December 08, 1985, by Susan Lewis.
11. Waterways Have Their Time In Court, By Robert Loerzel
12. Hobbs, Galena's Glory Days
13. The Settlement of Illinois Form 1830-1850—Pooley
14. Ibid

Chapter Seven
1. Galena, Illinois—A History—1937 Pg 34
2. Ibid
3. Galena, Illinois—A History -1937 Pg 35
4. History of Jo Daviess County, Page 482
5. Wisconsin Enquirer (Madison, Wisconsin), Monday, January 17, 1842 - Page 3
6. History of Jo Daviess County, Page 477
7. Galena Illinois, A History - 1937 Page 39
8. History of Jo Daviess County, Page 341
9 Ibid, Page 353
10. Wikipedia—Panic of 1857
11. Galena, Illinois—A History -1937 Pg 41
12. Across the Plains in 64', by John Sloan Collins, Page 141

Chapter Eight
1. Frank E. Grizzard, Jr., "George! a Guide to All Things Washington" (2005) p. 285
2. Galena, Grant and the Fortunes of War, Page 38, Kenneth N. Owens
3. Ulysses S. Grant: Memoirs & Selected Letters: Library of America #50
4. The Personal Memoirs of Julia Dent Grant (Mrs. Ulysses S. Grant), Page 90
5. History of Jo Daviess County, Page 488
6. The Galena Directory and Miner's Annual Register 1847-8
7. Personal Memoirs of U.S. Grant by Ulysses S. Grant, Page 211
8. The History of Jo Daviess County, Illinois, Page 624
9. Ibid
10. The Papers of Ulysses S. Grant: August 16-November 15, 1864, Page 16
11. Generals in Blue and Gray: Lincoln's Generals, by Wilmer L. Jones, Page 176
12. Personal Memoirs of U.S. Grant by Ulysses S. Grant, Page 630

Chapter Nine
(9) Section A Business District
1. The Building of Galena, An Architectural Legacy, by Carl H. Johnson Jr.
2. The Century Illustrated Monthly Magazine, Vol. 30, Page 951, 1885
3. U.S. Grant Historic Sites Website
4. History of Jo Daviess County, Page 527
5. U.S. Grant Historic Sites Website
6. The History of Jo Daviess County, Illinois, Page 481

Credits and References

(9) Section B Public Buildings
1. http://courthousehistory.com/gallery/states/illinois/counties/jo-daviess
2. History of Jo Daviess County, Page 338
3. Jo Daviess County Reference and Yearbook, 2013-2014, Page 8, by Jean Dimke, County Clerk
4. History of Jo Daviess County, Page 458
5. History of Jo Daviess County, Page 463
6. History of Jo Daviess County, Page 464
7. History of Jo Daviess County, Page 488
8. The Galena Directory and Miner's Annual Registry, 1847-8
9. History of Jo Daviess County, Page 488
10. Ibid
11. History of Jo Daviess County, Page 527
12. Genesis of Steamboating on Western Rivers With a Register of Officers on the Upper Mississippi. 1823-1870, Merrick and Tibbals, Pg 129
13. Galena, By Kay Price and Marian Hendricks, 2007, Page 49
14. History of Jo Daviess County, Page 528
15. http://www.usmarinehospital.com/HISTORY.html
16. Ibid
17. http://www.granthome.com/market_house.htm
18. http://en.wikipedia.org/wiki/Old_Market_House_%28Galena,_Illinois%29
19. http://www.granthome.com/market_house.htm
20. http://www.illinoisbeautiful.com/northern-illinois-tourism/50-old-market-house-galena-illinois.html
21. Ibid
22. Congressional Record Volume 145, Number 108 (Wednesday, July 28, 1999)][Senate][Page S9622]
23. http://galenahistory.blogspot.com/2012/01/post-officecustom-house.html
24. Ibid
25. John Stevens: The Man and the Machine by James Alexander Jr.
26. http://www.stourbridge.com/stourbridge_lion.htm
27. http://www.galenahistory.org/researching/galena-history/the-coming-of-the-railroad/
28. http://en.wikipedia.org/wiki/Horsebus
29. American Medical Directory, 1909, Pg. 225
30. http://turnerhall.com/history.htm
31. Ibid

(9) Section C Residences
1. Historic Galena, Yesterday and Today, Florence Gratiot Bale, 1939
2. Ibid
3. The Personal Memoirs of Julia Dent Grant (Mrs. Ulysses S. Grant), Page 83
4. Chicago Tribune, 09-20-1953—Article: "8 Historic Houses Will be Opened"
5. History of Jo Daviess County, Page 385
6. www.granthome.com
7. Ibid
8. Ibid
9. Galena, By Kay Price and Marian Hendricks, 2007, Page 42
10. The Galena Gazette, 09-21-2011—Bernadine's Stillman Inn Has Unique History, by Jan Smith
11. Ibid
12. Ibid
13. http://belvederemansionandgardens.com
14. The Biographical Dictionary and Portrait Gallery of Representative Men of Chicago, Page 143
15. The Spokesman's Review, April 13, 1909, "Days of Lincoln and of Grant" page 1
16. Ibid
17. Ibid

Credits and References

(9) Section C Residences—*Continued*
18. http://www.oldhousephotogallery.com/historicmansions/jamesryanmansion.html
19. Portraits & Biographical Album of Jo Daviess County, 1889 pg 610
20. Ibid
21. Portraits & Biographical Album of Jo Daviess County, 1889 pg 617
22. Ibid
23. Ibid
24. The Felt Genealogy, The Descendents of George Felt, Page 181
25. Ibid
26. Galena, By Diane Marsh, Page 115
27. Genealogy of the Loveland Family in the U. S. A. Vol. 3, By John Bigelow Loveland, George Loveland pg 37
28. Ibid
29. Freeport Journal-Standard from Freeport, Illinois · Page 4, Tuesday, February 24, 1959
30. John Brown Serendipity by H. Scott Wolfe, http://abolitionist-johnbrown.blogspot.com
31. Portraits & Biographical Album of Jo Daviess County, 1889 pg 499
32. Ibid
33. Ibid
34. Galena, By Diane Marsh, Page 119
35. Portraits & Biographical Album of Jo Daviess County, 1889 pg 483
36. http://www.hellmanguesthouse.com/
37. Trends in the American Economy in the Nineteenth Century, Page 462
38. http://www.granthome.com/washburnehouse2.htm
39. Ibid
40. Ibid
41. Ibid
42. Ibid
43. Misc. Documents of the Senate, Congressional edition, Volume 2823, By United States. Congress, Pg 201
44. Portraits & Biographical Album of Jo Daviess County, 1889 pg 499,500
45. Galena, By Diane Marsh, Page 122
46. Galena, By Diane Marsh, Page 111
47. From Research By Brad Davis and Roth Weaver

(9) Section D Churches
1. History of Jo Daviess County, Page 498
2. Ibid
3. Ibid
4. Ibid
5. http://www.firstpresgalena.org/A_Brief_Church_History.html
6. Ibid
7. Ibid
8. Ibid
9. Ibid
10. Ibid
11. History of Jo Daviess County, Page 506
12. The Diocese of Rockford 1908-2008, Page 193
13. http://www.gracegalena.org/history.cfm
14. History of Jo Daviess County, Page 504
15. Ibid
16. Ibid
17. Ibid
18. http://www.stmat.net/history-galena.htm
19. Galena, By Diane Marsh, Page 120
20. Galena, By Kay Price and Marian Hendricks, 2007, Page 23

Credits and References

(9) Section D Churches—*Continued*
21. Ibid
22. The Diocese of Rockford 1908-2008, Page 194
23. Ibid
24. http://www.catholicgalena.com/History_of_the_Parishes.html
25. http://www.wupcgalena.org/church-history.html
26. History of Jo Daviess County, Page 508
27. http://www.wupcgalena.org/church-history.html

Chapter Ten
1. http://en.wikipedia.org/wiki/Mississippi_River
2. Galena, IL. An American Heritage—1961
3. Sandusky Clarion Newspaper, Ohio, 09-06-1828, Page 3
4. Belvidere Daily Republican, Feb.. 28, 1948, Page 6

Photo Credits
Unless otherwise stated, all color photographs were taken by and are the property of Philip Aleo and Aleo Publications.

Chapter One	**Courtesy of:**
Page 1	Iowa Department of Natural Resources
Page 2	Ronald Tigges, DigitalDubuque.com
Page 3	Ronald Tigges, DigitalDubuque.com
Page 7	Black Hawk State Historic Site and Tom Willcockson, mapcraft.com
Page 8	Photos by Aleo Publications, with permission of Black Hawk State Historic Site
Page 9	Photos by Aleo Publications, with permission of Black Hawk State Historic Site
Chapter Three	
Page 19 Right	Scott Wolfe
Page 24	U.S. Grant Sites—Illinois Historic Preservation Agency
Page 25	U.S. Grant Sites—Illinois Historic Preservation Agency
Page 26,27	U.S. Grant Sites—Illinois Historic Preservation Agency
Page 28-29	U.S. Grant Sites—Illinois Historic Preservation Agency
Page 30	U.S. Grant Sites—Illinois Historic Preservation Agency
Chapter Four	
Page 33	Galena & US Grant Museum, Galena IL
Page 34, 35	U.S. Grant Sites—Illinois Historic Preservation Agency
Page 36, 37	U.S. Grant Sites—Illinois Historic Preservation Agency
Page 38 Upper	U.S. Grant Sites—Illinois Historic Preservation Agency
Page 38 Lower	Galena Public Library / Alfred Mueller Historical Collection Room
Page 39 All	U.S. Grant Sites—Illinois Historic Preservation Agency
Page 40	U.S. Grant Sites—Illinois Historic Preservation Agency
Chapter Five	
Page 58	U.S. Grant Sites—Illinois Historic Preservation Agency
Page 59 Up Left	U.S. Grant Sites—Illinois Historic Preservation Agency
Page 59 Lower	U.S. Grant Sites—Illinois Historic Preservation Agency
Chapter Six	
Page 74	Galena & US Grant Museum, Galena IL
Page 84	Creator: Edward Mendel Source: Chicago Historical Society (ICHi-00698) Wikipedia

Photo Credits

Unless otherwise stated, all color photographs were taken by and are the property of Philip Aleo and Aleo Publications.

Chapter Seven	**Courtesy of:**
Page 86	U.S. Grant Sites—Illinois Historic Preservation Agency
Page 87	U.S. Grant Sites—Illinois Historic Preservation Agency
Page 88	U.S. Grant Sites—Illinois Historic Preservation Agency
Page 91	U.S. Grant Sites—Illinois Historic Preservation Agency
Page 92,93	U.S. Grant Sites—Illinois Historic Preservation Agency
Page 94	U.S. Grant Sites—Illinois Historic Preservation Agency
Chapter Eight	
Page 99 Upper	Galena & US Grant Museum, Galena IL
Page 99 Lower	Galena & US Grant Museum, Galena IL
Page 100 Both	Library of Congress
Page 102	U.S. Grant Sites—Illinois Historic Preservation Agency

Chapter Nine
Section A Business District

Page 104	U.S. Grant Sites—Illinois Historic Preservation Agency
Page 105	U.S. Grant Sites—Illinois Historic Preservation Agency
Page 106, 107	U.S. Grant Sites—Illinois Historic Preservation Agency
Page 108	U.S. Grant Sites—Illinois Historic Preservation Agency
Page 109	U.S. Grant Sites—Illinois Historic Preservation Agency
Page 110	U.S. Grant Sites—Illinois Historic Preservation Agency
Page 111	Galena & US Grant Museum, Galena IL
Page 112, 113	Scott Wolfe Collection
Page 114	U.S. Grant Sites—Illinois Historic Preservation Agency
Page 115	Galena & US Grant Museum, Galena IL
Page 116	Galena & US Grant Museum, Galena IL
Page 117	U.S. Grant Sites—Illinois Historic Preservation Agency
Page 118	U.S. Grant Sites—Illinois Historic Preservation Agency
Page 121	Galena Gazette, Carter and Sarah Newton
Page 122	U.S. Grant Sites—Illinois Historic Preservation Agency
Page 123	U.S. Grant Sites—Illinois Historic Preservation Agency
Page 124	Galena & US Grant Museum, Galena IL
Page 125	U.S. Grant Sites—Illinois Historic Preservation Agency
Page 126	U.S. Grant Sites—Illinois Historic Preservation Agency
Page 127	U.S. Grant Sites—Illinois Historic Preservation Agency
Page 128	U.S. Grant Sites—Illinois Historic Preservation Agency
Page 131	U.S. Grant Sites—Illinois Historic Preservation Agency
Page 132	U.S. Grant Sites—Illinois Historic Preservation Agency
Page 133	U.S. Grant Sites—Illinois Historic Preservation Agency
Page 134	U.S. Grant Sites—Illinois Historic Preservation Agency
Page 135	U.S. Grant Sites—Illinois Historic Preservation Agency
Page 136	U.S. Grant Sites—Illinois Historic Preservation Agency

Photo Credits

Unless otherwise stated, all color photographs were taken by and are the property of Philip Aleo and Aleo Publications.

Chapter Nine   **Courtesy of:**

Section A Business District
Continued
Page 137   U.S. Grant Sites—Illinois Historic Preservation Agency
Page 138 Upper   U.S. Grant Sites—Illinois Historic Preservation Agency
Page 138 Lower   U.S. Grant Sites—Illinois Historic Preservation Agency
Page 139   U.S. Grant Sites—Illinois Historic Preservation Agency
Page 140   U.S. Grant Sites—Illinois Historic Preservation Agency
Page 144   Scott Wolfe Collection
Page 146   U.S. Grant Sites—Illinois Historic Preservation
Page 147   U.S. Grant Sites—Illinois Historic Preservation
Page 148   Einsweiler Family Collection
Page 150   U.S. Grant Sites—Illinois Historic Preservation Agency
Page 151   U.S. Grant Sites—Illinois Historic Preservation Agency
Page 152   Galena & US Grant Museum, Galena IL
Page 154   U.S. Grant Sites—Illinois Historic Preservation Agency
Page 156   U.S. Grant Sites—Illinois Historic Preservation Agency
Page 158   U.S. Grant Sites—Illinois Historic Preservation Agency
Page 160   U.S. Grant Sites—Illinois Historic Preservation Agency
Page 162   U.S. Grant Sites—Illinois Historic Preservation Agency
Page 163   U.S. Grant Sites—Illinois Historic Preservation Agency
Page 164   U.S. Grant Sites—Illinois Historic Preservation Agency

Section B Public Buildings
Page 165   U.S. Grant Sites—Illinois Historic Preservation Agency
Page 166   U.S. Grant Sites—Illinois Historic Preservation Agency
Page 167   U.S. Grant Sites—Illinois Historic Preservation Agency
Page 168   Diocese of Rockford 1908-2008
Page 170   Galena Art & Recreation Center
Page 172   U.S. Grant Sites—Illinois Historic Preservation Agency
Page 173 Upper   Galena Public Library / Alfred Mueller Historical Collection Room
Page 173 Lower   U.S. Grant Sites—Illinois Historic Preservation Agency
Page 174 Upper   Galena & US Grant Museum, Galena IL
Page 174 Lower   U.S. Grant Sites—Illinois Historic Preservation Agency
Page 176 Upper   Galena & US Grant Museum, Galena IL
Page 176 Lower   U.S. Grant Sites—Illinois Historic Preservation Agency
Page 177   Galena Fire Department
Page 178   Galena Public Library / Alfred Mueller Historical Collection Room
Page 179   Galena & US Grant Museum, Galena IL
Page 180   U.S. Grant Sites—Illinois Historic Preservation Agency
Page 182   U.S. Grant Sites—Illinois Historic Preservation Agency
Page 183   U.S. Grant Sites—Illinois Historic Preservation Agency
Page 184   U.S. Grant Sites—Illinois Historic Preservation Agency
Page 186   Galena & US Grant Museum, Galena IL
Page 187   Library of Congress
Page 188   U.S. Grant Sites—Illinois Historic Preservation Agency
Page 190,191   U.S. Grant Sites—Illinois Historic Preservation Agency

Photo Credits

Unless otherwise stated, all color photographs were taken by and are the property of Philip Aleo and Aleo Publications.

Chapter Nine	**Courtesy of:**

Section B Public Buildings
Continued
Page 192	U.S. Grant Sites—Illinois Historic Preservation Agency
Page 194	U.S. Grant Sites—Illinois Historic Preservation Agency
Page 196	U.S. Grant Sites—Illinois Historic Preservation Agency
Page 198	Scott Wolfe Collection
Page 199	U.S. Grant Sites—Illinois Historic Preservation Agency
Page 200	Galena Public Library / Alfred Mueller Historical Collection Room
Page 201	U.S. Grant Sites—Illinois Historic Preservation Agency
Page 202 Upper	U.S. Grant Sites—Illinois Historic Preservation Agency
Page 202 Lower	U.S. Grant Sites—Illinois Historic Preservation Agency
Page 203	U.S. Grant Sites—Illinois Historic Preservation Agency
Page 204	U.S. Grant Sites—Illinois Historic Preservation Agency
Page 205	Galena & US Grant Museum, Galena IL
Page 206	U.S. Grant Sites—Illinois Historic Preservation Agency

Section C Residences
Page 207	U.S. Grant Sites—Illinois Historic Preservation Agency
Page 208 Upper	Library of Congress
Page 208 Lower	U.S. Grant Sites—Illinois Historic Preservation Agency
Page 210	Library of Congress
Page 214	Harper's New Weekly Magazine Vol. 23 1866
Page 216	U.S. Grant Sites—Illinois Historic Preservation Agency
Page 217	U.S. Grant Sites—Illinois Historic Preservation Agency
Page 220	U.S. Grant Sites—Illinois Historic Preservation Agency
Page 222	U.S. Grant Sites—Illinois Historic Preservation Agency
Page 224	U.S. Grant Sites—Illinois Historic Preservation Agency
Page 226	U.S. Grant Sites—Illinois Historic Preservation Agency
Page 228	U.S. Grant Sites—Illinois Historic Preservation Agency
Page 229	Scott Wolfe Collection
Page 230	U.S. Grant Sites—Illinois Historic Preservation Agency
Page 232	Bob and Rita Wadman Collection
Page 233 Upper R	Bob and Rita Wadman Collection
Page 233 Center Color	Bob and Rita Wadman Collection
Page 234	U.S. Grant Sites—Illinois Historic Preservation Agency
Page 238	U.S. Grant Sites—Illinois Historic Preservation Agency
Page 240	U.S. Grant Sites—Illinois Historic Preservation Agency
Page 242	U.S. Grant Sites—Illinois Historic Preservation Agency
Page 244	U.S. Grant Sites—Illinois Historic Preservation Agency
Page 245 Center R	Brad Davis & Roth Weaver Collection
Page 245 Lower	Brad Davis & Roth Weaver Collection
Page 246	U.S. Grant Sites—Illinois Historic Preservation Agency
Page 248	U.S. Grant Sites—Illinois Historic Preservation Agency

Photo Credits

Unless otherwise stated, all color photographs were taken by and are the property of Philip Aleo and Aleo Publications.

Chapter Nine	**Courtesy of:**

(9) Section D Churches
Page 250	U.S. Grant Sites—Illinois Historic Preservation Agency
Page 251	U.S. Grant Sites—Illinois Historic Preservation Agency
Page 252	U.S. Grant Sites—Illinois Historic Preservation Agency
Page 253	U.S. Grant Sites—Illinois Historic Preservation Agency
Page 254	U.S. Grant Sites—Illinois Historic Preservation Agency
Page 255	U.S. Grant Sites—Illinois Historic Preservation Agency
Page 258	U.S. Grant Sites—Illinois Historic Preservation Agency
Page 259	Diocese of Rockford 1908-2008
Page 260	U.S. Grant Sites—Illinois Historic Preservation Agency
Page 261	U.S. Grant Sites—Illinois Historic Preservation Agency
Page 262	U.S. Grant Sites—Illinois Historic Preservation Agency
Page 264	Diocese of Rockford 1908-2008
Page 265	U.S. Grant Sites—Illinois Historic Preservation Agency
Page 266	U.S. Grant Sites—Illinois Historic Preservation Agency
Page 268	U.S. Grant Sites—Illinois Historic Preservation Agency
Page 269	U.S. Grant Sites—Illinois Historic Preservation Agency
Page 270	U.S. Grant Sites—Illinois Historic Preservation Agency
Page 271	U.S. Grant Sites—Illinois Historic Preservation Agency
Page 272	U.S. Grant Sites—Illinois Historic Preservation Agency
Page 274	U.S. Grant Sites—Illinois Historic Preservation Agency
Page 276	U.S. Grant Sites—Illinois Historic Preservation Agency

Chapter Ten
Page 280	Galena & US Grant Museum, Galena IL
Page 279	U.S. Grant Sites—Illinois Historic Preservation Agency
Page 280, 281	Scott Wolfe Collection
Page 282, 283	Scott Wolfe Collection
Page 284	Scott Wolfe Collection
Page 285	Galena & US Grant Museum, Galena IL
Page 286	U.S. Grant Sites—Illinois Historic Preservation Agency

Chapter Eleven
Page 288	Galena Jo Daviess Convention & Visitor's Bureau
Page 289 Upper	Galena Jo Daviess Convention & Visitor's Bureau
Page 289 Lower	Galena Jo Daviess Convention & Visitor's Bureau
Page 291	Galena Jo Daviess Convention & Visitor's Bureau
Page 292	Eagle Ridge Resort and Spa
Page 293 All	Galena Jo Daviess Convention & Visitor's Bureau
Page 294, 295	Pilot and Photographer James Schmidt

Index

LOCATIONS HIGHLIGHTED IN BOOK

513 S. Bench Westminster United Presbyterian 274-276
227 S. Bench, St. Michael's CatholicChurch 258-261
125 S. Bench, First United Methodist Church, 254-257
106 N. Bench, First Presbyterian Church 251-253
500 Bouthilliar St. Grant's Home 210 - 213
513 Bouthilliar Street - Stillman Home 214 - 215
106 S. Commerce 139
245 N. Commerce 140 - 143 Blacksmith Shop
216 Diagonal Street, Dowling House 234 - 239
343 Franklin 146
406 Franklin, St. Mary's Catholic Church 262-265
418 Franklin Street 199
1237 Franklin Street, Cloran Mansion 222, 223
516 Green Street, Kammerer Residence 229
318 Hill Street, John Hellman Mansion 232, 233
113 S. High, Habich Residence 228
121 S. High, Grant Home 208 - 209
127 S. High, St. Matthew Lutheran Church 270-273
209 S. High Street, Strode Residence 244
507 S. Main 109
401 S. Main 110
230 S. Main, Desoto House 111 - 120
222 S. Main 121
203 S. Main 122
130 S. Main 123
122 S. Main 124 Coatsworth Bldg.
109 S. Main 128, 129, 130
106 S. Main 126, 127
103 N. Main 125 Grant Store
115 N. Main 131
120 N. Main 132, 133
203 N. Main 134
208 N. Main 135
210 - 212 N. Main 136
213 N. Main 137
Corner of Diagonal & Main 138
407 Park Avenue, 246, 247
1008 Park Ave, The Belvedere Mansion 216 - 219
301 S. Prospect, Loveland Estate 226, 227
225 S. Prospect, Richard Seal Home 245
213 S. Prospect Street, John Fiddick Mansion 230, 231
125 S. Prospect, Felt Manor 224, 225
107 S. Prospect, Grace Episcopal Church 266-269
908 Third Street, Washburn Residence 240 - 243
11373 West U.S. 20, Ryan Mansion 220, 221
Belvedere Mansion 216 - 219
County Court House 166, 167
Feehan Hall 168 - 171
Fire Station No. 1 on Bench St. 174, 175
Galena High School on Prospect 180 - 183
Galena's Breweries 150, 151

Grant Park 184 - 185
Grant's U. S. House (First) 208 - 209
Grant's U. S. House (Second) 210 - 213
High School Stairs, The Old 183
Marine Hospital 186 - 187
Market House 188 - 191
Omnibuses 198
Post Office / Custom House 192, 193
Railroad Depot 194 - 197
Recreational Park 172 - 173
Spring Street Hose Co. No. 5 178
St Mary's Hospital 199
Turner Hall 200 - 206
Westwick Foundry 144,145

INDEX A—Z

1008 Park Ave, The Belvedere Mansion 216 - 219
103 N. Main 125 Grant Store
106 N. Bench, First Presbyterian Church 251-253
106 S. Commerce 139
106 S. Main 126, 127
107 S. Prospect, Grace Episcopal Church 266-269
109 S. Main 128, 129, 130
113 S. High, Habich Residence 228
11373 West U.S. 20, Ryan Mansion 220, 221
115 N. Main 131
120 N. Main 132, 133
121 S. High, Grant Home 208 - 209
122 S. Main 124 Coatsworth Bldg.
1237 Franklin Street, Cloran Mansion 222, 223
125 S. Bench, First United Methodist Church, 254-257
125 S. Prospect, Felt Manor 224, 225
127 S. High, St. Matthew Lutheran Church 270-273
130 S. Main 123
203 N. Main 134
203 S. Main 122
208 N. Main 135
209 S. High Street, Strode Residence 244
210 - 212 N. Main 136
213 N. Main 137
213 S. Prospect Street, John Fiddick Mansion 230, 231
216 Diagonal Street, Dowling House 234 - 239
222 S. Main 121
225 S. Prospect, Richard Seal Home 245
227 S. Bench, St. Michael's CatholicChurch 258-261
230 S. Main, Desoto House 111 - 120
245 N. Commerce 140 - 143 Blacksmith Shop
301 S. Prospect, Loveland Estate 226, 227
318 Hill Street, John Hellman Mansion 232, 233
343 Franklin 146
401 S. Main 110
406 Franklin, St. Mary's Catholic Church 262-265

Index

407 Park Avenue, 246, 247
418 Franklin Street 199
500 Bouthilliar St. Grant's Home 210 - 213
507 S. Main 109
513 Bouthilliar Street - Stillman Home 214 - 215
513 S. Bench Westminster United Presbyterian 274-276
516 Green Street, Kammerer Residence 229
908 Third Street, Washburn Residence 240 - 243
Adena 2
Allen, Leo E. 278
Allenwrath Diggings 42
Anderson 45, 95, 214
Anderson's Slough
Annunciation 168, 169
Anti-Beaureguards 96, 97
Appalachian Mountains 277
Apple River Fort 61-63
Appomattox 99
Army Corps of Engineers 284
artillery 54, 57, 95, 184
Asmus C. A. 132
Atchison 56
Babcock, Lieutenant - Colonel C. E. 100
Badeau, Lieutenant-Colonel Adam 100
Bader Grocery Store 146
Bader, Michael 146
Bargemen 85
Barnard, U.S. Gen 33
Bartlett, Sylvestor M. 121
Bastiau, Mary 230
Bates, David G. 24
Battle of Bad Axe 66, 68
Bean (River) 16, 29, 45
Belmont, Missouri 98
Belvedere Mansion 216 - 219
Bench Street 41, 86, 88, 104, 113, 131, 136, 148, 169, 176, 182, 201, 250, 251, 252
Bering Strait 1
Bill of Fare 115
Black Hawk 5, 6, 47, 48, 51-72
Black Jack Mine 26
blacksmith 15, 73, 140-143, 264
Blair, William A. 39, 40
Blakely 95, 185
Blewett, W.H. 119
blockhouse 57, 58, 61, 62
Bouthillier, Francois 18, 32, 89
breweries 90, 150
brigantines 11
British Band 54
Bronell Nursing Home 214
Brunswick-Balke-Collender Company 120
Buck Lead 18, 19

Burrichter, John 232
Business District 105
Cahokia 12
California Gold Rush 89, 230
Canedy-Otto Blower 144, 145
cannon(s) 58, 66, 95, 99, 116, 184, 185
carpenters 73
Carson, J. D. 89
Casper Bluffs Effigy Mounds 3
Casserly, Nicholas and Thomas 108
casualties 62, 65, 98
Catfish Creek 15, 21, 29
Catholic 47, 169, 199, 250, 258, 262, 263, 264
Chase, Rev, Philander 259
Chef Ivo 109, 127
Chetlain, General A. L. 86, 101
Chicago 12, 13, 18, 52, 81, 84, 86, 88, 89, 123, 147, 195, 196, 216, 217, 220, 241, 243, 258, 267, 287
Chicago Historical Society 241, 243
Chicago History Museum 243
Cholera 81. 84, 258
Church, First Presbyterian 251-253
Church, First United Methodist 254-257
Church, Grace Episcopal 266-269
Church, St. Mary's Catholic 262-265
Church, St. Matthew Lutheran 270-273
Church, St. Michael's Catholic 258-261
Church, Westminster United Presbyterian 274-276
Cigar 136, 242
Circuit Court 136
Clark, William 56
Cleveland Mine 24
Clingman Pharmacy 121
Cloran Mansion, 1237 Franklin Street, 222, 223
Cloran, John 131, 222, 223
Coatsworth 138, 139, 224
Coatsworth Bldg. 122 S. Main 124
Col. Bumford 31, 32
Coldwell Bankers Realty 110
Collins, Eli A. 124
Columbian Exposition 123
common schools 73, 74
Comstock 23, 42, 100, 139
Comstock and Hunkins Livery Stable 139
Comstock, Lieutenant - Colonel C. B. 100
Confederate 95, 99, 184
conical 2
Connor, James 24
Continental Divide 277
Cormack, Rivers 250
Corner of Diagonal & Main 138
County Court House 166, 167
Courthouse 96, 136, 166

Index

Crawford, W. S. 4
Cretors, Charles 122
criminal 79
cupola 167, 171
Cyr, Father St. 258
Damask draperies 219
Davenport, Col. 16, 18
D'Bois, Stephen 20
Dent, Lieutenant- Colonel F. T. 100
Desoto House 32, 89, 111-120, 139, 198 203, 214, 267
Dew, Rev. John 250, 255
Dixon 55, 62
Dixon, John 55
Dowling House 234-237, 238
Dowling, John 4, 42, 137, 234, 235
Dowling, Nicholas 42, 234, 235, 237
drag-ropes 74, 174
Dubuque 18, 20, 89, 203
Dubuque, Julian 20, 21, 22,
Duff, Lieutenant –Colonel W. L. 100
Duncan, James A. 23
Durley, William 56, 57
Eagle Saloon 136
Eckstine's Ice Cream 122
effigy 2, 3
Effigy Mounds National Monument, Iowa 1
Einsweiler, Frank 148, 278
electricity 143, 169
embankment 3, 285,
Emporium 79
engine 22, 35, 74, 75, 174, 175, 176, 177, 179
engineers 84, 147,166, 284
Eulberg 151
excursions 37, 38, 40,
Farrar, Amos 23, 24, 32, 42, 58
Farrar, Sophia Gear 24, 42, 59
Feehan Hall 168 - 171
Feehan Hall 168, 169
Felt Manor 224, 225
Felt, Lucius Sawyer 224, 225
Felt's Folly 224, 225
ferry 57, 88, 89
Fever River 7, 12-20, 22, 23, 24, 25, 29, 31, 32, 41
Fiddick Mansion 230, 231
Fiddick, John 230, 231
Fiddick, Richard H. 231, 244
Fire Station No. 1 on Bench St. 174, 175
First Presbyterian Church 251-253
First United Methodist Church 254-257
fish 6, 7, 32, 48, 52, 75
fishing 32, 75
Flood Gates 278, 279, 285, 286
flood(s) 89, 189, 277-286

Foley, John 56
Forsyth, Thomas 52
Fort Armstrong 52, 54, 56, 65
Fort Clark 52
Fort Dearborn 52
Fort Donelson 99
Fort Henry 99
Fort Johnson 52
Fort Lamotte 52
Fort Massac 52
Fort Sumter 95, 185, 209
foundry 148
Fulton Brewery 150
Gaines, General Edmund Pendleton 53, 54
Galena Advertiser 121
Galena Brewing Company 150
Galena Cellar's Winery 109
Galena Fairgrounds 172
Galena Flood Control Committee 285
Galena Gas Light Company 224
Galena High School on Prospect 180 - 183
Galena Pottery 237
Galena Recreational Park 172
Galena Shoe Company 109
Galenian 121
Galena's Breweries 150, 151
garrison 58, 95, 184
Gazette, Galena 121
Gear, Charles 42
Gear, Hezekiah H. 16, 24, 41, 82, 250, 267
Gear, Sophia 24, 42, 59
Gear, William O. 17
General Harrison 51
generosity 83
George Rogers Clark, Col. 13
German schoolhouse 255
glaciers 1, 2
Goodman, Lucella (Lucy) 245
Grace Episcopal Church 266-269
granaries 86
Grand Tower 31,
Grant Park 184 - 185
Grant Park 95, 184, 185, 279
Grant Store, 103 N. Main 125
Grant, Frederick 209
Grant, Jesse. R. 124, 125, 208
Grant, Julia Dent 96, 114, 209, 212, 213
Grant, Nellie 209, 213
Grant, Simpson 124, 139
Grant, Ulysses S. 96, 98, 100, 101, 116, 124, 125, 186, 205, 208-213, 217, 241, 243, 267
Grant's U. S. House (First) 208 - 209
Grant's U. S. House (Second) 210 - 213

Index

Gratiot, Adele   240
Green Bay   12
Green Street   32, 113, 116, 117, 152
Green, Capt. W. B.   55
Grey Eagle   40, 184
Habich Residence   228
Habich, Fred C.   228
Haile, Captain Asa   117
Haines, Jonathan   89
Hanover, Village of   3
Hardin, Isham   89
Harris farm   45
Harris, Daniel S.   15, 23, 31, 35, 65, 66, 184, 232
Harris, James   31, 32, 45
Harris, Wenona   232
Harrison   13, 42
Harvest Festival   253
Hauberg   8
Hawkins, Brigadier-General-Colonel J. A.   100
hearse   147
Heim, Terry   110
Heimerling Father   255
Hellman Mansion   232, 233
Hellman, John V.   232, 233
Hempstead, Charles S.   240,
Hempstead, William   66
Henry Erben Organ Company   259
Hernando de Soto   11
Hesselbacher Jewelers   125
Hesselbacher, Lisa   125
High School Stairs, The Old   183
Hopewell   2
horse   6, 47, 60, 62, 65, 81, 139, 140, 172, 198
hospitality   83
Howard, Captain Bushrod B.   96, 97
Hughlett, Thomas B.   210
Hunkins,   4, 139
Hunt, Bensen   31, 44
ice sleigh   89
Illinois Central Railroad   4, 89, 195, 197, 222
Illinois Central Railroad Depot   102,
Itasca   208
Itasca, Lake   277
Ivo, Chef   109, 127
jackscrews   84
Jackson, Alexander J.   210
Jackson, George E.   15
January, Thomas H.   24, 32, 41
Jefferson, Joseph   136
Jo Daviess Guards   96
Johnson, Col. James   22, 23, 32
Joliet   11, 12
Jones, Joseph Russell   216, 217

Kammerer, Willie   229
Kammerer, Xavier   229
keel-boat   31
Kelly, T.D.   223
Kemper, Rev. Jackson   259
Kempter, Frank   122
Kennedy Mine   25
Kent, Rev. Aratus   250, 251, 252
Keo-kuk   53
Keough Effigy Mounds   3
Kerry's Spreader Day Parade   164
kidnapped   23
kindness   83
Klindworth, Rev. John   271, 272
Knoebber, Frank   138
Kraehmer, O.C.   114, 123, 126, 127, 128, 130
La Fevre   16
La Pointe   16, 17, 42
Lake Michigan   12, 13, 55, 81, 216
Lancaster-Marshall   267
Lapham   2
Le Sueur, Pierre-Charles   15
lead   3, 13, 15-24, 28, 33, 41, 42, 45, 57, 76, 86, 87, 89, 90, 148, 188, 192, 234, 237, 240, 243, 258, 290
Leadmine Foundry   148
Lemfco   148
Lewis, T. H.   2
LIDAR   1
Lincoln, Abraham   96, 116, 211, 217, 241, 243
Livery Stables   139
Loring, Charles E.   121
Loveland Estate   226, 227
Loveland, Daniel Frazer   226, 227
Mah-cau-bee   16
Marine Hospital   186 - 187
Market House   86, 179, 188 -191
Marquette, Jacques   11, 12
Mazzuchelli, Father Samuel   166, 258, 259
McKenzie   136
McMahon, Father John   258
Meehan, Father
Meeker, Moses   31, 32, 41, 45
Meller, Mathias   150
Menominee   32
Merchants National Bank   224
Meskwaki   8, 9
Meusel   134, 135
Meusel, Albert   135
Meusel, Benjamin   134
Meusel, John   134
Mexican War   96, 208
militia   53, 54, 57, 58, 61, 66, 68, 95
Miller, John S.   15, 44

Index

million 1, 18, 19, 20, 26, 76, 86, 90, 98, 287
Mississippi Telegraph Company 116
Morningstar 39
mound 2, 3, 4, 16, 19, 54
Muir, Dr. Samuel C. 18, 32
mutinous 53
Nast, Thomas 99, 290
negro 23
Ne-o-Pope 55
New Orleans 33, 259, 277
New St. Paul 35
Newhall, Dr. Horatio 14, 57, 60, 205
Nominee 35
Northern Light 40
Odd Fellows 245,
Omnibuses 198
organ 123, 255, 257, 260, 267
Orville 25
Packet 35, 216
Paleo-Indians 1, 2
Parker, Captain Ely S. 100, 192, 193
Pearl Harbor 284
Perkins, C. R. 139
pew 251, 252, 255, 256, 259,
phonograph 125
piano (s) 123,
pig lead 87, 192
Pilcher, P. J. 65, 66
Pilot Knob 18, 19
Pittsburgh 73, 76, 79, 80, 226, 275
Pleistocene Epoch 1
Poor House 89, 90, 91
Pope, Nathaniel 13
Portage 4, 12, 16, 17, 24, 65
Porter, Lieutenant – Colonel Horace 100
Post Office / Custom House 192, 193
potatoes 78
Prairie Du Chien 18, 20, 45, 56,
Prohibition 150, 151
Prophetstown 54
Prospect Street 57, 58, 113, 150, 181, 182, 224, 226, 230, 231, 232, 245, 248, 250
Pui, Rev. James De 259
Quality Hill 19, 86
Railroad Depot 194 - 197
Rawlins 96, 101
Readel, Louis 142
rebel 95,
Recreational Park 172 - 173
Red Stripe Beer 150, 151
Reynolds, Governor John 53, 54, 56
Richardson, Willard 140, 141
Rinehart, Frank 10
Robinson, John 208
Rock Island 5, 6, 8, 33, 40, 47, 53
Rocky Mountains 229, 277
Roosevelt, President 284
Rowley, Louis A. 4
Rowley, William 101
Ryan Mansion, 11373 West U.S. 20, 220, 221
Ryan, James M. 220-221, 222
Saukenuk 5-7, 51-54
savage 53, 68
scalp(ed) 55, 56, 57, 67, 68
Scott, General Winfield 68
Seal, Judge Richard 245
Selye 74, 174
Seymour 18
Shiloh 99
Shull, Jesse W. 18, 32
sidewalk(s) 84, 102, 210
Sidney 37
silversmith 73
slavery 23, 95, 96
slaves 23, 24, 95
Slaymaker, John 89, 166
smelters 22, 23, 41, 76
Smith, Rev. John M. 275
Smith, V. A 145
Snyder, W. M. 4, 16
Sonderback, Rev. Alfred 259
Spring Street 178, 179
Spring Street Bridge 104
Spring Street Hose Co. No. 5 178
St Mary's Hospital 199
St. Louis Store 244
St. Mary's Catholic Church 262-265
St. Matthew Lutheran Church 270-273
St. Michael's Catholic Church 258-261
stagecoach 88
Stahl, Frederick 55, 56, 201
Standard Cigar Factory 136
Steamboat 15, 31, 35, 39, 40, 44, 65, 66, 79, 86, 89, 232, 251, 277
Stephenson, J. W. 56
Stillman, Major Isaiah 55, 56
Stillman, Nelson 214
Stillman's Run 56, 61
Strode, Col. J. M. 57, 58, 60
Strode, Mary 244
Suckers 42, 43
Sueur, Charles Le 15
Sullivan & Caille 147
Sunny Hill Nursing Home 214
supernatural 21, 22
Swanzy 23, 24,

Index

Symmes, B.   24
tanner   73, 98, 138, 139
Taylor, John I.   90,
Telegraph   116, 196, 205, 217, 242, 243
Telford, Henry C.   246
temperance   47
Thomas, Lieutenant   41
Tickner, Rich   144
Tiffany   259
tobacco   6, 136
tomahawk   57, 65, 69
Townsend, H.S.   55
tractor   25
train   4, 87, 89, 96, 125, 196, 197, 201
Transportation   7, 73, 79, 88, 197, 198
Trask, Kerry A.   68
treaty   13, 48, 51
Turner Hall   172, 179, 200-206
Turney, John   42, 121
undertakers   147
Van Buren, Martin   121
Vicksburg   99, 290
Vincent J. P. & Sons   147, 238

Vinegar Hill Township   22
Virginia   13, 23, 31, 33, 37, 95, 99, 100, 229
Virginia City Cemetery   229
Warrior, Steamship   66
Washburne, Elihu B.   98, 192, 212, 217, 240-243
waterfront   85, 86, 88
West Point   96, 101
Westminster United Presbyterian Church   274-276
Westwick Foundry   144, 145, 148
Westwick, John   144, 145, 148
Whig   121, 240, 241
White Cloud   54, 55
wigwams   7, 32
Wilson, Henry   138
Winnebago   32, 45, 54, 55, 65
Wisconsin Heights, Battle of   65
Wolfe, Scott   229
Woodland   2
woodwork   76, 135, 232
World War II   284
Yates, Richard   98
Zinc   26, 201

About the Author

Phil Aleo resides in the northwest suburbs of Chicago, Illinois. He has a passion for travel, history and photography.

He has always been an avid researcher that has documented projects on various subjects. Topics range from religion to ancient history with a prominence in local history. Phil tells almost forgotten stories of some of the most intriguing landmarks, buildings, and people.

Early in the year 2000, while sharing his then current project with others, Phil was encouraged to publish and share his work with the public. Following through, he published *Dundee Township, Moments Frozen In Time* in 2001.

The public response to Phil's first book was very positive. Having sold thousands of copies, he was encouraged to continue writing and publishing other historical photographic books. This book is his sixth and others are in the works.

Phil does all the research, modern photography, archive photo restoration, writing, formatting and design of the entire book.

www.aleopublications.com

This book has been made possible because of the generous support of the following individuals, organizations and companies:

Amelia's Galena Ghost Tours *Featuring* **The Ryan Mansion**		**LuLu's Clothing and Gifts**	
Baranski, Hammer, Moretta & Sheehy Architects		**Susan McKeague Karnes** *in loving memory of* **Gordon and Marea McKeague**	
Michael and Rachel Buckman		**La Vie En Rose**	
City of Galena		**LeFevre Inn & Resort**	
John and Marge Cooke		**Jamie Loso**	
DeSoto House		**The Market House Restaurant**	
First Community Bank of Galena		**Charles and Katherine Marsden**	
Don and Carol Fouts		**Libby Miller**	
Galena Brewing Company		**Terry Miller**	
Galena Candle Company		**Ken and Ann Robb**	
Galena's Kandy Kitchen		**Brian and Lisa Schoenrock, DDS**	
Ben Douglas Gay and Lene Graff		**Jerry and Susan Schurmeier**	
Grant Hills Motel		**U.S. Grant Historic Sites**	
Illinois Bank and Trust		**Vinny Vanucchi's**